Comparative Postcolonialism in the Works of V.S. Naipaul and Toni Morrison

Comparative Postcolonialism in the Works of V.S. Naipaul and Toni Morrison

Fragmented Identities

Alshaymaa Mohamed Ahmed

LEXINGTON BOOKS
Lanham • Boulder • New York • London

Published by Lexington Books
An imprint of The Rowman & Littlefield Publishing Group, Inc.
4501 Forbes Boulevard, Suite 200, Lanham, Maryland 20706
www.rowman.com
86-90 Paul Street, London EC2A 4NE

Copyright © 2022 by The Rowman & Littlefield Publishing Group, Inc.

All rights reserved. No part of this book may be reproduced in any form or by any electronic or mechanical means, including information storage and retrieval systems, without written permission from the publisher, except by a reviewer who may quote passages in a review.

British Library Cataloguing in Publication Information Available

Library of Congress Cataloging-in-Publication Data

ISBN 978-1-66692-162-5 (cloth)
ISBN 978-1-66692-164-9 (pbk.)
ISBN 978-1-66692-163-2 (electronic)

To the Soul of My Father

Contents

Acknowledgments	ix
Introduction	1
Chapter One: Postcolonial Literature and Comparative Literature	9
Chapter Two: Mimicry and Fragmented Identities in V.S. Naipaul's *The Mimic Men* and Toni Morrison's *The Bluest Eye*	31
Chapter Three: Memory as a Reflection of Cultural Identity in V.S. Naipaul's *The Enigma of Arrival* and Toni Morrison's *Beloved*	69
Chapter Four: A Journey from Unhomeliness to Hybridity in V.S. Naipaul's *Half a Life* and *Magic Seeds* and Toni Morrison's *Home*: Hybridity: What and Why?	103
Chapter Five: Gender in Naipaul and Morrison	137
Chapter Six: Naipaul and Morrison: Some Conclusions and New Comparative Outlooks	171
Bibliography	185
Index	199
About the Author	203

Acknowledgments

This book is based on my PhD thesis in English and comparative literature that was submitted to Brunel University London in 2020. Therefore, I am imbued with deep appreciation to all the people who have provided me with tremendous help and massive support during my doctoral pursuits. The most considerable debt of my heartfelt gratitude undoubtedly goes to my principal supervisor, Prof. William Spurlin, who has been supporting and guiding me through my writing process. I am profoundly grateful to him for his absolute trust in me and his great encouragement for me to carry out the present challenging but fascinating comparative study. Without his scholarly inspiration, insightful comments, constructive criticisms, a generous offering of research materials, and the most meticulous and patient reading and correction of my work, I could hardly imagine the completion of my PhD. I am thankful to him, as he has enlightened me to venture into the field of comparative study and has spent a tremendous amount of time on my book out of his busy schedule as the vice dean in the College of Business, Arts, and Social Sciences. My sincere and deep gratitude also extends to my second supervisor, Prof. Azza Ahmed Heikal, who has guided me to embark on the right track of doing my research. Her illuminating comments on my book and logical way of thinking have sharpened my critical perception and initiated me into the present project. I am thankful for her admiring wisdom, artistic taste, and kind personality. Her encouraging words helped me through the toughest time of my writing. She offered me professional suggestions while correcting meticulously even the tiniest printing mistakes. Her scholarly attainment and academic carefulness will always remain my goal of a lifelong pursuit. I would like to pay special acknowledgments to Prof. Bill Leahy, the vice-provost (Students, Staff, and Civic Engagement) at Brunel University London, for chairing my viva and for his substantial help. I am especially indebted to him for his being always supportive and helpful. He has always worked as my inspiration. His words were as the impulsive power that pushes me toward my goal. I would like to thank my examiners, for taking the time to read and examine my PhD, and for providing the rich, academic deliberative forum that vivas should provide doctoral candidates as the cumulative experience of their years of research and writing. Moreover, I want to thank my family members for their spiritual support and caring words. Nothing is enough to express my sincere gratitude to my mother for her everlasting trust. To her, I want to say, your love and care have been around me since the moment when I first began my book. Finally, I would like to express my special thanks of gratitude to the Arab Academy for Science, Technology and Maritime Transport for funding me for five years and for giving me an opportunity to do my PhD at Brunel University London.

Introduction

From a postcolonial comparative perspective, this book takes the form of a cross-cultural analysis of fragmented identities in selected novels by two eminent authors, V.S. Naipaul and Toni Morrison. Against the background of globalization and the features of cultural diversity and cross-cultural communication, comparative literature is playing an increasingly significant role in bridging the cultural void and developing an understanding of the uniqueness within, and the harmony between, different cultures. More significantly, comparative literature is an art involving bridging gaps between literature and other fields of knowledge through establishing relations of comparison, influence, and contrast. Comparative literature also combines, mingles, and co-relates literary texts, with attention to their cultural and historical differences, in order to reach a more comprehensive appreciation of those literary texts. Furthermore, comparative literature examines literatures and cultures relationally.

Comparative literature attempts to go beyond the confinements of national borders and examines cultures relationally. However, the modern trend of comparative literature studies has witnessed a move away from "the canonical great tradition to include literary texts and spaces previously marginalized," particularly "the writings of women, and the writings of ethnic minorities at the periphery of larger literary systems" (Dahab, 2004, xiii). Acknowledging the importance of raising the voices of the marginalized within the literary scene, this book studies two Nobel Prize laureates—West Indian writer V.S. Naipaul, and African-American writer Toni Morrison—as subjects of comparison, to explore their attempts at searching for, seizing, and reconstructing their marginalized identities via the medium of literature.

Comparative literature occupies a significant position among cultures and nationalities. It often explores the themes of displacement and complexity—common among people living in diaspora as well as for racial minorities—which can be found in the works of twentieth-century and contemporary authors, crossing the barriers of caste, creed, and nationality. As a result, comparative literature has changed its scope from traditional Eurocentric canons to a wider space incorporating literary works of marginalized cultures in its exploration of both particularities and commonalities. Thus, the book's objective is to locate comparative literature within a postcolonial milieu, paying more attention to indigenous cultures, and crossing frames and borders outside Eurocentric and American traditions.

Classically defined, the term 'comparative literature' denotes the practice of comparing any literary work or works to any other literary work or works. Hence, it can be defined as "the study of texts across cultures, that is interdisciplinary, and that is concerned with patterns of connection in literature across both time and place" (Bassnett, 1995, 1). Previously, comparative literature primarily focused on European and American literature; however, its "most recent development" is characterized by the move "to embrace the literature of the Orient as well as the West" (Aldridge, 1980, iii). Consequently, comparative literature has distinguished itself as an important academic discipline, enabling cross-cultural dialogues and mutual understandings, alongside the general development of cultural diversity and global integration.

On the other hand, the term 'postcolonial' refers to a particular historical period or epoch, which is suggested by the phrases 'after colonialism' and 'during colonialism.' The term 'postcolonial literature' has been used to refer to the writings produced both during and after the colonial period. Subsequently, postcolonial literary studies are an important response to a new literary development: the emergence of literature in European languages, produced in some areas of the world once colonized by European imperialist powers. This area of comparative literature includes literature written in European languages, given the impact of colonialism, and literature written in indigenous languages, which will be discussed further in chapter 1.

Although comparative literature in its earlier stages did not pay particular attention to marginalized literature, the primary interest of postcolonial literature is the literature of indigenous and marginalized cultures. Besides, postcolonial literature is concerned with the exploration of peoples and societies adjusting to life after their colonizers have left. Consequently, and with this framework in mind, I am more interested in exploring a new relationship that examines both comparative literature and postcolonial literature in new ways. The book argues that this new approach will merge the features of both disciplines in a weaving known as a postcolonial comparative approach to literary studies. The first chapter of this book will discuss in detail the intersectional relationship between postcolonial theory and the new comparatism. Various scholars, including Susan Bassnett, Gayatri Spivak, Haun Saussy, Edward Said, Homi Bhabha, and Robert Young, have debated such a relationship dynamically. They maintain that the postcolonial comparative approach is a new hybrid combination that claims the death of both kinds of literature as individual, separate disciplines.

A postcolonial comparative approach combines the features of the two disciplines in paying equal attention to the literature of people who were formerly colonized and to minority literature, in contrast to Western literature or the dominant canon of literary studies. Moreover, it will explore the history and culture of nations, along with rereading literary texts from a global or transnational point of view. Therefore, in this book, a postcolonial comparative critical approach will be used as a lens for a framework to analyze selected novels by V.S. Naipaul and Toni Morrison. Comparing Naipaul and Morrison based on Frantz Fanon's theory will allow the comparative literature to be more exposed to indigenous cultures, which dominant cultures have historically marginalized. Comparing Naipaul and Morrison in a historical and cultural contextualization framework will also shed light on both the differences and similarities between Naipaul and Morrison.

This book also depicts how Toni Morrison could be studied as a postcolonial writer, based on Ania Loomba's expansion of the term 'postcolonialism' to encompass groups who have been culturally and intellectually colonized by Western ideas and beliefs, such as African-American people. Postcolonialism refers to issues that are mainly related to people's responses to colonial superiority and domination; however, Ania Loomba, in *Colonialism and Postcolonialism*, states that African-Americans or people of Asian or Caribbean origin in Britain can be considered postcolonial subjects, even though they live within metropolitan cultures (Loomba, 1998, 16).

Grounded in Fanon's theory of identity, this book traces fragmented identities in Naipaul's and Morrison's selected novels. The close, contextualized, comparative examination of selected novels by both writers reveals that Naipaul's and Morrison's writings can exemplify the three main phases of Fanon's theory, which will be discussed in detail in the first chapter of the book. In *The Wretched of the Earth*, Fanon states that indigenous intellectuals assimilate into the dominant power in the first phase. In the second phase, indigenous intellectuals decide to return to their own history and the importance of their indigenous culture. In the final stage, a major effort is made to reawaken and inspire the marginalized through a cultural and literary revival (Fanon, 1968, 178–179). Also, this book will illustrate how Naipaul and Morrison depict gender in their novels. Comparing Naipaul and Morrison will prove that colonialism and slavery share a similar legacy of oppression. Colonialism and slavery generate spectrums of racializations in different contexts and societies. By continuously "separating human communities across line of dominance and subjection—lines of racial and colonial difference—[oppressed people] are made disproportionately more socially insecure as individuals, communities and intergenerational groups" (Manjapra, 2020, 10). Therefore, the significance of this book lies in its contribution to the body of knowledge in many disciplines, such as postcolonial studies, African-American studies, gender studies, and cultural studies.

By comparing Toni Morrison to V.S. Naipaul, the book will investigate the impact of the legacy of the dominant powers over the writings of both writers. However, Naipaul experienced the colonial era in Trinidad, whereas Morrison, who did not directly experience colonialism, is haunted by what happened to her slave ancestors in the past in the Middle Passage. Therefore, the book will probe whether Toni Morrison can be studied in a postcolonial context and compared to Naipaul. Furthermore, I will shed light on the impact of the two writers' fragmented social and cultural backgrounds, resulting from the impact of their "voluntary and forced diaspora" (Braziel and Mannur, 2003, 5) and their double consciousness. In other words, I will examine the two writers' three-phase journeys of reclaiming their identities, using Frantz Fanon's theory of claiming a cultural identity. These phases will be marked out in their novels, as influenced by their cultural backgrounds.

V.S. Naipaul (1932–2018) has been termed a West Indian novelist of a colonial experience. As a postcolonial novelist, Naipaul concentrated on significant themes related to the problems of postcolonial people. As an observer and interpreter of the former colonies, he exposed the inadequacies of such societies. Since colonialism "colonises minds to bodies and it releases forces within colonized societies to alter their cultural priorities once and for all" (Nandy, 1983, xi), postcolonialism is concerned with the political and cultural independence of people formerly subjugated under colonial rule. Postcolonialism is the study of the ongoing legacies of the era of domination, and the residual political, socioeconomic, and psychological effects of colonialism.

Naipaul discusses colonialism's damaging impact on the identity and psyche of indigenous people, explaining how it attempted to systematically erase and negate cultural differences and the identities of postcolonial people. Moreover, Naipaul argues that colonialism "creates feelings of inferiority and fosters bonds of dependency by the colonized people upon the colonizers" (Staples, 1987, 16) as colonialism can be considered the conquest and control of other people's lands, cultures, and minds. Hence, during and after colonialism, indigenous people became fragmented, alienated, isolated, and dislocated as a result of their assimilation into, and acceptance of, the dominant groups' values and culture. Naipaul is known as being a novelist with an overhanging sense of loss. Therefore, most of the characters in his novels grapple with the themes of fragmentation and alienation, rootlessness, finding and defining home and dislocation. Naipaul represents societies that have recently emerged from colonialism and are still suffering its devastating effects.

Postcolonial literary theory focuses on forces of oppression and coercive domination that operate in the contemporary world; the politics of anti-colonialism, race, gender, class, and ethnicities define its terrain. Accordingly, the term postcolonial denotes a particular historical period or epoch like those suggested by phrases such as 'after colonialism' and 'during colonialism.' Consequently, I assert that what I have discussed regarding postcolonialism relates to my first writer, V.S. Naipaul, because he experienced his homeland of Trinidad during and after multiple colonialisms. Still, the question remains: What about people such as African-Americans who did not pass through the classic colonial experience? Can the definitions of postcolonialism be related to the second novelist discussed in this book, Toni Morrison? How can her novels be read from a postcolonial perspective?

The above questions will be answered throughout the whole book. Toni Morrison (1931–2019) was born in Lorain, Ohio, and grew up in the American Midwest in a family that possessed an intense love and appreciation for their African heritage. However, she never went to her ancestors' African motherland. Morrison was awarded the Nobel Prize for Literature in 1993 because of her marvelous delineation of African-American community. Among many other awards, Morrison also received a lifetime achievement honor for Excellence in Fiction in 2018 from the Center for Fiction in the United States.

Toni Morrison's characters struggle to seek and establish a cultural identity. Moreover, her reference to her African ancestors' traditions and folklore gives her novels great strength and texture. In order to explore the complexity of the relationship between blacks and whites in Morrison's narratives, this book will refer to the work of postcolonial theorists like Frantz Fanon, Robert Young, and Homi Bhabha, who elaborate on postcolonial concepts of mimicry, past, fragmentation, discrimination, alienation, ambivalence, and hybridity, which I will discuss in relation to Morrison's novels. Morrison's novels can be read efficiently within the context of a postcolonial theory that deconstructs Western cultural hegemony, while still affirming a denied or alienated subjectivity and representing the lived experience of oppressed and marginalized people. Framing Morrison's fiction in the context of postcolonial literature, more specifically, this book will investigate how Morrison views the possibility of resistance and subversion in the American history of black oppression.

Naipaul and Morrison are diasporic writers who have lived far from their original cultures. Subsequently, I have chosen to compare Naipaul and Morrison because the primary concern of their fiction is to examine and reconfigure cultural identity, which ideological colonial and racist discourses have previously constructed. Thus, Naipaul's and Morrison's writings focus, more or less, on characters suffering from self-negation, or who are searching for their identity. The restoration of decolonized authentic identity is one of the essential politics in early postcolonial theory. Through their literary journeys focusing on cultural identities, Naipaul and Morrison have reconfigured cultural identity, not as a static entity that can be physically located, but as a shifting entity that can take different shapes in different (historical/sociopolitical/cultural/communal/spiritual) contexts. Furthermore, by dismantling the binary discursive system of white/black, colonizers/colonized, definer/defined, and binary gender/nonbinary gender, Naipaul and Morrison illuminate the possibility of agency for marginalized groups, thus the possibility of resistance, within their fiction.

These two writers explore the most common aspects of marginalized groups' neglected or buried past and an undocumented or misinterpreted history. They recall this past in order to produce new and better knowledge of their worlds, and attempt to reinterpret the historical past and re-envision the world. Morrison's ancestral history is the legacy of the Middle Passage unacknowledged in classic slave narratives, whereas Naipaul has neglected his ancestors' traditions, rituals, and history, suppressed by colonial rule. Thus, this book will try to assert that although Naipaul and Morrison address similar cultural issues, their approaches and techniques to handle these issues differ considerably.

Most comparative studies only compare writers from the same region instead of venturing into cross-cultural comparison. Therefore, by conducting a comparative study of Naipaul and Morrison, this book will invite the Western world to hear the voices of minorities and marginalized groups. By comparing Morrison to Naipaul and relating both to Fanon's three phases of the development of postcolonial indigenous intellectuals, the study's main contribution is to develop a postcolonial comparative approach to literary works. Moreover, the comparison will demonstrate that the colonial legacy is different from slavery, racism, or patriarchal authority. Discussions of power relationships between colonizers and the colonized are sometimes similar to studies on slavery and relationships between masters and slaves. After relating and comparing Toni Morrison as an African-American female writer to V.S. Naipaul, a more typical postcolonial writer, and relating both writers to Fanon's three postcolonial phases of identity, the last part of the book will investigate the assumption that Toni Morrison is a postcolonial novelist. In order to address the points of comparison between Naipaul and Morrison, this book has been organized into six chapters, as follows:

Chapter 1 discusses the intersectional relationship between postcolonial literary theory and comparative literature. It will also highlight the importance of using a postcolonial comparative approach in relating and comparing Naipaul and Morrison, and developing the points already made above. Chapter 2 presents the first phase of Fanon's theory in Naipaul's *The Mimic*

Men and Morrison's *The Bluest Eye*. In Fanon's first phase, indigenous writers attempt to imitate and cope with the colonizer's society by adopting and mimicking their values, which sublimate their original identity and culture. In their earlier novels, Naipaul and Morrison both attempt to neglect and undermine their differences in order to be accepted by the society of the dominant power in which they live.

Chapter 3 presents the second phase of Fanon's theory in relation to Naipaul's *Enigma of Arrival* and Morrison's *Beloved*. In the second phase, Fanon maintains that indigenous intellectuals grow dissatisfied with imitating the colonizers, or the dominant white culture, and instead celebrate their indigenous culture's authentic traditions and practices as a quest for identity. The writer addresses the past, history, memory, traditions, customs, rituals, and legends of their nations. However, Naipaul tends to neglect his history, culture, and traditions, whereas Morrison always celebrates her ancestral history and past.

Chapter 4 goes further by applying Fanon's third identity phase, known as the fighting phase. In this phase, indigenous intellectuals, after having attempted to lose themselves in their original cultures, will, on the contrary, turn themselves into awakeners of their people, bringing about a revolutionary literature that will lead to a new way of becoming. In Naipaul's *Half a Life* and *Magic Seeds* and Morrison's *Home*, both authors stress hybridity as a new way of becoming to resist any essential hierarchy created by a dominant group or society.

Chapter 5 is dedicated to discussing gender issues in selected novels by Naipaul and Morrison. It depicts different images of identities that have been fragmented as a result of gender oppression. Moreover, the chapter sheds light on Naipaul's and Morrison's means of resisting hegemonic powers. It also attempts to explain how Morrison, in most of her novels, deconstructs and challenges the traditional notion of binary gender, which will lead to developing new approaches to gender. In *Sula,* Morrison presents Sula as a revolutionary character who resists phallic patriarchal authority in a hegemonic world. Sula's defiant way of living and her rejection of her society's existing traditions and customs force her society to re-examine its norms and values. Thus, chapter 5 illuminates Morrison's tools of resistance to deconstruct the hegemony of phallic patriarchal power.

However, I argue that although Morrison presents the concept of black women's communities to resist oppressive gender norms in hegemonic societies, Naipaul presents normative masculinity as a tool to resist marginalization in dominant societies. Naipaul always represents sexual relationships between postcolonial migrant men and white women. In these relationships, postcolonial men dominate and humiliate white women who symbolize the dominant English culture.

Chapter 6 addresses Toni Morrison from a postcolonial perspective. It also includes a summary of the outcomes and findings of this study and address its limitations. Moreover, it sets out this book's implications for further research in the field of comparative literature seen from a postcolonial approach, as well as extend new venues and outlooks on the comparison between Naipaul and/or Morrison towards examining expatriate Egyptian and Arab women writers as well as Arab women writers.

Using the postcolonial comparative approach as the primary research vehicle in this book will help in establishing comparative literature in a new mold that goes beyond its Eurocentric conventional frame. Eurocentric notions of comparative literature will thus be challenged, leading to a situation where comparative literature has today become a multilayered and wide-ranging discipline, and where it has persistently attempted to create a dialogue between the so-called dominant and marginal literatures. A postcolonial comparative approach also helps in rereading literary texts, as any literary text will appear different in relation to other literature in different contexts, in much the same way as Morrison's novels are read from a postcolonial perspective when they are compared to Naipaul's novels. The study concludes that Naipaul's ongoing senses of fragmentation, alienation, and rootlessness, which always appear in his novels, can diagnose the economic, social, political, and psychological problems resulting from colonial legacies. Also, Morrison tries to offer African-Americans, through her novels, the possibility of a better connection between present black generations and their slave ancestors in order to understand and realize themselves better as African-Americans in America. Therefore, Morrison's novels emphasize the importance of reclaiming the past in the interests of recovering black women's communities and culture. By comparing Morrison to Naipaul, this book opens up the discussion for further studies in the field of comparative literature from a postcolonial perspective.

Chapter One

Postcolonial Literature and Comparative Literature

What is the relationship between postcolonial literature and comparative literature? The scope of postcolonial theory is to investigate the aftermath of colonialism. It can be a revision of the significations imposed through the process of the colonization of subjugated countries and societies; it can also be considered as the development of a theory for interpreting the consequences of colonial dependency within the space of language in the individual and collective consciousness, as well as historiographic thought and artistic expression. Nonetheless, despite all attempts to define the scope and interest of postcolonialism, the discipline has revealed its comparative foundations.

Regardless of where the origins of postcolonialism are located—whether it became an academic discipline in anticolonial movements, in the literature written in ex-colonies or metropolises by émigrés from former empires—comparative tendencies constitute the critical feature of postcolonial thought. To a great extent, comparativism in postcolonialism is evident in how it understands and analyzes power relationships between colonialism as a dominant power, with hegemony, compulsion, and subjugation on the one hand, and indigenous cultures' processes of resistance on the other.

Postcolonial authors are concerned with the violent historical burden of colonialism, which forced postcolonial societies and their literature into confrontation and marked differences. Therefore, postcolonial literature cannot be anything but comparative since it is written from the position of difference, in contrast to, or through a comparison with, two different politics, identities, languages, cultures, and perspectives. With the effects of postcolonialism, comparative literature finally comes into its own. As a result, postcolonial literature is haunted by its own comparatism, as it is a literature of relations. Consequently, postcolonial studies have developed as an inherently comparative discourse. More substantially, locating comparative literature in a postcolonial context widens the traditional scope of comparative literature to include the literature of marginalized groups, often excluded by dominant hegemonic powers.

Thus, I am concerned with a new relationship between postcolonial literature and comparative literature. Such a relationship will create a new approach to literature that will announce the birth of a new trend in literature—postcolonial comparative literature. This new integration between postcolonial literature and comparative studies will be used in the rest of this book as the basis of my approach to compare, contrast, and relate two eminent writers: V.S. Naipaul and Toni Morrison. Using a postcolonial comparative approach will lead to literary texts being read in relation to other literature, which means that any literary text can manifest differently outside its original context.

In this chapter, I argue that a postcolonial comparative approach combines the features of both disciplines, paying equal attention to the literature of postcolonial and marginalized in contrast to that of the dominant groups. The chapter is concerned with the history and culture of nations, and it involves rereading literary texts through a global or a transnational lens. Therefore, a postcolonial comparison will help comparative literature broaden its scope and shed its traditional Eurocentric trends. In this chapter, the following questions will be explored: What is comparative literature? What is postcolonialism? What type of relationship can combine both of them?

The term comparative literature denotes the comparison of any literary work or works with any other literary work or works. Hence, comparative literature can be defined as "the study of texts across cultures, that is interdisciplinary, and that is concerned with patterns of connection in literatures across both time and place" (Bassnett, 1995, 1). Therefore, it is essential that while conducting a comparative study, one takes into consideration sources, themes, myths, forms, literary strategies, social and religious movements, and the social and historical contexts of works and their various audiences. Additionally, comparatists should interrogate the existence of boundaries among different cultures, how they have been formed historically, and their implications for literary texts.

Comparative literature intrinsically "has content and form which enable the cross-cultural and interdisciplinary study of literature, and it has a history that validated this content and form" (Bernheimer, 1995, 2). Moreover, comparative literature has historically focused on European literature, and later on, American literature; thus, modern criticisms of the discipline's Eurocentrism are valid. At the same time, though, comparative literature has paid more attention to "Other" literature rather than other national literature. Furthermore, for the bulk of its history, comparative literature has kept "its distance from the Africanists and the Orientalists" (Young, 2013, 688), which means that comparative literature has kept itself aside from marginalized cultures and has paid more attention to European and American literature.

On the other hand, the term postcolonial denotes a particular historical period or epoch like those suggested by the phrases 'after colonialism' and 'during colonialism.' In other words, the former leads to the latter. The term 'postcolonial literature' has been used to refer to the writings produced both during and after the colonial period. The term 'postcolonial' covers all the cultures affected by the imperial process from the moment of colonization to the present day. This definition of 'postcolonial' is so broad that it does not cover the discussion of 'postcolonial' in recent scholarship. However, postcolonial remains marked by traces of violence, defiance, struggle, and pain, which represent the political ideals of community, equality, self-determination, and dignity that colonized peoples fought for.

Accordingly, postcolonial literature is one in which the "destructive cultural encounter is changing into an acceptance of difference on equal terms" (Ashcroft et al., 1989, 2). Thus, postcolonial literature is a literature of resistance that aims "to make a discernible impact on situations of injustice, exploitation and oppression within the world that it represents" (Burns, 2019, 3). Here, I would like to stress that because postcolonial thought emerged as a counterdiscourse regarding Western modernity, this resistance dynamic situates postcolonial studies as comparative from the beginning. First of all, colonizer/colonized encounter activates, enforces, and enhances comparative knowledge. Colonizers need to know the colonized for it to be seen as different from colonizers and to contain the colonized within the category of "Other." Consequently, colonial discourse appears to be legitimizing colonial power as historically and ethically necessary. Nevertheless, the semantic origin of the term 'postcolonial' might suggest a concern only with the national culture after the departure of colonialists.

Accordingly, postcolonialism can refer to the periods before and after independence: colonial period and postcolonial period. In other words, no postcolonialism without the historical precondition colonialism. In a sense, colonialism and postcolonialism state the obvious: the former is, of course, the determining condition of the latter. Thus, postcolonialism is always already contaminated by colonialism.

Postcolonial authors use their literature and poetry to solidify an emerging national identity through criticism and celebration, which they have taken on the responsibility of representing. The re-evaluation of national identity is an eventual and vital result of a country having independence from a colonial power or emerging from a fledgling settler colony. Postcolonial literary production has enriched English studies by offering challenging readings of texts created in colonial and postcolonial situations and enabling us to be more aware of the systems of representation that operate in postcolonial writing, which addresses and struggles with the legacies of colonial systems.

Moreover, postcolonial literature is also interested in emphasizing the distinctive features of a particular national or regional culture and identifies certain characteristics across various national literatures, such as the common racial inheritance in African diaspora addressed by black writers. Subsequently, postcolonial literary studies are, importantly, a response to a new literary development: the emergence of comparative literature in European languages, most significantly produced by people once colonized by European imperialist powers. Consequently, and with this framework in mind, I am more interested in exploring a new relationship that explores both comparative literature and postcolonial literature in new ways. I will argue that such a new relationship will merge the features of both disciplines to produce what I have called postcolonial comparative literature.

As a result, a postcolonial comparative approach as a new hybrid amalgamation proclaims the death of both kinds of literatures as individual, separate disciplines. Susan Bassnett supports this claim when she announces the death of comparative literature when stating in the early 1990s, in her *Comparative Literature: A Critical Companion*, "today, comparative literature in one sense is dead" (Bassnett, 1995, 47). Bassnett may be correct in that comparative literature in its traditional centers—France, Germany, and the United States—is undergoing both intellectual and institutional changes, and a certain loss of position, owing to some factors such as the takeover of theory by English studies, the impact of cultural studies, and the diminishing number of comparative literature professorships in comparative literature and students studying it. However, comparative literature lives under other guises in the radical reassessment of Western cultural models at present being undertaken in many parts of the world, in the transcendence of disciplinary boundaries, through new insights supplied by gender studies, queer studies, and postcolonial or cultural studies, and in the examination of the processes of intercultural transfer within translation studies.

By way of explanation, postcolonial theory has, in a sense, usurped the disciplinary space of comparative literature that European literature and criticism had reserved for themselves. This means that any work that looks comparatively at postcolonial cultures and their literary production, as Bill Ashcroft and others maintain, is indeed the way forward in the world in which we live today, so the strength of postcolonial theory may well lie in its inherently comparative methodology and the hybridized and syncretic view of the modern world which this implies.

The relationship between postcolonial theory and new comparatism has been debated vigorously by various scholars. In his *Comparative Literature in the Age of Globalization*, Charles Bernheimer demonstrates the decolonization of the discipline and calls for new paradigms of comparative literature that would reflect the contributions of postcolonial and cultural studies (Bernheimer, 1995, 39–48). As the report emphasizes, a new comparativism that connects with postcolonial studies should include comparisons between artistic productions usually studied by different disciplines; between various cultural constructions of those disciplines; between Western cultural traditions, both high and popular, and those of non-Western cultures; between the pre-and postcontact cultural productions of colonized peoples.

Therefore, developments in comparative literature beyond Europe and North America do indeed cut through and across all kinds of assumptions about literature that have come increasingly to be seen as Eurocentric. That is to say, comparative literature is now emerging and developing actively outside Western contexts, and this can be seen in the emergence of new comparative literature journals, new chairs in comparative literature, and a marked increase in publications. The growth of national consciousness and awareness of the need to move beyond the colonial legacy has led to the development of comparative literature in many parts of the world. Comparative literature in places such as China, Brazil, India, or many African nations is employed to explore both indigenous culture and hegemonic culture in a way to deal with both cultures equally. Accordingly, I agree with Susan Bassnett while suggesting that the arrival of the term postcolonial comparative on the critical scene must surely be one of the most significant developments in comparative literature in the twentieth century and in the present days.

In 2003, Gayatri Spivak's *Death of a Discipline*—a study by a renowned postcolonial critic who claims to provide an outline for a "new comparative literature" (Spivak, 2003, 33–35)—served as a starting point from which to critique a particular branch of postcolonial studies, as well as to outline some of its core issues briefly. In line with her book's title, Spivak pronounces that comparative literature is dead; however, I believe that this refers specifically to a strand of the discipline that most scholars in the field have abandoned. One might also say that Spivak's 'death notice' very much resembles the one Susan Bassnett posted ten years earlier (Bassnett, 1995, 47). In 2006, Haun Saussy supported Spivak while stating that comparative literature has always thought about difference, but inequality remains foreign to its usual vocabulary, transverse to its standing organization of differences. Our research nonetheless bridges domains on both sides of divides that we cannot ignore or assume to have been taken care of by the discipline's own inclusiveness. The more cosmopolitan our reach, the more evident the problem.

Saussy observes that the more comparative literature reaches out to its perceived Others, the more it fails to grasp them. Therefore, Saussy emphasizes the idea of changing the traditional cosmopolitan or Eurocentric direction of comparative literature so as to reach the literature of the marginalized. Combining Bassnett, Spivak, and Saussy's standpoints on new comparative literature, I argue that all of them have sounded the death knell for a discipline born out of nineteenth-century Europe. Also, this new discipline should give prominence to various regional literatures; their reformulation of the perception of literature itself will focus on a direct rapport between literature and regional identity. This may open the way to a new, more open, lively, politically aware understanding of the discipline beyond its historical, Eurocentric roots, and its relocation in the broader field of the study of intercultural processes.

I have the same opinion as Spivak, and while her approach to the merging of postcolonial studies and comparative literature is indeed not the only one, how she constructs and formulates her argument does in many ways lend itself to outlining a 'postcolonial challenge to comparative literature.' A claim she makes at the end of *Death of a Discipline* is, for instance, also very much in line with what scholars in postcolonial studies would by and large endorse. Spivak argues that the new comparative literature needs to undermine and undo the tendency of dominant cultures to appropriate emergent ones.

Overtly, I mean that comparative literature has to move on from its European context and relocate itself globally. In other words, comparative literature will need to move beyond the parameters of Western literatures and societies and reposition itself within a planetary context. This is indeed a sign of the 'politicized dimension' of comparative literature, which Bassnett has pointed out; however, the latter's suggestion that Spivak's idea of planetary in opposition to globalization involves the imposition of the same values and system of exchange everywhere is highly contestable. In *Death of a Discipline*, Spivak maintains that the field of comparative literature should go beyond its Eurocentric origins to pave a way forward for the discipline from its decline. I agree with Spivak when stating that new comparative literature should be born out beyond the limits of Western concepts to include the literature of indigenous and marginalized groups. Until recently, the terms of comparison have always been European concepts posed as universal values, resulting in recolonization, appropriation, distortion, or violence vis-à-vis non-European texts and traditions.

Therefore, I can assert that this new comparativism is a new way of studying, exploring, and analyzing the relationship between two different cultures through a new face of comparative literature, that is, postcolonial comparative literature, which emerged to reread both the colonized and the colonizer's literature equally in relation to each other. Supporting this point, Spivak claims that new comparative literature, which is related to postcolonial cultures, is needed to destabilize the tendency of dominant cultures to subjugate others.

Having a similar viewpoint as Spivak, and perhaps responding in some way to her claim, Edward Said's theory of contrapuntal reading has also established a sturdy base for a new comparative literature that has a powerful connection with postcolonial studies. Said's *Orientalism* does not discuss the history of postcolonialism, but it outlines the scope of a new postcolonial comparative thought. He writes in *Orientalism* that the Orient constituted the "Other" of the West and helped describe Europe as its contrasting image, idea, personality, experience. Orientalism is a discourse producing and sustaining a Western vision of the Orient, which has an undeniably comparative gesture, with the significant reservation that the West legitimates, through this comparative program, its own domination over the East. As an object of knowledge, the Orient serves to create a sense of positional dominance for the people of the West.

Through contrapuntal reading, Edward Said engaged in a reading back to uncover the immersed but critical presence of the empire in recognized texts and to prove "the complementarity and interdependence instead of isolated, venerated, or formalized experience that excludes and forbids the hybridizing intrusions of human history" (Said, 2000a, 367). Thus, I believe that unlike one-sided readings, in which the stories narrated by dominant groups become naturalized and acquire the status of 'common sense,' a contrapuntal reading demonstrates a simultaneous consciousness both of the metropolitan history and those other histories against which (and together with which) the dominating discourse acts.

In practical terms, and through reading Jane Austen's *Mansfield Park*, Said's contrapuntal reading outlines a postcolonial comparative approach targeting unsaid history that is missing from dominant or Eurocentric narratives. For example, Jane Austen's *Mansfield Park* is about an estate owned by the Bertram family whose prosperity derives from sugar plantations in Antigua. However, as Said records, there is almost no mention of Antigua in the text despite the fact that in a structural sense, the story depends on it because, without their properties in the colonies, the Bertrams would neither be as wealthy as they are, nor be obliged to spend a long time away from the manor—factors that open up the story possibilities that the novel explores. Said's approach, then, is to read the novel in light of this structural dependency, which means that the stability and order of the Bertrams' estate in England depend on Antigua, which Austen in the novel neglected. Therefore, Edward Said reads the forgotten other back into the text. This contrapuntal analysis is often used in interpreting colonial texts, considering the perspectives of both colonizers and the colonized as well. If one does not read the full historical background, one may miss the weight behind the presence of Antigua in *Mansfield Park*, that a colonial sugar plantation is seen as important to the process of upholding a particular style of life in England.

More critically, contrapuntal reading must take account of both processes, that of imperialism and that of resistance to it, which can be done by extending our reading of the texts to include what was once forcibly excluded by the authors. A contrapuntal reading wrenches texts from their natural situations to expose their complex colonial or historical affiliations and backgrounds. Said's foremost example of a sugar plantation in Antigua becomes, via contrapuntal reading, the principal affiliation of Austen's *Mansfield Park* and its position within colonial history. In *Mansfield Park*, Austen was trying to cover up the facet of the colonial policy by ignoring the significance of Antigua and a sugar plantation to the novel. However, Said's reading is considered an attempt to unveil what the author of the text purposefully left out. Interpreting or reading contrapuntally is interpreting different perspectives concurrently and seeing how the literary text interacts with itself as well as with other historical or biographical contexts.

More to the point, the vision of the world as overlapping lands and entwined histories was prefigured in the works of founders of comparative literature. However, contrapuntal reading will be influential in showing how the imperial project made a particular cultural vision. Contrapuntal reading necessitates and entails a vision in which imperialism and literature are viewed simultaneously. Thus, comparativism based on postcolonial studies does not want to verify the ample rejection and overcoming of colonialism, but, instead, exposes the ambivalent outcomes of colonialism and opens up a new perspective, in Edward Said's words, of nomadic and contrapuntal historiography and history of literature.

Postcolonialism as an examination of relations between culture and colonization sets for itself the task of revealing the mechanisms of establishing the hegemony of the West and the reverse mechanisms of resistance against processes of objectification and coercion, as critical components of the experience of the colonized. The comparative potential inherent in postcolonialism is apparent in how it deals with imperialism as a dynamic force field, where hegemony, oppression, and suppression are challenged by oppositional discourses ranging from mimicry through open resistance to a rewriting of history and a struggle for identity.

Edward Said claims in *Orientalism* that all cultures are involved in one another; none is single and pure, all are hybrid, heterogeneous, extraordinarily differentiated, and unmonolithic. In addition, Said maintains that *Orientalism* should be perceived as a complex, interactive, material, and imaginary archive whose use commands authority: each work on the Orient affiliates itself with other works, with audiences, with institutions, with the Orient itself. So, Said's critical perspective on *Orientalism* is itself a comparative endeavor where various traditions of studying and representing the

Orient are gathered and classified to expose *Orientalism*'s structural presence in the development of imperialism.

Even so, Said's most crucial impact on articulating new needs of the discipline has been through his re-evaluation of the very idea of comparativism so that in the perspective of a comparative reading of cultures and texts, there could emerge agents so far repressed in the imperial discourse or limited to stereotypical representations of the colonized. Therefore, comparativism operating within the horizon of postcolonial studies will not so much look for evidence of the final rejection and overcoming of colonial dependence but will reveal the ambivalent aftermath of colonialism.

Therefore, new comparativism underlying postcolonial theory disrupts binaries that are characteristic of the imperialist structures of identity and nationalism, which, like imperialism, feed on clear divisions and hierarchical oppositions. New comparative approaches will read the new national and imperial cultures from more balanced perspectives without subjugating or ignoring formerly colonized cultures. My argument about the multicultural reading of literary texts using postcolonial comparative approach is supported by Homi Bhabha and Edward Said's notions about comparative literature. For that reason, a comparative model developing from this local to worldly and secular criticism is a transnational literature based on a philosophy of reading that opens up the text to the world; an ethos of connecting things to each other to the changes that are upon us now socioeconomically, politically, and imaginatively through such things as television, migrations, demographic shifts, refugees, transnational finance.

In other words, my argument will stress that the new comparativism considers the history and culture of both colonizers and formerly colonized nations or indigenous cultures as well. In this sense, postcolonial literature and comparative literature are interconnected with each other for literary texts to be reread from a multicultural point of view. Homi Bhabha, drawing on Goethe's concept of multiculturalism and 'Weltliteratur' (world literature), claims that the possibility, even necessity, of world literature was born in a particular historical context. Moreover, he draws a plan of contemporary comparative literature with a focus transferred from national literature to the problem of unhomeliness or cultural dislocation that defines the postcolonial place. Homi Bhabha also traces otherness, which he derives from postcolonial contexts such as cultural displacement, migration, uprooting, and the marginality of minorities. Furthermore, Bhabha supports Said when he brings into view a concept of world literature—comparative by default—which will substitute the domination of the category of national literature, involving cultural hierarchy and historical prejudices, with the idea of a transnational comparative awareness and unity whereby "literature haunts history's more public face, obliging it to reflect on itself in the displacing" (Bhabha, 1992, 146).

As a result, I assert that Homi Bhabha, Edward Said, Gayatri Spivak, and Suzan Bassnett claim the postcolonial comparative as a new form of comparativism that moves beyond Eurocentric contexts in order to analyze the relationship between indigenous cultures and imperialism, and sets for itself the task of revealing not only the mechanisms that constitute the hegemony of the colonizer, but also the opposite mechanisms of resistance against processes of objectification and force, as permanent components of the experience of the colonized. According to Young, a postcolonial comparative approach goes further than putting hitherto incomparable traditions together disjunctively; however, the comparison takes place in the literature itself through form and content—not just in subsequent critical acts of comparison.

Not only does such writing compare the incomparable, but it offers a different and new model of comparison that I will use in my study when I relate a postcolonial writer to a female African-American writer. Postcolonial literature is naturally comparative, and substantially more comparative than other literature because it is characterized by its comparatism. Therefore, postcolonial authors have always written comparative literature. Hence, comparativism operating within the horizon of postcolonial studies will not so much look for evidence of the final rejection and overcoming of colonial dependence, but will reveal the ambivalent aftermath of colonialism. Theoretical reflection comes after literary works, which had been written and had been postcolonial long before the academic discipline qualified them as such. In such a way, postcolonialism would have its beginning when the writing of literature became a conscious act of self-realization through language and arts. This would be accompanied by a sense of an unsure cultural inheritance, mostly the language enforced through the colonial system of education and literary forms, such as the novel, short story, or epic poem.

The beginnings of postcolonialism in creative literary work from the colonies involved an awareness of its unique worth, which would be one's voice recovered from underneath the structure of the imperial literary canon, although it should also be seen as evidence of the comparative dimension of postcolonial studies. So, while writing occurs in the language of the colonizer, postcolonial writers emphasize concepts like hybridity, fragmentation, and diversity. Such concepts are the products of some cultural elements exemplified by the legacy of colonization, diaspora, race, religion, double identity, gender, sexuality, and indigenous traditions and customs. Subsequently, many postcolonial novelists, artists, and dramatists are usually affected by their fractured backgrounds whose effects appear explicitly in the ways of thinking, technical devices, splitting narrative, confused language usage, scattered themes, and ambivalent characters who are always torn between assimilating into the dominant colonial power and celebrating their cultural or indigenous identities.

Consequently, Spivak and Bassnett's death notice—which was for a discipline born out of an emphasis on national literature with its focus on a direct relationship between literature and national identity—has given way to a new understanding of the discipline beyond its traditional Eurocentric historical definition. In so doing, the new comparativism's underlying postcolonial theory disrupts the characteristic binaries that resulted from imperialist constructions of identity. Thus, the new comparativism necessitates thinking of the type Edward Said called contrapuntal reading to unveil literary texts' historical and cultural affiliations.

Postcolonial literature is not merely new comparative literature in criticism; rather, it involves a new comparative because its comparative gesture defines it. Postcolonial authors are deeply concerned with the violent historical burden of colonialism, which forced postcolonial societies and their literature into comparison in the first place. Postcolonial literature discloses its comparative, driving forward an understanding of imperialism as a dynamic force field where hegemony, oppression, and subjugation are faced and challenged with oppositional forms, from mimicry through open resistance, to the diversity of parodic renovations and textual reappropriations in the strategy of 'rewriting.'

Working from the view that postcolonial literature is a literature of relation, and emphasizing the idea of new comparativism calling for diversity, I will present a comparative study in a postcolonial framework to broaden the Eurocentric scope of comparative literature in order to embrace and pay more attention to marginalized groups. This book will compare and relate V.S. Naipaul and Toni Morrison from a postcolonial comparative perspective. This comparison will help in rereading Morrison's African-American novels from a postcolonial point of view. This book also assumes that although Toni Morrison is an African-American writer, she can be studied and compared to V.S. Naipaul, a postcolonial writer. My objective is to create a new postcolonial comparative approach to study the two writers in relation to each other because while all literature is in some sense comparative, no one writes without mentioning other literature.

Like other contemporary literary theories such as postmodernism, new historicism, and cultural studies, postcolonial theory and African-American studies have become primary critical practices in helping readers to understand the lives of marginalized groups regarding race, gender, and class in a different way. In the circle of literary criticism, though many scholars have been delving into postcolonial criticism and African-American criticism recently, limited research has been conducted on examining the interconnectedness between the two theories. My purpose in this book is to illuminate to readers a new comparison between Toni Morrison, an African-American writer, and V.S. Naipaul, a postcolonial writer.

Both postcolonial theory and African-American literature attempt to challenge the Western hegemony that incurred in the lives of indigenous people. Postcolonial and African-American criticisms are particularly useful in helping one to see connections among all the domains of experience: the psychological, ideological, social, political, intellectual, and aesthetic in ways that show us how inseparable these categories are in our lived experience of ourselves and our world. While African-American literature and postcolonial theory are different fields, both share a certain goal of destabilizing racial hierarchies. Views of power relationships between colonizers and the colonized are sometimes similar but not reducible to studies of slavery and the relationships between masters and slaves. This means that they form a site for comparative inquiry but are not the same thing, just very similar, which will enable me to study Toni Morrison through a postcolonial frame, since her ancestors were displaced through the slave trade and her writing focuses on the recuperation of cultural identity, similar to the issues that compel postcolonial writers. Therefore, postcolonial writing and African-American writing intersect but are not homogeneous.

After comparing the form and the content of selected novels by Toni Morrison as an African-American writer to V.S. Naipaul, a postcolonial writer, I investigate, near the end of my study, the assumption that claims that Toni Morrison is herself a postcolonial novelist. Therefore, I attempt to locate comparative literature in a postcolonial framework to help in developing a new approach to comparative literature that grasps marginalized literature. The book compares Toni Morrison and V.S. Naipaul, not to stress or show the similarities and differences between the two, but to study them in relation to each other to reread African-American literature from a postcolonial comparative perspective that compares the incomparable. After all, postcolonialism can be perceived as an actual struggle against colonial domination and its legacies. Consequently, I assert that what I have discussed about postcolonialism relates to my first writer, V.S. Naipaul, because he experienced his home of Trinidad, which witnessed multiple colonialisms.

V.S. Naipaul (1932–2018) was born in an impoverished rural Hindi-speaking area of Trinidad. His grandfather, a trained Brahman, indentured himself from India to teach among Trinidad's Indian cane-workers. Naipaul's father, Seepersad (1906–1953), was a local journalist and also a short story writer. Seepersad Naipaul introduced his son, Vidiadhar Surajprasad (V.S.), to literature and instilled in him the notion that he should become a writer. Vidiadhar sought and won a Trinidad government scholarship in 1948. In 1950, he left Trinidad to study literature at Oxford University and, since then, had lived in

England. So, Naipaul had eighteen years of colonial experience in Trinidad as Trinidad was under English colonialism from 1797 to 1962.

As a postcolonial novelist, Naipaul situates his novels in both colonial as well as postcolonial societies and gives a perspective account of the complexities inherent to such societies. The major themes that emerge from reading his novels are related to the problem of (post)colonized people: their sense of alienation from the landscapes, their identity crisis, the paradox of freedom, and the problem of neocolonialism in ex-colonies. In his early novels, Naipaul deals exclusively with the colonial society of Trinidad, the island of his nativity, and is preoccupied with the themes of dispossession, homelessness, alienation, mimicry, and the search for an authentic selfhood. The characters in these novels are continually in search of an identity and home. In his latest novels, he emerges as a novelist of postcolonial crisis. Naipaul makes it clear that independence has changed nothing and the imperialist states continue to retain their hold on the former colonies through the newer, more camouflaged methods of neocolonialism. However, the characters in Naipaul's later novels are even more lost and insecure than those depicted in the early novels.

Naipaul has written and produced many narratives and literary forms: short stories, novellas, novels, travelogues, reviews, essays, histories, and autobiographical accounts. He was awarded many literary prizes, including the Booker Prize in 1971 and the Nobel Prize in 2001. Naipaul's life has been rootless and adrift in many ways. The young Naipaul lived within an Indian community cut off from Trinidad. In other words, Naipaul lacked connections both to his Indian roots and to Trinidad's Creole society. Also, the administrative center of the colonial government, or London, was far away and had an image of inaccessibility. His sense of uprootedness was intensified by the fact that his family often moved from one place to another. Also, his leaving for England increased his sense of rootlessness as well. When he first approached England, he had a great sense of being adrift.

Many of Naipaul's characters choose to be away from their society for their own benefit. For individuals, the disconnection from society is both the source of their freedom and the cause of their distress. Even the characters under a forced exile see the advantages of their free situation. Naipaul's writing is caught up in a tension between a quest for personal freedom and a counter quest for a sense of belonging. Naipaul idealizes a society in which people are settled, share values, and have an organic relationship with the place as a rootless man. He also knows the joy of rootlessness and so is skeptical about whether anyone will appreciate any complete belonging to a particular land.

Thus, Naipaul simultaneously and paradoxically longs for individual freedom and a sense of belonging. He has multiple origins to which he only partially relates, which makes achieving a sense of belonging difficult for him.

The nature of a colonial education encouraged Naipaul in his identification with the values of English civilization. On the other hand, he is consciously aware of his ethnic roots as an Indian and reveals a Hindu morality in his works. His self-recognition as postcolonized is also strong. His postcolonial identification defines the destinations of his journeys. For instance, through the journeys to postcolonial nations, Naipaul reflects not only on postcolonial conditions but also on his own circumstances. However, Naipaul belongs to none of these origins entirely. Consequently, his search for his roots is caught in an unfruitful repetition.

These aspects of rootlessness, multiple heritages, and ambiguous belongingness are critical to understanding Naipaul. Naipaul is deprived of a consistent identity, a sense of security, and a sense of belonging to a particular culture as a consequence of cultural transplantation caused by imperialism. Naipaul embodies the aftermath of imperialism and the condition of postcolonial era. Much of the controversy over his works stems from how his sharp and honest vision is perceived. Feeling that he lacks his own settled culture and has no society to write about, he invariably undertook journeys to look for the material about which he writes. Thus, Naipaul's lack of society brings forth the spatial life of a traveler. Naipaul's fictional characters reveal ranges of spatial sensibility. Most of his characters are displaced, fragmented, and alienated.

Staying in foreign places or moving between different cultures, his characters feel the change in atmosphere instinctively or spatially. Naipaul is West Indian by birth but lives as an expatriate in London because of his migration. However, the question is—what about people such as African-Americans who did not pass through the colonial experience? Can the definitions of postcolonialism have any ramifications for my second writer, Toni Morrison? How can she be studied as a postcolonial writer?

In this book, I depict that Toni Morrison (1931–2019) be studied as a postcolonial writer based on Ania Loomba's expansion of postcolonialism to include culturally and intellectually diverse races' colonized Western ideas and beliefs, as are African-American people. Postcolonialism indeed refers to the issues that are mainly related to indigenous people's responses to colonial superiority and domination; however, Ania Loomba in *Colonialism and Postcolonialism* states:

> It is more helpful to think of postcolonialism not just as coming literally after colonialism and signifying its demise, but more flexibly as the contestation of colonial domination and the legacies of colonialism. Such a position would allow us to include people geographically displaced by colonialism such as African-Americans or people of Asian or Caribbean origin in Britain

as 'postcolonial' subjects' although they live within metropolitan cultures. (Loomba, 1998, 12)

Following the above assumption, this book compares Toni Morrison to V.S. Naipaul, who is well known for being a postcolonial writer. Naipaul and Morrison can be considered diasporic writers who have lived far from their original cultures. In *Theorizing Diaspora,* Jana Evans Braziel and Anita Mannur state that 'Diaspora' as a term once described Jewish, Greek, and Armenian dispersion. They also claim that diaspora refers to people who have been dislocated from their native homeland through immigration, migration, or exile. James Clifford supports Jana Evans Braziel and Anita Mannur when he mentions in his "Diasporas" that diaspora now shares meanings with a larger semantic domain that includes words like immigrant, expatriate, refugee, guest-worker, exile community, overseas, and community. However, many diasporas are born of flight rather than choice, in practice voluntary and involuntary migration, which is one of the main points that can differentiate V.S. Naipaul and Toni Morrison.

Morrison is forced to live in a different community rather than her homeland (Africa) as her ancestors were forced into dispersion from their original homes. She always felt a longing to return, thus demonstrating the existence of her homeland's memory, vision, or myth. Morrison is defined by her continuing relationship with her ancestors' homeland, which is always reflected in her writings. Therefore, Naipaul and Morrison together are considered emigrant exiled writers who live in diasporic exile communities. Nevertheless, Naipaul was an expatriate in London because of his self-chosen exile. He lived most of his life in England, but Toni Morrison was an African-American writer who was much affected by what had happened to her slave ancestors in the past. She was influenced by her ancestors who were sold into slavery and forcibly exiled to the new world during the almost 400-year period of legalized slavery which began in 1502. However, she had lived all her life in American society. Thus, both Naipaul and Morrison experienced fragmented identities as a result of being culturally exiled. This book will analyze the impact of diaspora and Naipaul's and Morrison's fragmented cultural backgrounds on their writings from a postcolonial comparative perspective. Comparing certain key novels of Naipaul and Morrison through relating postcolonialism to African-American literature will help in relating Morrison to postcolonial literary theory.

Therefore, I claim that although both Naipaul and Morrison share certain features, such as alienated and fragmented identities, in their novels because of their double consciousness, living in a diasporic world, and having fractured cultural backgrounds, the reactions of their protagonists toward reclaiming their identities are different. In other words, Naipaul's and

Morrison's novels intersect at the starting point, and then they will part company somewhat to resume their journeys in different ways. Consequently, I will explore a postcolonial comparative approach as a lens for a framework to analyze selected works by Naipaul and Morrison in form and content. I have started the book by declaring that African-American writers can be studied as postcolonial writers. To examine this assumption, I will compare Morrison, an African-American writer, to Naipaul, a postcolonial writer, with reference to selected works by both of them. Furthermore, the comparison will mark out the progression of fragmentation in their writings. One of the most prominent early theorists of postcolonial literary theory, Frantz Fanon set out three phases that he believed indigenous postcolonial intellectuals pass through to celebrate their cultural identities. Using Fanon's phases, it is possible to trace the development of fragmentation in Naipaul's and Morrison's novels. An initial examination of selected novels by both writers reveals that Naipaul's and Morrison's writings exemplify the three main phases of Frantz Fanon. In *The Wretched of the Earth*, Fanon describes the three phases as follows:

> In the first phase, the native intellectual gives proof that he has assimilated the culture of the occupying power.... In the second phase, we find the native is disturbed; he decides to remember who he is.... Finally, in the third phase, which is called the fighting phase, the native, after having tried to lose himself in the people and with the people, will, on the contrary, shake the people. (Fanon, 1968, 178–179)

The book consists of six chapters. Chapters 2, 3, and 4 will be based on Fanon's three phases of cultural identity, respectively. However, chapter 5 will shed light on the issue of gender in selected texts by Naipaul and Morrison. Chapters 2, 3, and 4 attempt to compare Naipaul's and Morrison's significant novels according to one of Fanon's three phases concerning each writer's themes, characters, and techniques. In Fanon's first phase, indigenous intellectuals attempt to cope with the colonizer's society by adopting the colonizer's masks and sublimating their identity and culture to that of the colonizers. In their earlier novels, Naipaul and Morrison, according to Fanon, are indigenous writers who attempt to downplay their differences to be accepted by the dominant power of the society, in which they live.

Homi Bhabha describes the phase of colonial mimicry in *The Location of Culture* as "the desire for a reformed, recognizable 'Other,' as a subject of a difference that is almost the same, but not quite" (Bhabha, 1994, 85–86). As mentioned before in Fanon's first phase, indigenous intellectuals try to cope with the colonizer's culture, traditions, and manners. Although they do not resemble their appearance, they act in 'Other' terms, so this first phase is considered the period of "unqualified assimilation" (Fanon, 1968, 178–179).

The book relates Fanon's first phase to Morrison's *The Bluest Eye* and Naipaul's *The Mimic Men*. However, there are differences between Naipaul and Morrison. Naipaul's characters imitate the colonizers, represented by British society, while Morrison's characters do not assimilate to a particular colonizer but instead the dominant power, represented by the dominant white American society. Unlike Naipaul, Morrison did not live in a colonial society but spent all her life influenced by her African ancestors who were forced to scatter from their homeland in Africa to America. Meanwhile, she has lived in and adapted to American society, which is considered a controlling power rather than an actual colonizer. Therefore, Morrison's characters imitate the colonizing gestures of controlling white American power.

In the second phase, Fanon maintains that indigenous intellectuals grow dissatisfied with mimicking the colonizers and instead they celebrate the authentic traditions and practices of their original culture as part of a quest for identity. They become concerned with their nations' history, memory, traditions, customs, rituals, and legends. Hence, they try to use these concepts as the primary step in their search for identity. Here, Naipaul and Morrison use memory and history as primary technical devices that tie their past to the present, but they use them differently.

Whereas colonialism intentionally devastated the precolonial history of the colonized by distorting this history to uncivilized evilness, Naipaul and Morrison employ history as a means to remember their roots. By recalling the history of her slave ancestors in *Beloved*, Morrison is addressing Fanon's second phase of constructing and questing for her black identity. She uses history and African folklore as significant technical devices to connect her ancestors' past with the present and the future of African-Americans. In other words, Morrison attempts to begin her reconciliation process and starts to heal the conflict between her past and present. However, in his *The Enigma of Arrival* (1987), Naipaul tends to deny his West Indian characters any sense of tradition and history. In one of his letters to his father during his first lonely years in England, Naipaul writes: "I hope I never come back to Trinidad . . . Trinidad has nothing to offer me" (Aitken, 1999, 37).

Naipaul also uses history to recall his country's traditions, rituals, and customs. In this stage, he compares his country to England to criticize his traditions and rituals. In *The Enigma of Arrival*, he sheds light on his country's educational, political, and economic systems in comparison to England. According to Naipaul, Trinidad is "a world of decay" (Naipaul, V.S. [1987] *The Enigma of Arrival*, 23, hereafter cited as *EA*). Further, Naipaul tends to deny his Trinidadian rituals and traditions, and he believes that the new generation has to move "further away from those sanctities" (*EA*, 354). Therefore, without a confrontation with the past, there could be no present or future. Whereas Morrison attempts to combine her past with her present, Naipaul denies his past and so is alienated in his present.

Finally, in Fanon's third phase of identity, which is called "the fighting phase," indigenous writers, after having attempted to lose themselves in their indigenous cultures, will, on the contrary, attempt to alter and shake their nations. They turn themselves into awakeners of their people and hence produce literature of struggle and revolution. The fourth chapter of this book will trace Fanon's third phase in Naipaul's *Half a Life* and *Magic Seeds* and Morrison's *Home*. By examining these novels, this book clarifies that Naipaul and Morrison try to guide their nations to hybridity as a new way of becoming to resist the alienation and marginalization in the dominant societies in which they live. Hybridity is considered as a residual of colonialism and a positive factor as it provides a space in which the subaltern seems to subvert the binaries of the colonial project. Consequently, hybridity can meet the criteria of Fanon's revolutionary literature in which indigenous writers, such as Naipaul and Morrison, resist the dominant Western discourses and essentialist categories that continue to write the colonized/subaltern as marginalized.

Moreover, in the third stage of Fanon's theory, indigenous writers try to expose the new generations to their original cultures and traditions. Although Naipaul remarked, "all my works are really one . . . I am really writing one big book" (Naipaul, 1973, 367), he maintains ambivalent themes, alienated characters, and fragmented identities in his latest novels, Naipaul guides his people to develop their indigenous culture. He criticizes some of his traditions, which hinder his nation's progress, such as Casteism, which scatters and divides Indian societies into subdivisions of religion. Moreover, Naipaul helps postcolonial people to find hybridity and cultural exchange as new ways of becoming in multicultural English society.

On the other hand, Morrison uses every means to assert her African-American identity and to integrate African culture and American society. She turns from the phase of mimicry to the phase of using history and African folklore to start her quest for identity. In the final phase, Morrison plays the role of her nation's awakener who guides and supports her nation to heal their fragmentation and find a new way of belonging. For example, in *Home,* Morrison's later novel, her characters' journey is summarized in just seventeen short chapters. According to Cee, the protagonist, her home is in black women's communities in American society. So, African-American protagonists choose to build their own community in the American land, which is considered their home.

This book also critiques gender issues in Naipaul's and Morrison's selected novels. Gender oppression is considered a major issue in marginalized communities. I describe how Naipaul and Morrison try to resist any hierarchical dichotomies created by dominant societies and groups. In parts of this book, I draw out the implications the construction of gender (and thereby the establishment of the norms of sexual difference) is achieved through continual reiteration and 'performance' of particular discourses. Later, in chapter 5, I explain how Naipaul's characters' performances of gender are more normative than in Morrison, as her characters, especially black women, resist normative gender roles. I argue that Morrison tries to change the conventional views of gender as a tool to resist white patriarchal authority and black male domination. For example, in *Sula*, the protagonist refuses to accept a life imposed by others, and she refuses prescribed gender roles in patriarchal societies. Furthermore, in most of her novels, Morrison emphasizes the concept of black women's communities as another means to resist marginalization and oppression in phallic hegemonic societies.

However, Naipaul stresses patriarchal domination as a means of resistance to marginalization in dominant hegemonic societies. In my view, Naipaul emphasizes the normativity of gender. In most of his novels, Naipaul makes sexuality a tool for oppressing women in general, and white women in particular. According to most of Naipaul's male characters, white women symbolize white English culture, which they want to dominate. While Morrison resists phallic patriarchal authority, Naipaul employs his patriarchal authority as his means of resisting the marginalization of postcolonial migrants in dominant societies. In other words, Naipaul's characters do not resist gender norms in the ways that Morrison's women do. Finally, my work on gender in chapter 5 produces a new kind of thinking out of the comparative.

Therefore, the book sheds light on oppression resulting from race, gender, sexuality, and ethnic group. Also, the book reveals how Naipaul and Morrison try to resist any essential practices. When employing a postcolonial comparative as an approach to relate Naipaul and Morrison, the book creates a new implementation of the theory by comparing two writers and discovering new conclusions concerning both of them. In other words, I scrutinize the assumption that posits African-American writers as postcolonial writers. Additionally, the comparison will demonstrate the similarities and differences between Naipaul's and Morrison's protagonists, who reflect, in some sense, perhaps, their writers' cultural backgrounds. Moreover, the study will assert that Naipaul's alienated, aimless characters do not gain any philosophical insight into their absurdist response to the world.

However, in this book, I also argue that Naipaul's fictional and nonfictional texts are the means by which he examines his people's reality in their new world, which is after that of colonialism. Therefore, while reading Naipaul's literary works, one finds that most of his novels promise healing of his characters' identities, but tend to degenerate into banality.

However, it can be concluded that both Naipaul and Morrison have their own types of resistance. Unlike Naipaul, Morrison creates a character who undergoes a process of becoming, of maturing, of finally reaching the point of self-realization. In other words, Morrison's characters are always in a mode of resistance and asserting their black identities in American society, while Naipaul's characters are always trying to belong. Therefore, I argue that Morrison uses positive resistance while Naipaul uses passive resistance to secure rights by personal suffering.

In this book, I will cross-examine how most of Naipaul's characters are fragmented and alienated. Naipaul has taken responsibility for West Indians and has become a spokesman for the colonial and postcolonial world. However, he is aware of the significance of his role as a writer, not only as a recorder of events but as a synbooking voice for others: "Living in a borrowed culture, the West Indian, more than most, needs writers to tell him who he is and where he stands" (Naipaul, 1962, 68). Seeing that people live in a disordered, fast-changing world, Naipaul believes they need help grasping, understanding, and controlling it. Moreover, this is how he can serve his nation.

On the other hand, Morrison documents her nation's history and explains how her nation struggles to root their black identities in American society by employing her various characters who play different roles in her novels. By choosing to relate Naipaul and Morrison using the postcolonial comparative approach, I have added a new contribution to the theory by suggesting that African-American writers can be considered postcolonial writers.

It is worth noting that postcolonial comparative literature is a journey of discovery and a journey toward self-awareness and self-recognition. That is to say, the value of the postcolonial reflection for comparative literature rests in slightly maneuvering between the process of close reading of literary texts and the need to place the literary text in its own intervening cultural and ideological context. This book asserts that postcolonial literature is derived from a comparative impulse and subsequently has developed as a form of comparative discourse.

Postcolonialism discloses its comparative drive the most in understanding imperialism as a dynamic force field where hegemony, coercion, and suppression are faced and challenged by oppositional forms, from mimicry through to open resistance and diversity of reclamations in the strategy of rewriting. A new comparativism informed by postcolonial studies, remarkably via Edward Said's work, disrupts fundamental binarisms—not only for imperial thinking about identity. Comparativism premised on postcolonial studies does not seek to prove the complete rejection and overcoming of colonialism, but, instead, reveals the ambivalent aftermath of colonialism and opens up a new perspective, in Said's words, of contrapuntal historiography and histories of literature. The foundational theoreticians of postcolonialism—Edward Said, Gayatri Chakravorty Spivak, and Homi Bhabha, to mention just the prominent figures—all recognized the significance of the tradition of comparative literature and have called for its borders to be expanded outside Europe. Similarly, each of them offers a different theory of comparativism enhanced by postcolonial sensibilities. The postcolonial intersectional relationship with comparative literature permits the creation of new literature, taking the literature of postcolonized and marginalized groups and the literature of colonizers and dominant groups into equal consideration.

Finally, postcolonial authors have always written comparative literature in so far as they are always in conversation with other literature. Postcolonial writers have been influenced by the historical imposition of colonialism, which forced postcolonial society and its literature into comparison constructs. Postcolonial literature is naturally comparative, and inherently more comparative than other literature because its comparatism defines it. However, there is a need for a dialogue between writers, theorists, and scholars working across cultures and languages so that a genuinely postcolonial comparative approach might emerge. However, postcolonial literature is comparative since it is written from the position of always having been put in comparison with other literatures. The focus of comparative literature has thus shifted to indigenous cultures of the now independent nations and a reaffirmation of national identities in a period of renewal in these countries.

Comparative literature in the global world is not just limited to studying two authors or texts across two different cultures and systems; it also considers the larger picture of nationhood, identities, and marginalization. Comparative literature is now an integral part of the various literary theorizations, and as a discipline, it has succeeded in acting as a conjoining force in postcolonial countries. In the following three chapters, this book employs Fanon's theory of decolonization to relate Naipaul and Morrison in order to examine comparative literature in a postcolonial framework.

NOTE

According to Fatemah Alzubairi in *Colonialism, Neo-Colonialism, and Anti-Terrorism Law in the Arab World*, neo-colonialism is "the forms of economic control, . . . Western financial aid to former colonies and developing countries and supranational financial supervision over states, organizations and banks" (Alzubairi, 2019, 27). Moreover, "neo-colonialism is seen as an adapted form of colonialism, which takes advantage of the weakness of the newly decolonised states in order to achieve economic, political and cultural benefits, mostly through relinquishing political power to favourable elites" (Martin, 1985, 189–190).

Chapter Two

Mimicry and Fragmented Identities in V.S. Naipaul's *The Mimic Men* and Toni Morrison's *The Bluest Eye*

When a person feels their only personality is of lesser importance in society, one option is to imitate another person's behavior and way of life—to become a mimic of someone else. In the context of immigration and under colonialism, mimicry is an expedient pattern of behavior: one mimics the person in power because one hopes to have access to that same power. Most probably, while mimicking the dominant power, one has to suppress one's own cultural identity intentionally. Thus, postcolonial migrants are left so fragmented and confused by their cultural encounter with a dominant culture that there may not be a clear preexisting identity to suppress.

This chapter is one of the three chapters that will trace, respectively, Fanon's three phases of identity. This chapter also sketches Naipaul's and Morrison's theme of mimicry or unqualified assimilation as an indispensable component in their earliest novels, *The Mimic Men* and *The Bluest Eye*. By analyzing structure, narrative techniques, language usage, settings, and symbols as they bear upon thematic considerations, I relate Frantz Fanon's first phase of celebrating a cultural identity, which is mimicry or unqualified assimilation, to Naipaul's *The Mimic Men* and Morrison's *The Bluest Eye*. According to Fanon, in the first phase, the native intellectual gives proof that they have assimilated into the culture of the occupying power.

Assimilating into the dominant power culture is considered one of the main reasons behind the fragmented identities in Naipaul's and Morrison's characters in their earlier novels. Therefore, I argue that mimicry creates a partial and incomplete identity of colonized people and that this partial identity leads to self-fragmentation and more alienation. I also focus on how Naipaul's and Morrison's earliest characters are eternally imprisoned in Limbo,[1] the first stage of Dante's *Inferno*. Those characters have "no hope and yet [they] live in longing" (Miller, 2006, 71; brackets added). In other words, they are locked into their wrong choices and deeds as they are longing for their hopeless wishes. Naipaul's Ralph Sigh and Morrison's Pecola Breedlove are torn in-between assimilating, mimicking the gestures of the dominant colonial power on the one hand, and celebrating their cultural identities on the other.

In my view, mimicry is considered a form of camouflage which is not a question of harmonizing with the background, but against a mottled background of becoming mottled—exactly like the technique of camouflage practiced in human warfare. However, it leads to ambivalence, which points to a fluctuating relationship between dominant groups and postcolonial people. Fanon is concerned with the psyches of oppressed people and their images of themselves. Furthermore, he examines the psychological effects of colonialism on colonized people who are forced to see themselves not as humans but as objects of ridicule and oddity and see themselves as the 'Other.' Colonized people are identified as inferiors because they are always imprisoned or torn between two different cultures. Fanon states:

> I took off from my significant presence, far indeed, and made myself an object. What else could it be for me but amputation, excision, the hemorrhage that spattered my whole body with black blood? But I did not want this revision, this thematization. All I wanted was to be a man among other men. I wanted to come lithe and young into the world that was ours and to help in building it together. (Fanon, 1952, 112–113)

Fanon asserts the desire of colonized people to cope with the dominant cultures by any means. Consequently, the ultimate hope of mimicking the colonizers or dominant groups controls colonized people who wish to live the colonizers' lives, to speak their language, and even to have their skin. Postcolonized people attempt to adapt to the dominant culture by adopting a mask, allowing them to hide their 'inferior' personalities and be accepted in the world of the dominant culture. Therefore, postcolonial people strive to escape their culture by embracing the so-called civilized ideals of the colonizers' atmosphere around them. They try to accept the education, values, language, and even the sexual affairs between them and their oppressors.

Accordingly, and with this framework in mind, I maintain that the works of indigenous intellectuals such as Naipaul and Morrison are developed and characterized by going through a panorama of three phases, of which mimicry or unqualified assimilation is the first. Fanon mentions that indigenous writers prove that they are assimilated into the dominant power culture in the first phase. Consequently, their characters are inspired by dominant or colonizer's culture and always search for their cultural identity. Therefore, indigenous people are fragmented and torn between their indigenous culture and dominant culture.

Similarly, Homi Bhabha, one of the leading voices in postcolonialism, supports my argument when he explains this phase as mimicry. Bhabha defines mimicry as one of the most elusive and efficient strategies within colonial power. He states that colonial mimicry is the desire for a reformed, recognizable 'Other' as a subject of a difference that is almost the same but not quite. Thus, marginalized groups learn to assimilate into the dominant power, but they are neither disempowered nor slavish individuals. They are invested with power to menace the colonizers, for they threaten to disclose the ambivalence of the discourse of colonialism, which the use of stereotypes tries to conceal. Therefore, the copying of dominant groups' culture, behaviors, manners, and values by marginalized groups contains both mockery and absolute menace. Hence, mimicry is not merely a resemblance that invites mockery, but it can also be a source of "menace and violence that invokes resistance" (Bhabha, 1994, 86).

For example, when the colonized do not become entirely like the colonizer, a failing that is quite menacing appears to the dominant power or the colonizer. This inappropriateness disturbs the normality of the dominant discourse itself. Then, the threat inherent in mimicry comes not from overt resistance but from how it continually suggests an identity not quite like the colonizer. This point of indeterminacy causes a great deal of anxiety in postcolonial literary characters' psyches. In other words, mimicry is the result of a colonial process through which the (post)colonized, denied an independent cultural identity of their own, have been coerced into seeking legitimacy by imitating Western models through the strategic adoption of "white masks." Bhabha thinks that this image of people who mimic the colonizer and dominant groups evokes an ambivalence that can be read not just as marking the trauma of postcolonial migrants, but also characterizing the workings of colonial authority as well as the dynamics of resistance. Thus, colonial authority is always uncertain, split between its appearance as original and authoritative and its articulation as repetition and difference.

Bhabha also states that the ambivalence of colonial authority repeatedly turns from mimicry—a difference that is almost nothing but not quite—to menace—a difference that is almost total, but not quite, because colonized subjects are never directly and entirely opposed to the colonizers. Therefore, I declare that colonial mimicry, in my view, is the desire for a reformed, recognizable Other, as a subject of a difference that is almost the same but not quite. Moreover, I mean when colonial discourse encourages colonized or postcolonized subjects to 'mimic' the colonizer or dominant society, by adopting the dominant groups' cultural habits, assumptions, institutions and values, the result is never a simple reproduction of those traits. Instead, the result is a distorted copy of the colonizer that can be quite threatening. Along these lines, mimicry becomes an anticolonial tool represented by the colonized in the colonizer's dominant society.

By way of explanation, mimicry relies on the colonized becoming like the colonizers but always remaining different. The ambivalence of mimicry (almost the same, but not quite) does not merely split the discourse but becomes transformed into uncertainty that puts the colonizer subject in a partial presence. By 'partial,' I mean both 'incomplete' and 'virtual.' It is as if the very emergence of the colonizer is dependent for its representation upon some strategic limitation or prohibition within the authoritative discourse itself. The success of colonial appropriation depends on the production of wrong objects that ensure its tactical failure so that mimicry is at once resemblance and menace. The menace of mimicry is in its double vision, which in disclosing the ambivalence of the colonizer's discourse, also disrupts its authority. Moreover, it is a double vision resulting from what I have mentioned as the partial representation/recognition of the colonial object. Mimicry unsettles and resists colonial discourse as it means excessive copying of the colonizer's language, culture, manners, and ideas. This exaggeration means that mimicry is repetition with a difference and is also a form of mockery because it mocks and destabilizes the ongoing pretensions of colonialism and empire.

Moreover, resistance is not necessarily an oppositional act of political intention, nor is it the simple negation or the exclusion of the content of another culture. The ambivalence of colonial authority continually turns from mimicry—a difference that is almost nothing but not quite—to menace—a difference that is almost total but not quite. Moreover, in that other scene of colonial power, where history turns to farce and presence to 'a part,' the twin figures of vanity and paranoia can be seen that repeat furiously and wildly. In this sense, Bhabha's notion of mimicry becomes a practice, which is clear in Naipaul's *The Mimic Men* and Morrison's *The Bluest Eye.*

Like Bhabha, Naipaul also believes in the ambivalence of colonial mimicry that disrupts the authority of imperial dominance. A postcolonial writer can create reality and identity by adopting colonial language. Naipaul takes the position that there is no alternative to becoming a 'mimic person' and a central tendency to imitate the colonial power. Naipaul's approach to mimicry bears some parallel to Homi Bhabha's work whereby mimicry's performance is masked by ambivalence. The ambivalent and multilayered notion of mimicry is found in the character of Ralph Singh—the protagonist and narrator of *The Mimic Men.*

In validating mimicry as a form of resistance, Morrison's narrative draws attention to how mimicry comprises the danger of internalizing the imposed images of the dominant culture. *The Bluest Eye* confirms Bhabha's notion of mimicry as a subversive strategy, especially when adopted by characters like Claudia MacTeer. Nevertheless, mimicry becomes a submissive practice, as exemplified in Pecola Breedlove's unrelenting attempts to absorb the imposed images of white culture. Therefore, in this chapter, I argue that mimicry is a strategy used in Naipaul's *The Mimic Men* and Morrison's *The Bluest Eye*. However, Morrison clarifies mimicry as a submissive and subversive strategy, whereas Naipaul emphasizes only the submissive side.

THE POLITICS OF MIMICRY

In *The Mimic Men*, Ralph Singh is a prototypical expatriate character, confused by the plural but unequal society in which he was raised, and for whom identity is a primary issue. Singh is a middle-aged man of Indian origin who was brought up in Isabella (a fictional British-dependent Caribbean island) and completes his education in England. The novel, therefore, takes place in two pivotal settings: Isabella (a disguised Trinidad) and London. *The Mimic Men* presents and examines a newly independent country in the Caribbean, the island of Isabella, with a pessimistic view: the former colony has now become independent, but the formerly colonized people of the island are unable to establish order and govern their country. The colonial experience has caused colonized people to perceive themselves as inferior to the colonizer. Colonial education and cultural colonization have presented the English world, with its rich culture, as a world of order, discipline, success, and achievement.

As a result, people of Isabella consider their own culture, customs and traditions, religion, and race to be inferior to those of their former colonizers and try to identify themselves with British empire. Since some of postcolonial people might be far away from their original homeland, their own original traditions and religions have become meaningless to them, and thus, they cannot identify themselves with those remote rules and codes. Therefore, they suffer from dislocation, placelessness, fragmentation, and loss of identity. People of Isabella try to imitate and reflect the colonizer's lifestyle, values, and views. In my view, as these psychological problems cannot be solved after independence is achieved, political independence itself becomes a word but not a real experience. The story is about Trinidad, but Naipaul has preferred to use the name 'Isabella' instead. In choosing the name Isabella for an island closely modeled on his native Trinidad, Naipaul forces the reader to remember Trinidad's colonial past—conquered first by the Spanish before its long colonization by the British (1797–1962). Thus, after being politically independent, the formerly colonized see themselves as lost in their postcolonial society that fails to offer a sense of national unity and identity.

Ralph himself is a disguised copy of Naipaul because his life, as depicted in the novel, is very similar to Naipaul's as both Naipaul and Ralph experienced eighteen years of English colonial authority in Trinidad (Isabella) before traveling to England. At the beginning of the novel, Ralph is in exile writing his memoirs in a quiet hotel in the suburbs of London. He documents his memories in an attempt to give his life meaning and order. He adopts 'European' or 'Western' views, and mimics memoirs, stories, lives, and landscapes that are not his own. Ralph's identification with the West affects his identity. He abandons his family, gets married to an English woman, and adopts a colonial education. His mimicry creates alienation from his culture, which results in fragmentation and the vulnerability of his inner self. Naipaul has always found to position himself as a lone, stateless observer, devoid of ideology or affiliation, a truth-teller without illusion. He has been building upon his experience of colonial and postcolonial trauma in his native island, Trinidad, and looking for his home and social construction in all the sites of dying colonialism and fallen imperialisms in the world. Much of Naipaul's writing issues are from his personal experience of being a displaced member of a minority race and religion in Trinidad. However, his multiple heritages place him in a position that makes it possible for him to render a detached account of his subjective experience. Being an Indian by ancestry, Trinidadian by birth, and English by intellectual training and residence, Naipaul is indeed a man with a broader perspective.

The title of the novel is taken from Ralph Singh, the protagonist's, meaningful statement: "we mimic men of the New World" (Naipaul, V.S. [1968] *The Mimic Men*, 146, hereafter cited as *MM*; emphasis added). The title of the novel—*The Mimic Men*—on one level describes characters who copy the actions and mannerisms of others, as Ralph Singh does. So, the title of the novel serves, furthermore, as a means of orchestrating the mimetic theme that gives the novel its chief significance. Thus, mimicry and its relationship with the characters' fragmented identities become clear in Naipaul's central themes, characterization, conflict, narrative techniques, and language usage as well.

Similar to Naipaul's significant title, which reflects the central theme of his novel, Morrison's title is also substantial. The title refers to Pecola's only and foremost desire in life, which mimics the white American myth of beauty by having blue eyes. These eyes, she believes, will change her gloomy life by making her cute and beautiful, so others' attitudes toward her will be changed positively. The novel takes place in Lorain, Ohio, which is Toni Morrison's place of birth. Morrison took on the task of writing *The Bluest Eye,* which involved "working out of her memory of what Lorain, Ohio, had been like in 1940, [and] she reconstructed her own childhood" (Rosenberg, 1987, 345; brackets added):

In that young and growing Ohio town whose side streets, even, were paved with concrete, which sat on the edge of a calm *blue* lake, which boasted *an affinity* with *Oberlin*, the underground railroad station, just thirteen miles away, this melting pot on the lip of America facing the cold but receptive Canada—What could go wrong? (Morrison, Toni [1970] *The Bluest Eye*, 91, hereafter cited as *BE*; emphasis added)

This context is significant in that it marks a time when Southern African-American women and men were migrating to the northern USA in search of work and formal liberation. While this migration north incited and reflected the establishment of new black middle- and working-class populations, it also denoted a particularly complicated time in African-American history. During the early to mid-twentieth century, the movement of black populations to major northern urban centers, such as those in Ohio, was coupled with intense urbanization and industrialization; this urban growth opened up possible employment opportunities and better living.

In contrast to Morrison's *The Bluest Eye*, Naipaul's *The Mimic Men* takes place between London and Isabella (Trinidad). Naipaul sets his novel in the two locations between which he and his characters are torn and lost. Alternatively, at the beginning of her literary life, Morrison tried to settle in Ohio, the place in which she lived. So, *The Bluest Eye*'s setting is in America, where Morrison's characters try to assimilate without any reference to their origins or roots. Meanwhile, Naipaul's characters in *The Mimic Men* are lost and confused between London, the colonizer's dominant culture, and Trinidad, the original homeland. Therefore, I maintain that Naipaul and Morrison have different politics of mimicry that are clear in their two texts.

Mimicry of Dominant Cultures

Mimicry is a dominant theme in *The Mimic Men* and *The Bluest Eye*. However, Naipaul's characters mimic the English colonizer. On the other hand, Morrison did not experience any actual colonial experience. However, she creates characters assimilating into dominant white American society. In this society, white is seen as the only thing worth offering credence, watching, idolizing, and respecting—this is devastating to African-American characters in the novel, especially the characters who are weak and completely unable to live up to the cultural image of white perfection. Therefore, Naipaul's and Morrison's different backgrounds affect their characters.

In *The Mimic Men*, mimicking English culture creates an inner conflict in Ralph's psyche. The conflict is between Ralph's dream of order and the disorder of his colonial experience—between his desire to imitate English society or return to his cultural identity. Like Naipaul, Ralph is a victim and an artist who seeks personal and aesthetic order in the chaotic colonial world. However, Ralph is not Naipaul; he fails to interpret and understand the nature of his fragmented society. He is unable to detach himself from the colonial situation; hence, he remains a victim of the system: "Yet how can we see, when we were part of the pattern?" (*MM*, 25). Ralph cannot bring order to the world, which is without order. The novel emphasizes the problems Ralph faces as he grapples with the formlessness of his experience. Ralph understands that to find the "perfect" culture, he must escape the "disordered" and corrupted world of Isabella.

In Naipaul's *The Mimic Men,* imitating English culture creates a conflict in Ralph's psyche. He is torn between his West Indian roots and the English society in which he has been educated. Pecola has the same conflict as Ralph; however, her conflict has two main dimensions. The first one is between her and her black family. The second is between her and the dominant white society on one side and the mimic light-skinned characters, on the other hand, who humiliate her blackness. This conflict is a disaster for her; she continually yearns to change her identity by mimicking white beauty to be accepted by both her family and white society. Kathy Russell, Midge Wilson, and Ronald Hall discuss the effects of white beauty standards among black children: "Every American black girl experiences some degree of shame about her appearance. Many must submit to painful hair-combing rituals that aim to make them look, if not more 'White-like,' at least more 'presentable'" (Russell et al., 1992, 43). Ralph and Pecola live with the illusion that they belong to elsewhere. Therefore, escape has become a way of life and displacement a permanent condition as "political independence solves no problem. A kind of cyclic determinism makes it impossible for them to find a home. Neither colony nor mother country provides a matrix, so dependency and displacement are the ultimates" (Thieme, 1975, 16). Consequently, marginalized groups persistently try to secure their lost culture, which cannot be recaptured, rather than come to terms with the present environment. Ralph, for example, believes that London, the center of Western culture, a place of tradition and order, will provide the security he seeks.

Ralph, therefore, exemplifies the permanently uprooted individual, who refuses to establish a connection or a sense of belonging to a new world. He is convinced that he was born in the "wrong" place and is merely "shipwrecked" on the "tainted" island. Throughout the novel, Ralph's situation is dominated by the "shipwreck" metaphor. It describes his Isabellan predicament as "a kind of Indian castaway" as well as his sense of abandonment in London so that even as he begins his memoir, he feels that he does so as a man whose journey has ended in the shipwreck which all his life he had sought to avoid. London turns out to be a place of even greater disorder, and the city underlines Ralph's sense of homelessness even further. The novel relates the various forms of escape Ralph undertakes to deny his island existence and his abortive attempts at finding order.

Morrison summarizes *The Bluest Eye* in her first prologue in the novel. She wants to say that the novel will start and end at the same point. Also, the familiar elementary school story of Dick and Jane provides an ironic frame for Pecola's life.

> Here is the house. It is green and white. It has a red door. It is very pretty. Here is the family. Mother, father, Dick and Jane live in . . . the house. They are very happy. (*BE,* 1)

For each segment of this idealized, secure, white, family life, Morrison offers in counterpoint the bleak specifics of Pecola's life: her shabby home and bitter and hostile parents who are the primary cause of her fragmented identity. Pecola's journey of searching for an ideal and acceptable face, that is to say, self, as she shrinks under the mask of ugliness, is the center of the novel. Her journey starts in the autumn as she is entirely obsessed with the dominant white culture, which is symbolized by a Shirley Temple cup and Mary Jane candies. Pecola's sense of ugliness will lead her to mimic the ideal white culture by aspiring to possess blue eyes. Pecola worships white culture and takes any opportunity to drink milk from her Shirley Temple cup to see Shirley's blue eyes and "sweet face" (*BE,* 22).

She also spends every penny she has buying Mary Jane candies, which wrapped in paper, bear a smiling white face with "blond hair in gentle disarray, blue eyes looking at her out of the world of clean comfort . . . [and where] to eat the candy is somehow to eat the eyes, eat Mary Jane, love Mary Jane, be Mary Jane" (*BE,* 43; brackets added). While eating the candy, Pecola tries to assimilate into the image of Mary Jane. Pecola's unquestioned acceptance of the idealization of white beauty is symptomatic of self-rejection. Also, when she drinks milk out of a cup bearing the image of the American actress, Shirley Temple, Pecola is unconsciously negating her blackness and trying to take on the mask of the dominant culture. While eating Mary Jane candy, Pecola is symbolically absorbing the white culture. She thinks that if she eats the candy of the blue-eyed Mary Jane, she will have blue eyes like hers. Therefore, while Pecola and Ralph are trying to assimilate into the dominant cultures and values, they internalize those values and aspire to be equal to the splendid model of the colonizer. Through this step, "which actually presupposes admiration for the colonizer, one can infer approval of colonization . . . [an attitude which] is subtended by a complex of feelings ranging from shame to self-hate" (Memmi, 1965, 121; brackets added).

Ralph's name-change, which marks a form of escape, testifies to this conclusion: "at school, *I was known as Ralph*. This name I chose for the sake of the initial, which was also that of my real name *Ranjit*. In this way, I felt I mitigated the fantasy or deception. . . . This was one of my *heavy secrets*" (*MM*, 113; emphasis added). Hence, Ralph's private world and his supposed security are merely part of a general pattern. He is torn between the need for cultural perfection in the metropolitan tradition, which exists only in dreams, and the sense of and fear of the inferiority of the immediate society. Ralph was positive that placelessness was part of his youth and that it would disappear once he left the disordered world of Isabella.

His escape to London, "the city of magical lights," with its "snow," which Ralph refers to as his "element," does not, however, solve his problem of disorder and homelessness. Instead, it leads to "a greater shipwreck" and to "the final emptiness" (*MM*, 90). Ralph discovers that London has its own set of mimic people as the city harbors uprooted people from every corner of the world. He soon learns that he is not the only "lost" soul, and his society is not the only society lacking unity and order.

Ralph's journey to London, to the place that existed in his imagination as a whole and pure culture, is a journey into higher disorder. Aligning himself with the "true, pure world" does nothing to dispel his inner hollowness. Instead, he must come to terms with the idea that he has merely exchanged one form of confusion for another. Ralph's rootless isolation is merely transplanted to another environment: "In the city as nowhere else . . . we are individuals, units" (*MM*, 36). London has quickly soured for Ralph. In the big city, the center of the world, where so much has been promised in terms of physical aspects, Ralph had hoped to find the beginning of some order. His shattered dreams led him to a nervous breakdown and forced him to return to Isabella: "I abolished all landscape to which I could not attach myself and longed for those I had known. I thought of escape to that which I had so recently sought to escape from" (*MM*, 36).

Ralph's escape from his Hindu roots to mimic metropolitan society in London is not different from Pecola's escape from her black roots to assimilate into American beauty. Pecola's obsession with the white-blond faces is the consequence of other people's rejection of her and the result of the awareness of her invisibility in the community, of her existential nonbeing: a metaphor that has been deployed recurrently to depict black identity in mainstream society. When Pecola goes to the candy shop of Mr Yacobowki, a white immigrant, he denies Pecola's self. He does not see her because "for him there is nothing to see" (*BE*, 36). Furthermore, "Pecola's story demonstrates, the socially mandated charade of being something one is not (white) and of not being something one is (black) makes one invisible" (Grewal, 1997, 122). Pecola can perceive the destruction of her subjectivity, her unbeing, in other people's gaze: "She would see only what there was to see in the eyes of other people" (*BE*, 35). Pecola represents African-American community, which is unseen and marginalized. She prefers silence to words and points at her candy without saying a word. In this scene, Pecola believes that "her blackness is static and dread. [So], it is the blackness that accounts for, that creates, the vacuum edge with distaste in white eyes" (*BE*, 42; brackets added).

Therefore, Pecola met the shopkeeper's negative attitude toward her with silence because she thought that this was better than saying anything. For Pecola, silence is a negative defense mechanism because, for white society, she is invisible, weak, and ignored. Pecola forgot the shopkeeper's behavior with her once she had three Mary Jane candies in her hand. She prefers the paper image of a blond Mary Jane rather than her self-image and identity.

The shopkeeper is a white character created by Morrison to represent the dominant white masculine culture that marginalizes and despises African-Americans. This central scene in the novel shows "the total absence of human recognition—the glazed separateness" (*BE*, 42) in the shopkeeper's blue eyes. A careful examination of the encounter between Pecola and the white shopkeeper reveals a central trope in the novel: eyes, and their essential significance, which is found in the shopkeeper's eyes. Like "Medusa's[2] look, which was capable of turning people to stone" (Bhandari, 2017, 34), the shopkeeper's humiliating look devastates Pecola, making her powerless, symbolically dead, unseen, or nonexistent.

Therefore, I would argue that the total absence of recognition seen by Pecola in the shopkeeper's glance corresponds to her negative self-perception. She can only be a thing, object, and being for others. Pecola seems able to respond only with shame, which allows herself to be defined by the other. Pecola can easily choose anger to be her reaction toward the shopkeeper's contemptuous glance. However, rather than choosing this creative act, Pecola is consumed by the evidence that: "the anger will not hold; the puppy is too easily surfeited. Its thirst too quickly quenched; it sleeps. The shame wells up again, its muddy rivulets seeping into her eyes what to do before the tears come. She remembers Mary Jane" (*BE*, 43). In her state of self-denial and self-hatred, Pecola takes consolation in shame, abnegating her responsibility for herself to the white shopkeeper. Pecola fails to be recognized and admitted by American society. In this regard, Pecola and Ralph, therefore, fail to mimic the dominant cultures.

After Ralph fails to mimic any of the roles that he tries to perform, he decides to withdraw from his "active" life, taking on the identity of a writer. He fails in adopting the role of a dandy, a student, a husband, a man of affairs, a businessman, and a politician. Therefore, he writes his memoir, not to discover more about himself, but "to impose order on my own history" (*MM*,

85). His first inclination is to write a history, to record the historical experiences which have shaped him and his society:

> It was my hope to give expression to the restlessness, the profound disorder which the great explorations, the overthrow in three continents of established social organizations, the unnatural bringing together of peoples who can only achieve fulfillment within the security of their own societies and the landscapes hymned by their ancestors. (*MM*, 38)

Ralph does, indeed, give expression to the restlessness, but it is not history that he writes but a memoir. He admits that he is too much a victim of disorder to rewrite history. He was hoping that he could pin down the historical disease, and recreate the history of his island, as Naipaul himself does in most of his fiction. Unfortunately, Ralph lacks the historical consciousness that is essential in helping him work out his order. Ralph's rage for order finally draws him into himself, where he must reach a still, calm center before he can write his memoir. However, Ralph's writing of his memoir, far from genuinely clarifying anything, appears finally to represent no more than an insincere ordering of experiences by a man who, temporarily or permanently, has given up the duties of adult life.

Ralph feels estranged from his lived cultures and experiences, a crisis of identity from which he never fully recovers. The result is a persistent and pervasive sense of emotional emptiness. His identity has no culture to center around, and he becomes a double yet hollow hybrid colonial subject that Homi Bhabha examines. He loses a feeling of place or his sense of identification with a place, and he equates placelessness with loss and disorder. Like Naipaul's Ralph, Morrison's Pecola is also broken and fragmented as she now has two selves: one she perceives as her true self—with blue eyes—and one who is her imaginary friend. Even though she does believe she possesses blue eyes now, that still does not seem to be enough. Morrison shows how trying to achieve white beauty standards will never work for Pecola or African-American people: they will be chasing them forever. If blue eyes—the white concept of beauty—cannot work for Pecola and make her loved, it seems not to be the correct answer for the healing of African-American identity.

Naipaul's characters must recognize and accept the reality of their environment; failure to do such results when, as they say, "moving out of ourselves, we look for extensions of ourselves in others" (*MM*, 22). Ralph does not "belong" anywhere, either in England or Isabella. Pecola as well is also rejected by both black and white communities. The difference between Pecola and Ralph is that Ralph chooses not to belong to anywhere, but Pecola is forced not to belong. Thus, the responsibility for order and belonging falls on the individual, not on society, and escape is not from society but from the self. Through *The Mimic Men*, we shall see how Naipaul's narrator, Ralph, indulges in pretence and mimicry as a means of avoiding or denying his society.

For Naipaul and his characters such as Ralph, the only way of finding order and tradition is by escaping, either through fantasy, escape from, or denial of the present environment. However, all options prove unsuccessful. There is no escape, and the disorder which Ralph attempts to escape is not, according to Naipaul, external: "The chaos lies all within" (*MM*, 40). The desire for life elsewhere or the desire for escape indicates two points at once: the rejection of one's own society and embrace of the reality other than one's home. This disjunction between past and present, between here and there, makes home seem far-removed in time and space, available for return only through an act of the imagination. Ralph and Pecola create fictions, not actual places or villages, but invisible ones, imaginary societies, and communities of the mind. In this formulation, home becomes primarily a mental construct built from the incomplete odds and ends of memory that survive from the past. As Iain Chambers explicates:

> To live *"elsewhere"* means to continually find yourself involved in a conversation in which different identities are recognized, exchanged and mixed, but do no vanish. Here differences function not necessarily as barriers but rather as signals of complexity. To be a stranger in a strange land, to be lost, is perhaps a condition typical of contemporary life. (Chambers, 1990, 18; emphasis added)

Indigenous people do not regard their homelands as originary, so they reconstruct an imaginary community and expect to resort to a dominant society where they hope to find their place in the world. To long for a reality, which lies elsewhere, is to assume fragmented and contradictory identities engaged with a multiple-identifying existence. Given simultaneous fascination and rejection, it is unavoidable that Ralph and Pecola should endlessly negotiate between two modes of identification—Western culture and their indigenous culture. Therefore, Ralph and Pecola's identities are so dispersed that they cannot be expressed via one role. The result is that a breakdown follows every role imitated by Ralph. Similarly, Pecola's obsession with white American beauty is followed by her madness and breakdown. Therefore, they move from one state to another, all the time experiencing the same feeling of meaninglessness, uncertainty, disorder, chaos, fragmentation, and in-betweenness, which means that indigenous people cannot be like the dominant power or like their own culture. They become incomplete reducible copies that menace and mock the dominant power.

In-betweenness and Ambivalence/Naipaul and Morrison

Struggling in-between the cultural root or the past and the diasporic notion has assumed a kind of cultural plurality and has created a sense of "unhomeliness or in-betweenness" (Bhabha, 1994, 86). Thus, mimicry, displacement, alienation, marginalization, search for identity, and location of culture are the principal streams in *The Bluest Eye* and *The Mimic Men*. Morrison's novels focus on African-American communities entangled in mimetic desire. They desire what dominant culture possesses—dominant position, power, privilege, wealth, and white beauty. The inability to have power, wealth, and white beauty creates in them a sense of self-hatred and self-denial. Consequently, Pecola, an African-American girl, hates her ugliness, which is represented by her black skin.

Pecola suffers first-hand from constant psychic violence from African-Americans who ignore and disdain her. She becomes the community scapegoat: Pecola will never be an insider in the black community and cannot possibly hope for acceptance beyond that community. However, she seeks acceptance and approval in a community that has internalized dominant white values. That is why she wants, more than anything, to be beautiful and to fantasize about having blue eyes. Pecola's wish for blue eyes epitomizes her internalized racial self-contempt. In contrast to Morrison, the majority of Naipaul's characters are displaced individuals who cross cultural or national borders occasionally. Staying in foreign places or moving between different cultures, the characters feel changes in atmosphere instinctively or spatially.

It can be said that Naipaul's life has been rootless and adrift in many ways. The young Naipaul lived within an Indian community cut off from Trinidadian society. In other words, Naipaul lacked connections both to his Indian roots and to the Trinidadian community. Also, the administrative center of the colonial government, or London, was far away and had an image of inaccessibility. Such background information brings forth one of the universal themes of rootlessness in his work. Many of his characters are adrift. They are away from their society or lack such a community from birth. For individuals, the disconnection from society is both the source of their freedom and the cause of their suffering.

Unlike Naipaul, Morrison's background is not represented directly by her characters. Nonetheless, she describes the lives of her African-American community, who live in America and try to fit in and adapt to the dominant society. She respects the difficulties that her characters endure because of their race, class, gender, and economic status, and yet holds them responsible for their actions. She does not imply that all characters have the same opportunities but portrays the strong characters as those who have made the most out of what they were given. Many of the characters in *The Bluest*

Eye experience isolation from the norm and from the ideal, which often results in isolation from the self. She also "questions the instant reactionary myth-making" (i.e., "Black is beautiful") in which power depends on white beauty (Morrison, 1974, 89).

Pecola's conflict with the dominant white society is not the main reason for her dilemma; she is also rejected and humiliated by African-Americans or light-skinned people as well as whites. Pecola is the symbol of the weak and humiliated blackness, which is objectified and oppressed by both whites and African-Americans as well. Whites oppress blackness because of the white myth of beauty. Meanwhile, African-Americans, who mimic the dominant white power, reject blackness because they do not want to remember their history. They mystify their identities by acting or playing the role of the white master who humiliates African-Americans and blackness. Frantz Fanon describes how oppressed people, who have no other alternative, vent their frustration and anger on each other:

> If this suppressed fury fails to find an outlet, it turns into a vacuum and devastates the oppressed creatures themselves. To free themselves, they even massacre each other. The different tribes fight between themselves since they cannot face the real enemy—and you can count on colonial policy to keep up the rivalries; the man who raises his knife against his brother thinks that he has destroyed once and for all the detested image of their common degradation, even though these expiatory victims don't quench their thirst for blood. (Fanon, 1968, 18–19)

While mimicking the dominant white culture, colored-skinned people in Morrison's novels deny their tendency to focus their anger and humiliation on the weaker members of their communities. Mrs Geraldine and Maureen Peel represent light-skinned people and their mimicking of the role of white elites. Mrs Geraldine is one of the characters who mimic dominant white society. By denying her own blackness, Geraldine feels that she can escape African-Americans' experience in the dominant white culture. Moreover, her hatred of herself is infectious—a destructive legacy that she passes on to her children, who victimize others. Geraldine is "a character who projects onto others her own fears and misgivings about herself and her race" (Davis, 1999, 177). According to Geraldine: colored people were neat and quiet; "*niggers were dirty and loud*" (*BE*, 87; emphasis added).

Accordingly, Pecola's alienation, abandonment, and isolation will lead her to complete self-fragmentation and withdrawal. The schizoid individual may have fantasies of being invisible, as being a visible object means to be constantly exposed to danger, accusation, or oppression. Therefore, self-alienation is Pecola's shelter or weapon against any oppression she faces in her life. Being rejected by the more affluent segments of black society is bad enough, but her family casts out Pecola—the main reason for her fragmented identity and abyss. So, womanhood, like blackness, is Other in this society, and the dilemma of a woman in a patriarchal society is parallel to that of blacks in a racist society. Therefore, disappearing and folding inward is the direction her quest takes. Pecola's only response is to "disappear" (*BE*, 39). She wants to have blue eyes because she thinks that if she can beautify her eyes, she would be different, and she could fit in the society in which she lives.

Naipaul describes and draws an image of two landscapes of the two cultures between which his main character, Ralph, is torn. Like Pecola, who desires to have blue eyes to change the world around her, Ralph wants to change his world by ordering the chaos around him. However, moving from one place to another increases the chaos and disorder around Ralph. Living in limbo and being fragmented because they fail to imitate the societies in which they live alienates both Ralph and Pecola. Their sense of alienation makes them withdraw and escape.

Consequently, one of Naipaul's chief accomplishments in the novel is Ralph's search for identity, which is linked to the landscapes he traverses. Thus, settings and their symbolic meanings become an essential means of Ralph's understanding of self in time. Landscape functions as a reliable measure in *The Mimic Men*, at first epitomizing inauthenticity and mimicry but later signifying acceptance of self. Ralph first leaves the twin prisons of his childhood house and Isabella and sails for London, where his temporary "home" is the Kensington boarding house—a paradigm of a fragmented society, peopled by immigrants, owned by an exiled Jew named Shylock. Ralph's room is "tall, multimirrored, book-shaped with a coffin-like wardrobe" (*MM*, 7), the adjectives revealing Ralph's emotional state. The mirrors symbolize his growing self-consciousness, lack of genuine identity, and adoption of a mask to cover an essential hollowness. In London, he finds no link between his present and past; he no longer knows who he is and ceases to feel himself a whole person. So he affects the "fixed, flat" character of the dandy, the two-dimensional figure in the mirror, and becomes the role he sees reflected in the eyes of others.

Naipaul admitted that he made three false starts on *The Mimic Men* before he realized "it needed a physical center," which would be "the place where the man was writing his memoirs" (Naipaul, 1968, 57). Thus, the London room becomes the unifying symbol of *The Mimic Men*. England, the dreamed-of ideal landscape, also fails Ralph when he discovers only a greater disorder and more significant shipwreck there during his student days. Ralph fails to root himself in the city, remaining "spectral, disintegrating, pointless, fluid" (*MM*, 52), returning to Isabella as adrift as before. This sense of personal incompleteness grows to almost destroy him. Ralph is affected by the corruption he perceives all around him. In fact, apart from all the external disorder, Ralph comes to realize that the "chaos lies all within" (*MM*, 192). Reflecting on his adult years in Isabella as a businessman and politician, Ralph writes, "I see that all the activity of these years existing as I have said in my own mind represented a type of withdrawal" (*MM*, 52).

Finally, moving and transferring from one place to another reinforces Ralph's sense of alienation and fragmentation, which lead him to his willed self-exile. The position of postcolonial people is no better than exile. Edward Said claims that exile is strangely compelling to think about but terrible to experience. It is the unbearable rift between a human being and their native place, between the self and its true home: its essential sadness can never be summoned . . . the achievements of exile are permanently undermined by the loss of something left behind forever (Said, 2000b, 173). Ralph and Pecola represent fragmented personalities, the psychologically disoriented and displaced victims of historical and political accidents. They are unable to create identities for themselves and to bring order to their lives. The problematics of mimicry lay in the fact that it repeats rather than represents, which further leads indigenous people to realize their own nothingness and insignificance. Ralph shows his awareness of this ambivalence: "We pretend to be real, to be learning, to be preparing ourselves for life, we mimic men of the New World" (*MM*, 146).

Naipaul's dislocation from his roots enables him to understand the alienation and self-fragmentation of marginalized people. Ralph and others can deal with the outer chaos. The meaninglessness and chaos are not just out there but exist because the characters fail to identify the real problem within. Ralph and Pecola are always in a Homi Bhabha's third space, in which they are neither the self nor the other. They do not know where to belong, and Pecola is positioned in the space between black and white humiliating communities, in which she is unaccepted and alienated from both. Failing to adopt the English colonizers' roles or going back to his Isabellan (Trinidadian) culture, Ralph is stuck in a space between the English and Isabellan (Trinidadian) cultures. In this sense, failing to achieve a reformed, recognizable Other, leads to Pecola's schizophrenic state and Ralph's final and chosen exile.

NAIPAUL'S AND MORRISON'S CIRCULAR AND FRAGMENTED NARRATIVE STRUCTURE

Circular and fragmented narrative structures in *The Mimic Men* and *The Bluest Eye* crystallize the alienation and fragmentation that causes the characters to mimic the dominant societies in which they live. It can be seen that the cyclical structure of *The Mimic Men* in some respect resembles that of *The*

Bluest Eye. Morrison's narrators are like Naipaul's narrator and also continuously backtrack in pursuit of elusive points of origin, even as they attempt to pursue forward, linear development. Claudia, Pecola's friend, is Morrison's narrator. She represents the voice of resistance to the mimicry of the dominant society. Ralph and Claudia backtrack in the events to join the past with the present. Discarding straightforward chronology, Ralph and Claudia create a narrative in which past and present combine to bring about meaning in keeping with the workings of memory. Morrison's novels suggest that there is never enough information available to complete the narrated moment; the narrator must consistently begin again at some new place as if to force the various discontinuous sequences to converge upon the truth.

However, in Naipaul's novel, it is not so easy to bring order to a nation, or a man, so utterly confused by identity, chronically unable to make connections with anyone or anything. The disjointed narrative reflects these tragic senses of self-fragmentation and alienation, which are the key themes of *The Mimic Men*. The novel is not a narrative with a straightforward chronological sequence, and so it does not have a direct linear movement. It is instead a narrative of displacements and disjunctive repetitions. *The Mimic Men* is a novel that undermines coherent narratives. The *Mimic Men* is incredibly disjointed. Ralph's political career almost feels like an afterthought and is only sketchily addressed in the latter portions of the novel, after an extremely long section on his childhood, which sneaks up on the reader with no warning. One section has little relevance to the next, focusing on characters and situations (although the overall themes remain intact), while Ralph himself is the primary element that binds everything together.

The plot bounces from his student days to his return to the island, his childhood, and his halfhearted political career. Characters, once so influential in one section, such as his wife Sandra during his student days, are barely mentioned in the novel's latter half. However, the chaotic, ever-shifting feel of the novel is part of the more significant theme. Ralph is writing his memoirs to bring order to an inherently disordered existence, but the historical period he is intimately connected with does not lend itself to such an endeavor. Like his native land, the chaos lies everywhere.

However, if one cannot tell a single story, as these novels imply, then one must tell many stories that, held together synchronically in the reader's mind, might consequently illuminate one another. So, Toni Morrison's technique here is not that of the traditional family story, in which the lives of many characters lighten one another. According to Morrison's characters, the thread of origins disappears and fractures in the backwards expanse of generations, and a statement of failure forewords the story.

Naipaul's narrative technique in *The Mimic Men* is confusing and fragmented. In contrast, Morrison's narrative in *The Bluest Eye* is a complex, multiformed narrative. *The Bluest Eye* integrates several different forms of textuality. It opens with three different forms of its master epigraphic primer, several lines taken from an elementary school primer. That is followed by an italicized overture introducing the primary narrator, Claudia, and the different motives of the novel.

The novel consists of two related kinds of texts, variously intermingled: four seasonal sections, narrated in the first person by Claudia, and seven primer sections (employing various narrative voices), so named because each section is set off by an epigraph taken from the master epigraphic primer. The novel has a double point of view, both first and third person. In *The Bluest Eye*, the narrator, Claudia, conveys the child's painful point of view while an omniscient voice gives perspective.

Claudia reviews the history of the Breedloves' storefront apartment, she moves successively through the minds of the members of the Breedlove family during a violent morning confrontation. The primer sections are dedicated to Pauline, and Cholly Breedlove and Soaphead Church, and those sections focus on the *what* and *how* of their featured protagonists' experiences. However, even those sections are multivocal; here lies the difference between Naipaul's and Morrison's narratives: Morrison uses multivocal narration while Naipaul uses a single narrator. A single character narrates *The Mimic Men*, but wholly in the first person. The narrator is indulged in his self-deception as he always struggles for identity. The narrator's youth comprises only part of the novel, however. Naipaul prefers a more subtle narrative method and works with nuance and irony to create a sophisticated portrait of an emerging postcolonial migrant. Ralph, the narrator of *The Mimic Men*, expresses the pain, confusion, the compulsion to imitate other cultures, and the inability to create a satisfactory definition of self, which Naipaul believes the person (and nation) emerging from a colonial to an independent state must suffer.

Ralph's narrative procedure becomes the chief instrument of his recognition and the means of his transcendence of mimicry. Abandoning straightforward chronology, Ralph constructs a montage-like tripartite narrative in which past and present, in keeping with the workings of memory, interpenetrate to bring about meaning. The overlapping chronology serves to orient the readers in historical time and space while providing them with the narrator's personal story at the same time. Ralph, the first-person narrator, travels in memory from his studying days and marriage in England back to his childhood and political career in Isabella, a barely disguised Trinidad. Then he comes back again to his exile in London. Therefore, a circular journey prevails throughout the novel. The circular, confusing, and fragmented pattern of *The Mimic Men* artfully counterpoints the underlying psychological process. Ralph's memory becomes vaguer as his memory seems to shadow as the novel moves closer to the present. Facts become dense, and events become shadowy contingencies as Ralph himself withdraws further and further into the private world that casts him into shaded relief. Ralph tells his story to discover something—he wants to see whether it is possible to create some sense of order in his world out of the chaos of his memories.

The Bluest Eye is also fragmented, not only in its structure but also in its narrative voices. In the novel, there are the voices of Claudia as a little girl, Claudia's adult insights, and a third-person narrator who tells stories of the Breedlove family and the community around them. Also, there is the point of view of characters like Soaphead Church, Cholly and Pauline, the presence of Pauline's first-person narration and, by the end, a dialogue (or monologue) of a descended-into-madness Pecola and her imaginary friend. These fragmented structures and voices incite the reader to put together the pieces of the story, reflecting on the different perspectives presented to understand what happened. For example, Cholly, putting together his memories, shows him from a different point of view: he is not merely a perpetrator of violence but a victim himself. The multiplicity of voices and stories also work to avoid a totalizing view, which Morrison considers essential, given the diversity of African-American people and their culture.

Regarding voice, however, the primer sections are very different from the seasonal sections. In the former, Morrison employs the figural narration that is the continual usage of the third person. The authorial narrator here does not say "I," except when copying or impersonating one of her characters. From an authoritative position, Morrison reviews and highlights the biographies of Geraldine, Pauline, and Cholly. Therefore, the figural presentations are frequently qualified by authorial commentary, and the narration shifts from authorial to figural to the first person. This shifting in the narration reflects the fragmentation in the novel's structure.

The Bluest Eye was first published in 1970 when Morrison was thirty-nine years old. Like Claudia, Toni Morrison was born in Lorain, Ohio; exactly like Claudia, she would have been nine years old in 1940–1941, the year in which the events of the novel take place. Those similarities suggest that Claudia MacTeer is Morrison's persona in the novel—her fictional "second self." However, the primer sections, which make up about two-thirds of the novel, contain almost no reference to the speaker's person, and certainly no explicit identification of that authorial speaker as the grown-up Claudia MacTeer; therefore, no apparent linkage is evident between the primer sections and the seasonal sections. I would argue that the eye in the title contains multiple meanings: it is at once the eye longed for by Pecola Breedlove, and the "I" that authorizes the novel as a whole—the "bluest I" that witnesses Pecola's fate, Claudia MacTeer.

Now, one question that inevitably arises whenever an author writes using the first-person point of view is the extent to which the narrator represents the author's views and the extent to which he or she is a separate individual. This has been one of the problems to which critics have devoted much discussion in the case of Naipaul. Karl Miller writes:

> Perhaps the most important consideration is this: if Naipaul dissociates himself from his character, there is no way of being sure how far he dissociates himself. In the end, we must go by what is mostly there, by what the book will be read for. It will be read in the West Indies and the world at large for the feelings by which it is governed. It will not be read for its disclaimers and its cautionary touches. (Miller, 1977, 332)

By way of explanation, Ralph is a filter for his story, but his viewpoint may be Naipaul's. Naipaul's usage of the first-person point of view expresses his identification with his character. There is a similarity between Ralph's life and Naipaul's life. Both of them adopt 'European' or 'Western' views and imitate memoirs, stories, lives, and landscapes that are not their own. Ralph's identification with the West affects his identity. They abandon their own families, get married to English women, and adopt an English education. Also, both of them struggle to establish identity. Yearning for home, for identity, and stability, is deeply embedded in the human psyche. Naipaul, Ralph, and most of Naipaul's characters carry around a yearning for the wholeness of home to address the crisis of the self-questioning at heart. They seem to bear all the layers of their history and past: their Indian roots, their difficulty of being born in Trinidad, and their cosmopolitanism, which make them uprooted persons, adrift in two worlds to neither of which they could really belong.

Meanwhile, Morrison uses Claudia as her "I" and her mouthpiece in the novel as she is the rebellious African-American girl who is considered Morrison's hope. Consequently, Morrison identifies herself with the first-person voice of Claudia, who attempts to put on the white mask and to adapt to American society, but without absorbing its values and while keeping her blackness. Naipaul and Morrison identify themselves with the characters that are close to their lives and their nations. Gloomily, Claudia's "I" testifies to the community's pain and complicity in the destruction of Pecola, who is the symbol of African-American characters who are obsessed with and destroyed by the white myth of beauty.

Morrison clarifies this gloom and sadness in the title of her novel, *The Bluest Eye*. Morrison's title, like her point of view, has multiple layers of significance. As has been mentioned earlier, quite evidently, the title alludes to Pecola's only desire in life: to have blue eyes. These eyes, she believes, will bring about significant changes in her life by making her pretty and consequently change other people's attitudes toward her. However, Morrison is also punning, while indicating the "gloomy ego" of Pecola. Morrison wants to focus on the gloomy, depressed, and miserable self created while mimicking the dominant society. One cannot help thinking that the title also alludes to Claudia, Morrison's mouthpiece, who tears apart her hated white baby dolls to see what is behind their blank blue eyes to discover the secret of their lovability.

"Blue," in this case, does not merely mean "gloomy"; it means the Blues—the sweetly sad songs of loss and reconciliation originated by African-Americans in the United States. Also, the "eye" or "I" alludes to Pecola's insanity and fragmentation's impact on Claudia's understanding. In addition, the bluest eye may be a pun on "the bluest I," which means the most gloomy and miserable self. African-Americans often feel blue because of the oppression to which they are exposed from early on in life. Then, the novel is a blues song, enunciating the pain of African-Americans in America and an attempt to struggle with a pain that is sometimes existential. Therefore, the superlative "bluest" implies that other groups are "blue" and "bluer"—and, of course, the black race is the "bluest." Therefore, Naipaul and Morrison select words in their novels to mirror their ideas and cultures. Notice the diction, which underlines Ralph's fragmentation, failure, and weakness: "exhausted," "oppressed," "waste," "helplessness," "nothing to do," "drifted," and "dully." Moreover, after this unusual outburst of exclamations, Ralph emphasizes his dissociation from that which prompted them: "I belonged to none of their associations" (*MM*, 41).

His memories and culture include parts of himself, which he does not wish to acknowledge. Ralph narrates his story in a distanced, enervated monotone. He seems incapable of feeling anything toward the events of his life, which he describes as follows:

> After each of these journeys, I came back more *exhausted* than before, more *oppressed* by a feeling of waste and *helplessness* . . . having *nothing to do,* I *drifted* into the School and . . . I stood dully. (*MM*, 41; emphasis added)

Naipaul's narrative begins with a confusing and fragmenting succession of ideas and images from his memory, with no sense of chronology. There is seemingly no order to his presentation of this material (except the "order" of the unconscious). The chaos threatens Naipaul and Ralph in their minds. It becomes questionable whether living in London allows Naipaul and his Ralph to explain their worlds in a way that is helpful to the society from which they have departed, or, it may be said, to the community to which they have attached themselves. Ralph believes himself to be whole, complete, and "free," yet the tone of his narration remains that of the same enervated, disengaged discourse with which he began his writing project.

Naipaul's and Morrison's narrative techniques express the two writers' fragmentation and confusion, which are reflected in the representations of their characters. If Naipaul's and Morrison's characters' lives do not cohere, and if they defy attempts to structure them, their fragmented methods of narration and language themselves help in explaining the fragmentation of their nations that was caused by the mimicry of the dominant societies in which the writers and their characters live.

LANGUAGE AND MIMICRY

Naipaul's adoption of the English language while narrating his novel is also momentous. He adopts and imitates the English language in his writing, but he appropriates it in such a way that it can reflect his thoughts and the local reality. Postcolonial writing takes the dominant language, often English, and uses it to express the most profound issues of postcolonial social experience. This form of imitation thus becomes a form of resistance. Here, the most compelling interpretation of postcolonial resistance is resistance to the dominant language's absorption, appropriation, and transformation to represent postcolonial cultural identity. Language is, therefore, a significant element of identity and representation.

Naipaul adopts the English language but transforms it to bear the burden of his local realities. Naipaul's displacement from his roots enables him to understand the alienation and self-fragmentation of postcolonial people. Mimicry of the dominant societies' languages is a strategy by which indigenous writers of different backgrounds seek to interrogate the dominant literary and cultural traditions that give shape to their work. Naipaul, on the other hand, argues that Caribbean writers are themselves fictional characters because "their second-hand existence living in a borrowed culture" (Naipaul, 1962, 68) and their substitute literature make them "mimic men" of "the new world" (*MM*, 146). These writers start to represent themselves in the literary forms they have adopted from Europeans, and they successfully avoid the position of the silent object in colonialist representation.

I argue that, in literary forms, mimicry remains a critical approach to resistance and recreation. Many postcolonial writers now use English. They customize the language 'to bear' the burden of their cultural experiences. Moreover, one has to convey in a language that is not one's own. One has to communicate the various shades of omission of creation through movement that looks maltreated in an alien language. Therefore, postcolonial writers' imitation of the English language after independence is criticized as colonial betrayal. However, Naipaul's mimicry of the English language in his writing is not a betrayal of his origins, but a discovery of one's possibilities on an aspect of the inevitable of the Caribbean and postcolonial literature.

Thus, I would argue that Fanon and Naipaul agree that the one who has a language consequently possesses the world expressed and implied by that language. Therefore, Naipaul's adoption of the English language helps to reveal the most profound issues of postcolonial social experience. This form of imitation becomes a kind of resistance to the dominant language to celebrate a postcolonial cultural identity. Fanon emphasizes the critical role of language in the colonial relationship between imperial possession of language and the colonized's mimicry of that language:

> To speak means to be in a position to use a certain syntax, to grasp the morphology of this or that language, but it means above all to assume a culture, *to support the weight of civilization* . . . [a person] who has a language consequently possesses the world expressed and implied by that language. What we are getting at is plain: Mastery of language affords remarkable power. (Fanon, 1952, 17–18; emphasis and brackets added)

Fanon emphasizes the ordeal of colonized people, and their acculturation, through language. Fanon briefly explains that language cannot be quarantined from the world or culture in which it is embedded. It is this embeddedness in an imperial language and culture that Naipaul seeks to address in *The Mimic Men*. It is useful to approach Ralph's existential crisis through Fanon's understanding of the phenomenon of language and the colonized. In his essay "The Negro and Language," Fanon explores how involvement in an imperial culture and discourse results in a self-division of the colonized, played out through conditions of schizophrenia, cultural dislocation, and alienation. In Fanon's view, colonized persons inherit an inferiority complex when forced to surrender their local culture (language) and accept an imperial discourse (see Fanon, 1952, 17–40), and that is what happens to Morrison's Pecola in *The Bluest Eye*. She suffers from a schizophrenic state in which she is deeply concerned about achieving the white beauty she needs to be loved and to overcome her lack of presence. In this way, the better acculturated postcolonial people become in the "civilizing" discourse and cultural standards of the metropolis, the closer they are to becoming like the dominant group or the colonizer. The colonizers' education enforces and encourages such forms of mimicry. Implicit in the act of mimicry is the desire of the colonized to appropriate models of power to overcome their primal lack of power, of discourse, and presence.

Therefore, I agree that many postcolonial writers, whose primary language is not English, have chosen to write in English not because they regard their mother tongue as insufficient, but because the colonial language has become a useful means of expression, and one that reaches the broadest possible audience. Chinua Achebe also supports this argument concerning Naipaul when stating:

> For me, there is no other choice. I have been given this language, and I intend to use it. . . . I feel that the English will be able to carry the weight of my African experience. But it will have to be a new English still in full communion with its ancestral home, but altered to suit its new African surroundings. (Achebe, 1975, 103)

Naipaul and Morrison have adopted the English language as it is notably the new world language whose power derives from its historical use across the largest of the modern empires and from its use by the United States. However, Morrison shifts between "Black English Vernacular (BEV), which is the language of many African-Americans" (Yule, 1996, 243), and Standard English. Morrison employs the English language to cherish her African culture and folklore, and mixing Standard English, and BEV creates new means of communication that link the two societies—the dominant and the marginal.

Shifting between BEV and Standard English is clear in Pecola's language. Morrison uses Standard English to accomplish changes in voice, rhetoric, and narration to make the language express African-American culture she is describing. In so doing, she uses a rare grammatical construction in BEV in which some verbs have irregular past forms in Standard English so that Morrison reflects the vividness of her African-American society. These verbs have the same form for past and present tenses in "Black dialect" (Fasold and Shuy, 1970, 60). This dialect of alienation, difference, and disease directly reflects Pecola's state of mind, which mixes both BEV and Standard English.

In *The Bluest Eye*, the shift between BEV and Standard English marks the in-betweenness in which Pecola lives. Little Pecola presents an example; she speaks Standard English when she dips into insanity and BEV when she is not insane. Therefore, Pecola's language is fragmented as she tries to imitate Standard English when she is insane, which means when she thinks that she has blue eyes. However, as long as she is black Pecola, she speaks BEV because she believes that she is still the inferior black Pecola. For example, Pecola speaks to her friends, Claudia and Frieda, about the prostitutes:

> She *don't know I go* . . . *She don't bother nobody.* Then how come *your mama don't* let you go in her house if *she so nice?* . . . *She say* she's bad, *but they ain't bad.* (*BE*, 8, emphasis added)

In BEV, the "s" suffix is deleted from the word "don't" in the present tense when the subject is in the third person singular. Such is the case when Pecola states: "She don't know I go," instead of the standard, "she doesn't know I go." The verb "to be" is also missing from her declaration, "They all nice." She uses the familiar multiple negations in her sentence, "she doesn't bother nobody." She loses the third-person suffix "s" in "she say she's bad . . . ," (*BE*, 140). Here, as has been previously stated in the chapter, Morrison adopts Homi Bhabha's notion of mimicry as a menace to the dominant authority as mimicry of English language disfigures the standard form of the English language. Now Morrison uses (BEV) as a means of resisting the language of the dominant society in which she lives.

Pecola's language here is different from the language she uses in the last chapter when she goes mad. This passage imagines that she gets what she has always wanted: a pair of blue eyes, which symbolize her acceptance in a white world that demeans her black skin and culture. To convey the onslaught of this new blindness, Morrison depicts a scene in which Pecola has a conversation with an imagined friend whose words are rendered in italics. Absent from her syntax are the markers of black dialect. She omits multiple negations and the word "ain't" from her lexicon, and she uses subject-verb agreement and the verb "to be" correctly:

You're just jealous.

I am not.

You are. You wish you had them.

Ha. What would I look like with blue eyes?

Nothing much.

If you are going to keep this up, I may as well go on off by myself. (*BE*, 152)

This conversation evokes the image of a hall of mirrors. First, it represents Pecola's split and fragmented mind externalized. Her newfound imaginary friend verbalizes the doubt that Pecola has about her new eyes when she mocks this prized possession. Secondly, the friend functions as a mirror, not of conscience, but of imagined admiration, when Pecola refuses to consider the words of sarcasm and opposition. Finally, there is a linguistic mirror, and the conversation mimics dialogue without ever becoming it. After all, since the friend is not real, perhaps this conversation does not exist in the form it assumes on the page. Pecola's language thus articulates the chaotic and the fragmented psychological experience of seeing this self through the eyes of white society. I would expand this concept to add that Pecola's linguistic acquisition of two voices accompanies this shift in her mental vision. Not only are there the two voices (Pecola and her imaginary friend), but there are also the two dialects, Standard English and BEV, which Pecola uses before and during her madness. The Standard English voice marks a permanent shift; a shift in which her self-image is torn apart, and her self-identity is permanently criticized and judged through the eyes of the other. Therefore, Standard English signifies the fantasy and the ideal world of those with blue eyes.

Meanwhile, BEV is used by the characters who yearn to replicate the dominant white power. Therefore, language and style, as well as methods of narration, reflect Naipaul's and Morrison's central themes of fragmentation and mimicry. Morrison ranges from authorial commentary to figural narration to dramatic monologue. The absence of "I" in the primer sections can be taken as a sign of the unwillingness of the superior authorial persona to call attention to herself. Morrison also shifts to differing first-person narratives in this novel to portray how the various characters have become the way they are, thus providing understanding without insensitivity. Morrison cleverly emphasizes her conclusion by opening *The Bluest Eye* with what appears to be a paragraph from a child's reading primer: "Here is the house . . . " (*BE*, 1)

As mentioned before, the master epigraphic primer, or, more precisely, thematic heading, is repeated twice, each time becoming more chaotic as punctuation, capitalization, and spacing disappears, until the final version appears utterly incomprehensible. Morrison chiefly uses this domestic paradigm to focus attention on the difference between being brought up in dominant white American community as opposed to growing up in African-American community. The breakdown and fragmentation of the epigraph structure reflect the breakdown of home and family in *The Bluest Eye*. The novel's African-American and often broken, fragmented, and fractured families exist in stark contrast to the white middle class—the family in the Dick and Jane narrative. The lack of clarity and feeling of turbulence created by the unstructured paragraph mimics the sense of pressure that these outside ideals—which they can never live up to—place on the young, fragmented African-American characters.

Hereisthehouseltisgreenandwhiteithasareddoor.Itisveryprettyhereisthe familyMotherFatherDickandJaneliveinthegreenandwhitehousetheyare veryhappy. (*BE*, 2)

Similarly, *The Mimic Men*'s chaotic and confusing narrative structure mimics the sense of alienation, chaos, and disorder in the characters' psyche. Thus, Ralph feels he cannot write about the horrible experiences of the colonized because of the ineradicable pain in his soul. However, although Ralph is the protagonist, this is an account of that restlessness, which has created that sense of chaos and disorder in the psyches of all postcolonial migrants. Also, the motive behind such an endeavor is essential to note: as mentioned previously, to construct a new self—a new identity out of that chaos and disorder. Postcolonial migrants attempt to escape into an ideal, static vision of the self and deny their indigenous culture: "we mimic men of the new world" (*MM*, 146).

Like Morrison, who highlights her African-American culture using the English language, Naipaul also situates himself with a European tradition, but at an angle. His mimicking of the English language in his writing is not a mere imitation of the dominant colonial language, but a subversion of the authority of colonial language. By using the English language, Naipaul introduces the local reality, cultural identity, history, sorrow, suffering, and pains of postcolonial migrants and establishes his identity as a postcolonial writer all over the world. For Naipaul, adopting the English language is a mode of resistance.

Naipaul is aware of the harmful effects of mimicry in his novel, *The Mimic Men*; he uses English language to present a comic but sad view of the terrifying position and contradictions and defects of the mimic people, such as Ralph. These fragmented characters lose their identities and ability to think by imitating the imperial authority's values, traditions, and norms. Mimicry gives them partial and fragmented identities that make them alienated from their communities, family, and inner selves. Their alienation is the consequence of the vivid, imaginative life created and sustained by the alien influence of imperial knowledge and power. They attempt to escape into an ideal, static vision of the self and deny the continuity of life in postcolonial societies. Similarly, Morrison's Pecola decides to reject her life as an inferior African-American girl, and she decides to escape into an imaginary, ideal, and beautiful world of American white society.

MIMICRY BETWEEN SUBMISSION AND RESISTANCE

Mimicry as Submission: Naipaul and Morrison

Naipaul and Morrison represent two patterns of submissive characters who are entirely dedicated and attached to the dominant societies in which they live. In *The Mimic Men*, Naipaul portrays Ralph Singh as an intelligent and sensitive person confused by Isabella's history of slavery that has left the island with a "taint." Naipaul also stresses the fact that Ralph wishes to escape from his East Indian immigrant history, in which he "is the late intruder, the picturesque Asiatic, linked to "neither" (*MM*, 8), and serves to complete a "little bastard world" (*MM*, 122). As a result, the inhabitants of Isabella (Trinidad) compose "a haphazard, disordered and mixed society" (*MM*, 55).

In *The Bluest Eye*, Morrison creates Pecola to be a prominent symbol of African-Americans that cannot put down roots in American soil. More universally, Morrison is writing about the human soil, a soil perhaps "of the entire country" (*BE*, 160). Because she is dealing with Pecola's dead baby as if it is the fruit of the human soil, she arranges the course of her novel according to the four seasons. In *The Mimic Men,* Naipaul portrays a vivid picture of postcolonial migrants who lose their autonomous cultural identity under the influence of mimicry. Naipaul opens his novel with a very vivid description of the mimicry:

> I paid Mr Shylock three guineas a week for a tall, multimirrored, book-shaped room with a coffin-like wardrobe ... I thought Mr Shylock looked distinguished like a lawyer or businessman or politicians ... I offered Mr Shylock my fullest, silent companion. (*MM*, 7)

This profoundly ironic passage uncovers the way mimicry works. The complexity of the potential insurgency of mimicry emerges in the above passage. Ralph, the main character in the novel, copies the habits of the landlord and mimics his manners. Naipaul's allusion to Shakespeare's Jewish Shylock suggests both the tenor of the colonial experience and the vagaries of diasporic condition. In other words, Naipaul wants the reader to correlate Ralph to Mr Shylock because both of them have similar colonial and diasporic experiences. Therefore, Shylock is not a model to imitate, but Shylock is a historical correlative for Ralph.

The novel begins with Ralph as a student in England in his multimirrored room. Naipaul summarizes Ralph's psyche in the previous sentence. The multiform of the mirror reflects the pluralized selves that Ralph encounters. His recognition of his splitting self and the multiple positions he occupies foregrounds the ambivalence of his subjectivity. Ralph faces the problem of being utterly unable to create an original identity caught between helplessly imitating and submitting to the colonizer or returning to the colonizers' roles imposed on the likes of him. Ralph's awareness of himself as someone trapped in a position of dependence on the dominant power for his identity is gained when he is in London.

As on a theatrical stage where every action of the player originates from a playwright, Ralph's actions also arise from the influence of the colonizer. Bhabha discusses the adoption of roles by persons with a postcolonial past via the notion of mimicry. This mimicry describes well the tendency of the colonized to imitate roles typical of the culture of the colonizer. In Ralph's case, those roles are exemplified by the roles of a student, a dandy, a husband, a businessman, and a politician. Ralph throws himself into the roles listed above, and each time he thinks that he has found order and stability in his life, or that he has finally been able to find a harmonious identity, although the truth is that these roles represent only a part of his identity and consciousness.

Pecola also tries to submit to and to imitate white culture but is incapable of struggling anymore through her painful and frustrating life and retreats into schizophrenia. Pecola goes deeper into a world of fantasy, rejecting the everyday world as a result of the dangerous circumstances of her life. She is, therefore, shown to be weak-minded, backwards, and powerless. She is assassinated by her family and white American dominant society because she simply does not exist. As Morrison states: even the self-appointed psychic is "wholly convinced that if black people were more like white people, they would be better off" (Morrison, 1977, 473). Soaphead Church, in a god-like manner, "grants" Pecola her only wish of having blue eyes, which only she will see. She prefers to escape and to withdraw from her fragmented society, which refuses her and chooses to believe that she has blue eyes.

Naipaul's Ralph also chooses to throw himself into escaping from his fragmented and chaotic Trinidadian culture, and the idea of living in disorder and chaos prevails throughout the novel. Naipaul reflects his feelings toward his homeland in the novel. Naipaul always emphasizes that Isabella (Trinidad) is the source of anarchy, and it is a fragmented and inorganic community in which there is no relationship between the land and its inhabitants. He means that formerly colonized people are not loyal to their land because the colonizers are the source of unity and order. Therefore, postcolonial people live in a conflict in which they struggle between imitating the colonizers and celebrating their identities. By showing the fragmented social structure of society in *The Mimic Men*, Naipaul portrays postcolonial migrants as being trapped in the various threads of multicultural interactions and colonial mechanics. Here, in a colonial society, the hybridization of cultures does not mean sharing different cultures, but establishing one particular dominant culture.

The dispossession and displacement that the uprooted, marginalized, diasporic, and indigenous people are subjected to bring them into a state of anguish, and they find that mimicry is the only way out. Caught up in that limbotic situation, immigrants lose not only their native place but also their identities. Consequently, the sense of alienation, fragmentation, and confusion controls their lives and minds. Their efforts to establish their identity by putting down roots in culturally alien society prompt them to try various alternatives to gain status. Naipaul and Morrison seem to believe that in such a society, evolving out of slavery and colonialism, no balanced or comfortable acculturation is possible, and mimicry of the colonial authority is evident.

There exists no opportunity to start anew, and there are no new and unsettling conceptualizations of identity to discover. Imitation of the colonizer's cultural habits, values, and assumptions makes them hollow people and dehumanizes and alienates their social, cultural, political, and linguistic identity. The anguished awareness of this cultural dislocation and the quest for a coherent social identity inadvertently seduces indigenous people to appropriate the value systems of the dominant society. Ralph's submissive fascination with colonial culture, subtended by feelings of shame and self-loathing, leads him to refer disdainfully to his Indian name. His family name is Singh and his father's name is Kripal. However, his own name is Ranjit, and his birth certificate says that his name is Ranjit Kripalsingh. "*I broke Kripalsingh into two, correctly reviving an ancient fracture* . . . gave myself the further name of *Ralph* . . . and signed myself R. R. K." (*MM*, 100; emphasis added).

Ralph accepts the Western European view as the only correct one. He disdains his given Indian name, Ranjit Kripalsingh, breaking it into two parts and adding Ralph's Western name. Here, Ralph is devastating his present from the very beginning of his life by separating himself from his past. When he changes his name to Ralph, he is mystifying his present. Moreover, by breaking his family name into two parts, he declines his history and splits his identity. Ralph, therefore, in this way, denies his present and his past to mimic the colonial power. This mimicry only serves to disorientate Ralph and dislocate his sense of place and history, creating a permanent dualism within him.

Therefore, one should not be surprised at his inevitable failure. He finds himself in a cycle of action and reaction that continually feeds on mimicry. His failure in imitating English culture leads him to a fragmented and confused identity. The colonized "can never succeed in becoming identified with the colonizer, nor even in copying his role correctly" (*MM*, 124). Ralph continues to try and play this role because he finds no authentic alternative identity, no matter where he travels, what company he keeps, or what he does. His world reaches the end foretold by T. S. Eliot in "The Hollow Man" (1925):

> This is the way the world ends
> Not with a bang but a whimper.

Pecola's tragedy is the dramatic consequence of the internalization of the system of values of dominant white society, which leads to the marginalization and self-fragmentation of black individuals. These values are perpetuated through the scapegoating of the weakest and most vulnerable members of the community. Pecola also tries to find shelter and a way out. She finds this way out in a fantasy world—a way to carry on. Her imaginary friend is a survival strategy. That is why when she asks her alter ego why she did not come before, it answers her, "You didn't need me before" (*BE*, 154). Pecola can deny her painful experiences in her dream world, especially those of sexual and physical abuse. When Pecola has a monologue with her fragmented self about her incestuous rape, she denies that it happened: "He just tried, see? He didn't do anything. You hear me?" (*BE*, 157).

Pecola's society has taught her not merely to want to be beautiful but to be the most beautiful of all, for only in such supremacy can she erase the lack of affection, the constant lack of approval. At the end of the novel, Claudia realizes how both the community and themselves have failed Pecola and have been participants in her victimization: "All of our waste which we dumped on her and which she absorbed" (*BE*, 162–163). Pecola is not the only victim of self-denial, yet she is the only character that falls into madness as a result of her desire to mimic American beauty. Alternatively, Ralph's life of mass culture has made the process of self-denial a satisfying experience. His position as a person, who mimics the colonizer, is not something that he willingly chooses; rather, he mimics English culture because he has no alternative. However, he enjoys moving from one role to another role. Ralph comes to London with the aspiration to search for an original identity, but finds himself reduced to an unreal, insubstantial character walking about in a too solid, too real city. Indeed, the Pecola and Ralph characters are represented as either double or Other through their internalization of colonial discourses. Nevertheless, instead of (consciously) mimicking the colonial authority, Pecola becomes a total "double" of her desired object with the bluest eye, but only through her schizophrenic identification.

Naipaul represents the submissive face of mimicry exemplified in Ralph's attitude toward adopting the colonizer's roles. Naipaul's Ralph and Morrison's Pecola try hard to establish accepted identities by mimicking their dominant societies but fail. When they fail, they escape and withdraw from their communities as a strategy to defend themselves against the dangers of their being that are the consequences of their failure to achieve a secure sense of their own identity. There cannot be a healing process for Pecola if she does not learn to accept and love herself. Like the marigolds that Claudia and Frieda plant, she cannot grow. Throughout the novel, Pecola does not gain awareness of the psychological origins of her split-off self. Morrison claims that an individual or community identity cannot be acquired as long as those individuals and communities acquiesce in and conform to the oppressive definitions of mainstream culture. Pecola is one of Morrison's irreversible lunatics who cannot bear it anymore. Such characters go crazy because the inhumane situations they have to live in finally break them. Naipaul and Morrison present two submissive characters who are caught in limbo, and they learn mimicry as their first strategy to escape their fragmentation. However, Morrison is different from Naipaul, as, at one point, she represents the two faces of mimicry, which are exemplified by the submissive Pecola and the resisting Claudia.

Mimicry and Morrison's Resistance

Claudia MacTeer epitomizes Bhabha's conception of a successful mimic—the one who adopts the mask of the dominant culture without absorbing its values. Unlike Pecola, Naipaul's Ralph, and other submissive characters, Claudia is the narrator and Pecola's friend who refuses to mimic white culture. When she recalls her former disenchantment with white idols like Shirley Temple, Claudia also imparts her awareness that white beauty does not exist, that it is valorized, and therefore that it exists only through its effects. She even vents her hatred of white idols onto white baby dolls by dismembering and deconstructing them to eagerly know "the secret of the magic they weaved on others. What made people look at them and say, Awwwww, but not for me? The eye slide of black women as they approached them on the street and the possessive gentleness of their touch as they handled them" (*BE*, 22). Claudia remembers:

> I destroyed white baby dolls.... The truly horrifying thing was the transference of the same impulses to little white girls. The indifference with which I could have axed them was shaken only by my desire to do so. (*BE*, 23)

Nonetheless, Claudia finally submits to society's adoration of white beauty when she develops a liking for Shirley Temple. Ironically, she utilizes her new dedication to expose the mechanism through which the dominant society, both directly and indirectly, forces mimicry on African-American culture. Claudia remarks: "I learned much later to worship [Shirley Temple], just as I learned to delight in cleanliness, knowing, even as I learned, that the change was an adjustment without improvement" (*BE*, 22; bracket added). I can relate Claudia's adjustment to the conflict trick of camouflage: in the same way as the child hides behind a nonexistent wall, the mimic seeks false resemblance of the dominant culture. Claudia's headstrong acceptance of white beauty is understood in her awareness of its "mottled" presence, mottled in the sense that, like camouflage, it takes advantage of absent spaces.

Significantly, the form of mimicry present in Morrison's *The Bluest Eye* affects a covert disruption of the binary opposition of black and white. In intentionally adopting the mask of whiteness, Claudia becomes more aware of its existence as a valorized social construct. While Claudia's narrative does not support any form of beauty based on skin color, it does show women's obsession with the myth of white beauty. For example, the secret of the ugliness endorsed by girls like Claudia, her sister Frieda, and Pecola is to be found in the way publicized images enforce hierarchies of beauty. Hence, African-American girls with thinner features and lighter skin color have a better chance of being recognized because they bear a resemblance to a prioritized form of white beauty.

In contrast to Pecola, Claudia refuses to conform to the dominant culture's model of beauty. Indeed, in a ritualistic act, she even tears apart a white doll she has received as a present for Christmas. Unlike the Breedloves, Claudia's family, the MacTeers, still keep common values. They take Pecola in when she is raped, even though their financial situation is complicated. In the MacTeer family, Morrison illustrates that the values that can sustain and provide the guidelines for growth are not alien to the community. Therefore, Claudia herself displays her family values when she defends Pecola from some boys who are bullying her or when she despises Maureen's sense of superiority for being light-skinned.

Claudia and her family demonstrate the ability of African-Americans to confront and rebel against an oppressive system. Claudia explains how it is hard to escape from the cultural images (inscribed on commodities) that idolize blue-eyed white faces and white values: "all the world had agreed that a blue-eyed, yellow-haired, pink-skinned doll was what every girl child treasured" (*BE*, 20). Without understanding the racism that makes the world adore white baby dolls, as a young child Claudia dismembers her white baby dolls to discover the secret of their desirability and beauty. Even though Claudia is a resistant character who "questions the impulse to mimic" (Grewal, 1997, 118), Claudia does not keep herself apart from the commodity/consumer culture validating racism.

Despite the hatred that she expressed for white baby dolls in her childhood, the novel reveals that Claudia eventually succumbs to the pleasure of consuming white cultural images. The novel does not specify how Claudia got to adore white images, but her narration clarifies that the transformation of her psyche has been achieved through commodities like Shirley Temple cups. "I learned much later to worship her" (*BE*, 22). In other words, Pecola and Frieda are African-American characters who try to imitate and to absorb cultural icons depicting physical beauty: dolls, magazines, movies, window signs, billboards, newspapers, and drinking cups. Claudia [I] could not join Pecola and Frieda in their adoration because 'I' (Claudia) hated Shirley. To the girls, Shirley Temple represents everything that society finds adorable—everything worth having. Frieda and Pecola innocently long for Shirley's attributes but—quite as innocently—what Claudia "felt at that time was unsullied hatred" (*BE*, 19; brackets added).

The adult Claudia says that she had not yet arrived at the turning point in the development of her psyche which would allow her to love Shirley Temple. This juncture, to be sure, is the point when we become mature, when we accept the material reality of the world around us and so learn to adjust to our physical and mental surroundings. Looking back at her development, the adult Claudia thus reasons that her hatred for Shirley Temple and blue-eyed baby dolls are not unfounded: "What was I supposed to do with it? Pretend I was its mother?" (*BE*, 20).

Such a question wittily dramatizes the psychological complexity of growing up as a black child. Where Frieda and Pecola find the experience of playing with dolls pleasurable, Claudia, encountering nothing but pain and mortification, is understandably moved to rebel. Claudia tells us how she destroyed white baby dolls, and how those same impulses could then have led her to axe little white girls. "What made people look at them," she asks, "and say, 'Awwwww,' but not for me?" (*BE*, 36).

In *The Bluest Eye*, Claudia survives all the forces that so tragically destroy Pecola. Although Claudia is puzzled and persistently frustrated by the ubiquitous daily messages which tell her that she is also a nothing, she is Pecola's antibook, for the former has the essential family support that the latter lacks. Bombarded by white images on cultural products, African-Americans are repeatedly introduced into colonial discourses, justifying African-Americans' inferiority in American society.

In the novel, Morrison adequately explains that contemporary black individuals internalize racist ideologies: "The *master* has said, You are *ugly* people" (*BE*, 34, emphasis added). Here, the master does not mean white colonizers anymore but refers to racist ideologies inscribed on commodities and every poster, every movie, every glimpse that interpellate black individuals as spiritually colonized subjects.

In *The Bluest Eye*, Claudia MacTeer can be described as a rebellious character who speaks of alternative culture and resistance. For example, by revisiting her childhood rage against blond, blue-eyed dolls, "Claudia highlights her resistance to the socialization and acculturation that cripples Pecola and other characters." Moreover, she questions the impulse to mimic, accurately perceiving it as a desire the environment persuades her to internalize. Claudia's narration assists the reader in better understanding the social process of white culture, mystifying its values and colonizing the minds of African-Americans. However, Claudia is by no means a defiant character who shows an alternative culture or any form of freedom to black communities. The MacTeer household is not the site of "true funk" in that they give white dolls to the girl at Christmas and laugh at Mr Henry's joking identification of Claudia and Frieda as Greta Garbo and Ginger Rogers.

More specifically, despite her childhood rage against white dolls, the novel makes it clear that when Claudia learns to adore white images, she learns only to feel ashamed of the curiosity that led to her disinterested violence against white dolls/girls and that her failures to accept without question the standards of white America is considered repulsive. The most hopeful message which Claudia's narration conveys to readers is her awareness that she has made "adjustment without improvement." Claudia's ability to articulate her awareness more or less reveals that she is once again critical of the structures of society that create racial self-loathing. However, Claudia is not a heroic rebel who speaks of change and resistance, and I think Morrison does not intend to create such a politically conscious character in her first novel. Morrison and Claudia share an authorial mission, which is recording the reality of African-Americans, not through the political lens of the Black Power Movement but via an artistic gaze.

At the end of the novel, Claudia realizes how both they and the community have destroyed Pecola and have victimized her: "All of our waste which we dumped on her and which she absorbed" (*BE*, 162–63). There is advancement in her recognition of their part in Pecola's ordeal. Morrison shows Claudia's passage to adulthood as a contrast to the unfortunate Pecola's entrapment in trauma. Whereas Naipaul's Ralph and Morrison's Pecola represent only the mimetic patterns that withdraw and escape from their society, Morrison's Claudia is one of the true survivors of this story and, in her awareness and honesty, we can expect some hope for the future.

To conclude, unexpectedly, Naipaul is still plagued by the same feeling of placelessness in London. Naipaul states: "London is my metropolitan center, it is my commercial center, and yet I know that it is a kind of limbo and that I am a refugee in the sense that I am always peripheral" (Hamilton, 1997, 126). His "shipwreck" is still greater, still more disastrous in the "promised land" of London; no place is home. Ralph's position between home and homelessness reflects that his identity is unfixed, unstable, and changing. He has gained an identity as a permanently exiled writer without a fixed home; his identity is open, not limited. However, his "open" and fluid identity brings not ecstatic freedom but exile's ultimate trauma. Similarly, Pecola's isolation from herself, from who she is, from what she looks like, surfaces again in the recognition that she cannot even see her worth or beauty, nor will she ever be able to see it. The lack of awareness of her beauty contributes to her destruction. If she did not accept other people's idea of beauty, she would see her raw human beauty. Again, her opportunities to see it, to struggle for growth, remain minimal, although present.

Fanon's first phase of unqualified assimilation or what Bhabha calls mimicry is presented differently in Naipaul's and Morrison's texts. For Naipaul, the stage of mimicry is expected; it is a dilemma that constitutes postcolonial experience, and even though it makes it easier for postcolonial people to maneuver in the dominant culture, part of the colonial's past experience has to be sacrificed in the process. According to Naipaul, while mimicking the colonizer, "the past has to be denied, the self-despised" (Naipaul, 1962, 67). In *The Mimic Men,* Naipaul portrays how white European culture mimicry becomes natural to postcolonial people. Naipaul asserts his unique colonial experience through his writing; he represents mainly postcolonial migrants very much like himself. Ralph's life, to a great extent, mimics Naipaul's life, whereas Pecola and Claudia do not mimic Morrison's life.

Naipaul experiences an actual colonial life, whereas Morrison does not. Morrison recalls her ancestors' painful experience of slavery. Naipaul and Morrison both suggest that the marginalized who aspire to the world of the colonizer or the dominant culture will experience the torments of hell. Naipaul and Morrison present the characters who try their best to imitate the dominant societies in which they live, but this mimicry fails to determine identity as these characters tend to withdraw. However, the difference between Naipaul and Morrison at this stage is that Morrison presents the two faces of mimicry—the submissive and the subversive aspects. On the one hand, she presents Pecola as representative of the oppressed black race who are humiliated by the dominant white society. On the other hand, Morrison gives her readers hope by creating the character of the rebellious Claudia—an African-American girl who refuses the concept of mimicry and praises her blackness.

Naipaul provides the example of Ralph Singh, the main character in his novel, who fails to perform any of the roles he adopts. Although he fails to reconnect himself to India, the homeland, or to connect himself to London, the metropolis, by writing his memoirs, Ralph Singh finally takes control of his sense of dislocation as he realizes that there is no ideal place with which he can identify himself. His final detachment is an expression of a distance from any clear-cut national identity or notion of home. Hence, in *The Mimic Men*, home can never ultimately be more than the books that Ralph writes or, perhaps more precisely, the action of writing them.

Slavery, the Middle Passage, colonialism, and migration caused people to dislocate from their country or place of origin (old world) to undergo the traumatic experience of alienation in areas of the 'new world.' They struggled to relocate and feel at home and to have experiences in the 'new world.' The intense feeling of alienation did not facilitate their belonging to the new space or cultivate an urge to rebuild the notion of home. Thus, they resort to mimicking the new world to challenge the ambivalent nature of their existence.

Ralph and Pecola attempt to mimic the dominant communities in which they live. Unreceptively, Ralph seeks order, and Pecola seeks white beauty. Order and beauty are the two primarily sought characteristics of the dominant societies. After many attempts to mimic the dominant power or culture, Ralph and Pecola fail to assimilate into the dominant culture or to celebrate their identities. In conclusion, Ralph and Naipaul examine and analyze the colonial and postcolonial periods, historical, cultural, and political backgrounds, economic problems, and psychological conflicts and finally conclude that writing can be decolonization itself. Ralph realizes that formerly colonized societies like Isabella suffer from lack of cultural, historical, and racial homogeneity. Pecola believes that she has the blue eyes needed to assimilate into white society, but still has black eyes and skin. By the end, their sense of fragmentation and loss are still sustained. Although *The Bluest Eye* and *The Mimic Men* can be related to Fanon's first phase of mimicry, Morrison's mimicry is different from Naipaul's, as while Morrison represents submission and resistance, Naipaul only represents the submissive side of mimicry.

NOTES

1. According to Wallace Fowlie, in *A Reading in Dante's Inferno*, "Limbo is the first circle of the Hell in which the suspended spirits who are excluded from Heaven and from the other parts of Hell. They live in desire but without hope" (Fowlie, 1981, 42).

2. Medusa was often imagined in [Greek] mythology as a powerful, serpent-like woman who is said to be a symbol of woman's power. In most myths, Medusa is ugly, with snakes and serpents as hair tendrils/locks curling round a hideous face which never saw the sun. She had the power to turn whoever looked at her into stone. (Whitt and Perlich, 2014, 129; brackets added)

Chapter Three

Memory as a Reflection of Cultural Identity in V.S. Naipaul's *The Enigma of Arrival* and Toni Morrison's *Beloved*

In their published work, and especially their historical novels, Toni Morrison and V.S. Naipaul have attempted, and to some extent have succeeded, in a worthy endeavor of rewriting the past as well as redescribing the world from their respective positions of nationality, cultural tradition, and indigenous experience. Whereas the first phase of Fanon's theory, mimicry, emphasizes that indigenous writers are entirely assimilated into the dominant power, indigenous intellectuals return to their memories to revive their past in the second phase of the theory.

After discussing mimicry in the previous chapter, I will focus on the second phase of recalling the past, which Naipaul and Morrison have recreated in their works, specifically in their historical novels: Morrison's *Beloved* and Naipaul's *The Enigma of Arrival*. I will shed light on the second phase of Fanon's theory, where he maintains that indigenous intellectuals grow dissatisfied with imitating the colonizers or the dominant power and instead celebrate their own original culture's authentic traditions and practices in their quest for identity. Indigenous writers become concerned with the past, memory, folk traditions, customs, rituals, and myths and legends of their nation and try to use these concepts as an initial step toward the formation of a new identity. Here, Naipaul and Morrison use memory, vision, and indigenous culture as the primary technical devices that tie their past to their present from different perspectives.

Memories have always had a substantial effect on persuading and mobilizing people into collective adventures, such as battles, wars, alliances, diasporas, or genocides. How people define themselves, what they believe in, and what they do with their cultural and political power depend on their response to past experiences. Stressing the close relationship between identity and memories, John Gillis maintains:

> The notion of identity depends on the idea of memory and vice versa. The core meaning of any individual or group identity, namely, a sense of sameness over time and space, is prevailed by remembering; and what is remembered is defined by the assumed identity . . . identity and memories are highly selective, inscriptive rather than descriptive, serving interests and ideological positions. (Gillis, 1994, 3–4)

Memory can bridge a temporal distance between past, present, and future. Furthermore, both memory and identity can be understood as the symbolic interplay of past experiences in the sense that individuals, groups, and communities manage a selection of past events to validate present choices. 'Who we are' and 'who we want to be' are questions often answered while searching for and constructing a cultural identity. Consequently, the appearance of memory is not possible without the negotiation of conflicting meanings and the legitimization of memory narrative. In the course of rendering their past, Naipaul and Morrison imagine, as well as repattern, actual and fictional materials to recreate and reconstruct the reality of a historical past that might not otherwise be reached. Naipaul's and Morrison's use of memory as a resource thus brings together the communal past and the present. Resorting to narrative strategies commonly practiced in fiction writing, historians construct the past by narrating historical and past experiences in the form of a meaningful story.

Approaching the past from a different direction, fiction writers come by and sort out actual and historical materials to translate and recast them in an imaginary setting. Therefore, repatterning history manifests a process of re-defamiliarising and readjusting documentary data into various kinds of matrices. One kind is not more correct than the other, but rather a different constituent of the same and coherent picture of the historical past. The importance of going back to the past lies in its significance as an effective way of resistance against mimicry or assimilation. Hence, Fanon's second phase of constructing a cultural identity relies on recalling the past of indigenous people. Stuart Hall and Fanon state that the past continues to speak to us. But it no longer addresses us as a simple, factual 'past,' since our relation to it, like the child's relation to the mother, is always-already 'after the break.' It is always constructed through memory, fantasy, narrative, and myth.

In other words, the quest for a cultural identity on the part of the newly emancipated subject has evoked a rephrasing of past and forgotten communal histories. The process of past recovery has been achieved through the (re)construction of erased ethnic and cultural traditions, which are exemplified by myth, fantasy, and memory. In so doing, Morrison, and Naipaul present an alternative vision of the world and reality that challenges the organization and authority of dominant social groups. By inventively interpreting and repatterning historical documents, Naipaul and Morrison have recreated a historical reality that transmits and incorporates their personal and cultural experience. In my view, personal memory as history puts pressure on dominant historical narratives—history itself is always a narrative and never a mere collection of objective data about the past. As thus stated, history is continually rectified and transformed to fulfill individual interpretations and the requests of today and tomorrow. Living in a "community . . . away from home [will make] the communal mind remember, [and] memory is active . . . in exile" (Farah, 2009; brackets added).

Explicitly, Morrison's novels take advantage of "ripping the veil" and "masking African-American history" (Morrison, 1987b, 110), which has been discredited and has been "quiet as it's kept" (*BE,* 4). Similarly, Naipaul is committed to seeing one "little chasm filled" (Naipaul, V.S. [1987] *The Enigma of Arrival,* 149, hereafter cited as *EA*) after another in his literary journey to light up "areas of darkness" in the history of his diasporic worlds (Naipaul, 2004b, 183). In Naipaul's semiautobiographical *The Enigma of Arrival,* a middle-aged unnamed Indian writer leaves his homeland of Trinidad and ends up in a cottage on the grounds of a Victorian country estate in Wiltshire, England. He invents an unnamed protagonist who mediates freely between the living and the dead.

The title of the novel is borrowed from an early surrealist painting by Giorgio de Chirico, an Italian surrealist artist. De Chirico's painting *The Enigma of the Arrival and the Afternoon,* chosen to serve as the title of the novel, seems to inspire the whole of Naipaul's *The Enigma of Arrival.* With its depiction of an ancient Mediterranean seaport, as the narrator interprets it, the painting suggests the story of a visitor who arrives at an ancient port city and begins a journey of self-discovery that moves toward an unforeseen ending. In other words, the painting represents "the scene of desolation and mystery; it speaks of the mystery of arrival" (*EA,* 98).

The Enigma of Arrival is a narrative of the discoveries and changing perceptions of its unnamed narrator as he lives in this English cottage for ten years. Learning to see the countryside and its seasonal changes, he finds himself feeling a sense of harmony with a place that contrasts sharply with the dislocation and estrangement that have marked most of his previous life, both as a child in Trinidad and as a student and eventually a successful writer in England. For the first time, he can accept the realities of change and death.

Morrison's *Beloved* is set against the background of slavery in the American South in the period at once before and following the Civil War (1861–1865). Toni Morrison looks at the writing of her novel, *Beloved,* as a revisionist history, where she projects a truthful account of the fugitive slave mother Margaret Garner, who killed her daughter to save her from the horrific life of the institution of slavery. *Beloved* is a story about the ghost of a baby girl killed by Sethe, her mother. The baby receives her name only after her death. As a ghost, Beloved also has the features of a real person. She can eat, drink, and love. There are some other ghosts in the novel, for example, the souls of the ancestors roaming in the valley. Morrison uses the relationship between the past and present, death and life, and between the spirit and the material world. *Beloved*'s narrative is mainly concerned with the painful rebirth of buried memory and repressed psychological motivation. *Beloved* is thus significantly informed by the dualities of master and slave, colonizers and the colonized, power and powerlessness, which have dominated the lives, identities, and relationships of all *Beloved*'s main African-American characters, for example, Paul D. and Sethe. The character of Beloved is a symbol of the painful slavery memories that are forgotten and buried.

By imagining and repatterning historical materials, Morrison gives voice to those collective memories that are unspoken in classic slave narratives. These collective memories can be defined as the conscious historical and cultural knowledge common to a group of people. This shared knowledge is transmitted from generation to generation through the use of traditional oral forms. It is a function of telling stories that provide living testaments to ensure the group's continued survival. In an interview with Bonnie Angelo, Morrison remarked that the enslavement of African people is something that no one wants to remember. She stated:

> It . . . got to be the least read of all the books I'd written because it is about something that the characters don't want to remember, black people, don't want to remember, white people, don't want to remember. I mean it's national amnesia. (Morrison, 1989, 120)

Morrison's notion of 'rememory'—a hybrid of 'remembering' and 'memory'—describes her approach to the past as being a stable, active power in the present that helps African-Americans to root themselves into American society. However, *Beloved*'s main characters, such as Sethe, must take a journey back to the past to confront their trauma and thereby discover their primal place and to be able to find a place and a home in the present. Morrison uses this connection between place and trauma to illustrate individual traumatic memories as representations of a larger historical trauma: If Sethe's memories exist in the world as fragments of a historical memory, then, by extension, the individual process of recollection or 'rememory' can be reproduced on a historical level.

The resistance of memories is confirmed by Sethe, who consistently fights back the painful events of the past in her "rememory." This struggle with the brain that keeps her "not interested in the future" can be seen in the following passage where Sethe chides her memory for its persistence of recalling disturbing things:

> I just ate and can't hold another bite? I am full, God damn it of two boys with mossy teeth, one sucking on my breast, the other holding me down, their reading teacher watching and writing it up. (Morrison, Toni [1987a] *Beloved*, 8, hereafter cited as *B*)

These painful memories create the necessary bridge that leads to the characters' healing, the central point of the novel. Memory, a phenomenon of primary importance in an oral tradition, becomes a political and cultural statement in *Beloved*, evidenced by Morrison's combination of folktale and remembered history. Also, Naipaul transforms authentic blackness or darkness into a historical knowledge of the different cultures that have made him. For example, Naipaul's view of history and time is repeated and utopian, and his vision remains apart from the revolutionary aspects of postcolonial discourse. Naipaul's comprehensive view of time and history sees how empires and kingdoms rise and fall. In this way, Naipaul evades becoming trapped in dualism and in-betweenness, choosing instead to make the dialectic of cultural politics his subject.

In *The Enigma of Arrival*, Naipaul stresses that a land of decay and junk replaces the English pastoral countryside in the literary world. Lamenting the death of British empire in a place with its glory gone, the unnamed narrator looks at the hedge around Jack's garden as "a vestige, a memory of another kind of house and garden and street, a token of something more complete, more ideal" (*EA*, 16). What causes his disillusionment is a stranger's expectation of perfection and of "an unchanging world"—an opinion he will soon revise (*EA*, 32). With the notion of "flux and constancy of change," the unnamed narrator learns to overcome distress in death or a departure and to rethink the "idea of ruin and dereliction, of out-of-placeness" (*EA*, 54) and rootlessness.

However, the traumatic memories of the past will not quickly become lighter or die suddenly; they are reinforced instead in the growing wish and effort to address them in the world of literature. In their texts, *Beloved* and *The Enigma of Arrival*, respectively, Naipaul and Morrison investigate the mazes of the infamous Middle Passage and slavery, of dislocation and diaspora, and of precolonial, colonial, and postcolonial experience, each of which has the potential to evoke traumatic memories. Interestingly, each title provides a critical metaphor that foregrounds the concept of past that the novels perceive—that is, a historical past can be assumed as Morrison's dearly beloved and Naipaul's unresolved enigma.

It is also worth noting that when the state of enigma or beloved is associated with and superimposed by time past, present, and future, a degree of understanding rises to the surface. In other words, history can be interpreted as an enigmatic picture of past experience, which will be valued and taken into the future. To be more specific, in *Beloved*, history and past are the legacy of slavery unacknowledged in classic slave narratives. In *The Enigma of Arrival*, history and the past could represent the ignorance of the diasporic self, community, and the whole world. The main difference between Naipaul and Morrison lies in their cultural backgrounds. By way of explanation, and as mentioned earlier in the first chapter, Toni Morrison does not have an actual colonial experience, but Naipaul experiences actual English colonialism. However, Naipaul seems to be more fragmented—as are all his characters—than Morrison. One can notice that Morrison tries to be connected to her roots, although she has not been to her original native Africa before. Nevertheless, Naipaul does not have a sense of belonging to his cultural backgrounds as much as Morrison. Therefore, Naipaul's negligence of his nation's past and Morrison's interconnectedness with her ancestors' past will be apparent in their novels' themes, characterization, and literary techniques.

The Enigma of Arrival expresses Naipaul's reaction to England and supplies images, which both conform to and defy traditional conceptions of it. It embodies a complex of conflicting attitudes toward England, based partly on a distinction between past and present, town and country, fantasy and reality because it is the former imperial center. The novel narrates the process of an initial disillusionment with England. The unnamed narrator states: "I was still in a kind of limbo" (*EA*, 7). Nonetheless, the preconceptions with which Naipaul emigrated are exposed as inadequate. Naipaul's preoccupation with historical facts enables him to interweave his personal past into his diasporic worlds' sociocultural and geopolitical histories.

Beloved reveals the oppressed history of slavery, as depicted in the novel, and discusses how female characters are oppressed in both patriarchal societies as well as within slavery. The novel traces out this figure's origins in the shameful act of Sethe's prostitution; explores Beloved's parasitical existence; shows the chaos wrought by wholesale resistance to memory, and points toward the possible cure afforded by memory. Morrison confronts and gives life to slavery as an essential yet forgotten moment in American history. Giving life to that past requires a creative effort that is itself a proper function of memory. However, Morrison's creative memory goes further, calling for general resistance to the past to aid in discarding much of it and selecting what is significant to preserve.

RECALLING THE PAST

Naipaul and Morrison represent in their fiction the forgotten, suppressed, and untapped past through the creation of memory and writing. Morrison tries to recall the past that she never experienced, and Naipaul recalls his past from different cultures to which he himself was exposed. The past is brought up through rememory in Morrison's *Beloved,* in the sense that rememory imagines in the present what happened or what might have happened in the past, and that rememory is a reservoir of historical experiences that need to be continuously reinterpreted and healed. The past is built from traces left by the memories and unwritten stories about a place or a person in Naipaul's *The Enigma of Arrival,* which celebrates his search for identity through documented interpretations of historical traces and imaginative stories.

Whether it is slavery, diaspora, or postcolonial experience, to render the past frequently associated with displacement, dislocation, or chaos stirs up traumatic memories that stop possibilities and hopes for the present and future. A memory of the past depends on dynamic, cognitive, social, and neurological factors in complex interaction. What is remembered is what one intends to remember. Memory examines, selects, assembles, and constructs past experience, and all of these activities cannot be done without imagination—that is, imagining which memories are most pertinent to represent a particular aspect of reality in the past. As such, memory is gifted with a narrative quality and an artistic freedom for literary re-creation.

Naipaul and Morrison have demonstrated different ways of fictionalizing history. Working on fragmented and broken memories to different degrees, Naipaul and Morrison discover an interest in imaginatively recasting the past to overcome and move beyond it. Hence, memory is envisioned "less as a pure source of illumination than as an enabling context, a prelude to insights generated by the imagination in the present" (Jay, 1984, 147). Motivated by the memory of the past alongside the present need, history always takes on new meaning and significance. In short, Morrison turns to rememory, and Naipaul works on historical traces of British empire. In other words, Naipaul hesitates between his past and present, but Morrison incorporates her past with her present.

Evoking the Past in Naipaul's In-betweenness and Ambivalence and Morrison's Rootedness

Whereas Naipaul's unnamed narrator in *The Enigma of Arrival* moves to the imperial or to the global capital to find out about his past, in *Beloved,* Morrison's Sethe goes deep into her black ancestors' roots to find her identity. Meanwhile, Naipaul's enigmatic past creates his major sense of in-betweenness, and Morrison's dedication to her beloved past emphasizes her rootedness. In chapter 2 of this book, Naipaul's and Morrison's in-betweenness is emphasized. However, in the following section, I will explore the differences between Naipaul and Morrison through comparing Naipaul's continual state of in-betweenness and Morrison's rootedness. Naipaul and the unnamed narrator of *The Enigma of Arrival* are the amalgamation of cultures and civilizations: Hindu, Trinidadian (West-Indian), and English. Their fragmented identities have been shaped by their ethnic heritage and their experiences as intellectuals and writers—by their travel and life around the world—in the Caribbean, South America, Africa, Asia, England, and the United States. Naipaul and his narrator retain ties with Trinidad, where they were born and grew up, and with England, where they studied and lived, on and off, during their adult years, but these ties do not fix their identity. Naipaul's unnamed narrator maintains: "I had lived with the idea of change, had seen it as constant, had seen a world in flux" (*EA*, 57).

In *The Enigma of Arrival*, then, the old dualistic separation between the metropolitan world and postcolonial world that has dominated human relationships in Naipaul's work has lost its force and no longer dominates the author's consciousness. Naipaul embraces a postcolonial humanism that does not refute the shaping power of place and culture but goes beyond national and local boundaries in its allegiances to life and human struggle. The world today is becoming a global world of branching communities, mixing, and hybridity that defies borders. In this sense, and from the very beginning, Naipaul and his narrator recognize and examine the special "incompleteness" (*EA*, 157), or in-betweenness of subject position and identity.

In the world of Naipaul and his narrator's childhood, this incompleteness comes from their incomplete knowledge of their native Trinidad; from their equally fragmented connection to a Hindu community far from India, which struggles to preserve its attachment to an India of nostalgic imagination; and, finally, from their bookish and abstract knowledge of England acquired through their colonial education. Homeless in all places, the unnamed narrator ultimately arrives at a different sense of home, and this is the true "arrival" referenced in the title of *The Enigma*:

> [Human beings] need history; it helps them to have an idea of who they are. But history, like sanctity, can reside in the heart; it is enough that there is something there. (*EA*, 353–354; brackets added)

In Morrison's journey of waking the dead from the past in her *Beloved*, the characters, as though on a slave ship, are "suspended between the nastiness of life and the meanness of the dead" (*B*, 3–4). The novel is full of characters without a sense of time, unable to tell linear narratives. Morrison says that she prefers to "develop parts out of pieces . . . preferred them unconnected—to be related but not to touch, to circle, not line up" (Morrison, 1987b, 123). The failure to remember and to gather the fragments of their damaged pasts leaves the characters, particularly Sethe, locked in their particular houses of memory. Ironically, they remain unable to remember, bereft of stories to pass on, at the mercy of the underworld. If the underworld goddess, Persephone, is the Greek queen of the place of memory, then Morrison not only enters her domain in *Beloved*, but she arrives there in much the same manner. Morrison will go "narrow and deep" into her ancestors' past to awaken the dead, painful memories (Morrison, 1988, 5).

Although Sethe's murder of her child appears to be the main action of *Beloved*, the way she learns to remember and shape her story is equally important. Her struggle becomes a model for all of those who are drawn into the dynamic of memory. Slavery is an ancient and dreadful experience, which had adverse effects on those enslaved physically and psychologically. Morrison depicts Sethe as a heroic woman who sheds a positive light on resistance to slavery. As not everything from the past needs to be part of the present, some painful memories ought to be warded off and resisted. The final warding off of *Beloved* allows a new paradigm of memory to emerge for a dispossessed people reluctant to remember, and in danger of being consumed by the past. Because the written history of the slaves as recorded in their narratives does not "give total access to the unwritten interior life of these people" (Morrison, 1987b, 111), Morrison divines and imagines that interior life because she did not experience slavery herself.

In contrast to Morrison's writings, most of Naipaul's fiction and nonfiction writings depend on an autobiographical substance to provide the overlapping accounts of his diasporic and fragmented life. In my view, the writing of an autobiography is shaped by the interaction between the desire to state a connection between the past and present self—to establish endurance over time, which could be thought of as defining the very notion of identity—and an opposing sense of distance from the earlier self. Therefore, *The Enigma of Arrival* combines elements of fiction and nonfiction and blends autobiography with fictional material not directly concerning the personality of the author. However, Naipaul states in *The Enigma of Arrival*: "my journey, the writer's journey" (*EA*, 309). The novel intertwines a description of Naipaul's development as a writer with a detailed narrative of rebirth in the Wiltshire countryside. However, by creating an unnamed narrator as the protagonist, Naipaul symbolizes all postcolonial migrants, including Naipaul himself, who leave their homeland and choose to be attached to their new, dominant culture. Moreover, making his protagonist a writer (of memoirs, of novels), Naipaul problematizes, more thoroughly and self-consciously than in previous novels, the process of writing the past, showing how human memory misremembers the past, and portraying "Englishness" as a literary and textual construct. Naipaul uses the consciousness of homesickness to point out the pitfalls of building an identity based upon the dominant culture and portrays the lives of most migrants who try to build an identity in the dominant society in which they have come to settle. He shows how they tend to feel alienated and adrift. Naipaul asserts:

> We had made ourselves anew. . . . There was no ship of antique to take us back. We come out of the nightmare, and there was nowhere else to go. (*EA*, 352)

Like Naipaul, while depicting the fragmented life of most postcolonial migrants, Morrison's *Beloved* depicts the painful life of Sethe, who represents black slaves both before and after the end of slavery. Morrison, in *Beloved*, more intensively and overtly addresses the issue of black identity than in any of her other novels by delineating a process of self-liberation within the colonial context of slavery, which makes it possible to read the novel as a postcolonial text.

The portrayal of Sethe's life represents the lives of various slaves. Thus, *Beloved* is taken to look through the traumatic situation carefully, recognize where the damage has been done, and then finally live without denying its scars.

Beloved's narrative, which is primarily concerned with the painful resurrection or rebirth of buried memory and repressed psychological motivation, is thus crucially informed by the paradigms of master and slave, colonizer and colonized, power and powerlessness, which have dominated the lives, identities, and relationships of all the African-American characters who are always unhomely, humiliated, dislocated, and confused. Sethe states: "Masters not only work, kill, or maim you" (*B*, 215).

Likewise, Naipaul's characters always have a sense of dislocation and unhomeliness and live in a state of fragmentation, so they move from one place to another, hoping to find somewhere to belong. Naipaul stresses these themes of loss and in-betweenness through his unnamed narrator in *The Enigma of Arrival*. The narrator is unnamed to emphasize that he has no identity and he has no home. After lamenting the death of the old British empire, the unnamed narrator tries to find a home in Trinidad. Naipaul's past experience will be clear in his narrator's first trip back to Trinidad after six frustrating years as an unpublished writer in England. Despite the temporal distance, Naipaul's first homecoming voyage is re-enacted and repatterned in the text. In *The Enigma of Arrival*, the narrator recounts:

[At] that first return, I had moved from place to place, to see it shrink from the place I had known in my childhood, and adolescence. (*EA*, 166; brackets added)

This quote reveals an epiphanic moment for the unnamed narrator and perhaps for Naipaul himself, who once thought that his home country's geographical and intellectual smallness not only confined but also threatened his ambition to become a writer. Naipaul emphasizes the theme of in-betweenness while explaining his narrator's transformation from place to place as if he does not feel safe. For Morrison, then, the return of the dead past is an overture to burial. A refusal to bury leaves the dead uncovered, nearby, exposed, and in a place between the living and the dead. This in-between state is similar to Naipaul's and is very much present in *Beloved* when Sethe refuses to let the child she has killed remain unburied. However, in the form of the figure Beloved (the killed child), the forgotten past is also trying to seize and consume the present ordinary concerns of the characters, particularly those of Sethe. If the resistance to memory is something to overcome, it may also be what protects the self from returning from a past that threatens revenge. Resistance is a reminder that going back to the past is dangerous, as doing so might turn African-Americans' vision so far inward that they can no longer live out their lives in the present. Thus, Morrison's swinging between waking her past and burying it does not go on, as she prefers to wake up her ancestors' past rather than bury it. Here lies the difference between Naipaul and Morrison—Naipaul shifts between his past and his present, but Morrison's past leads her to a sense of rootedness.

By emphasizing her African-American characters' memories in *Beloved*, Morrison unveils an American historical landscape of trauma and thus offers new possibilities on unspeakable American history. History is intrapsychic in Morrison's *Beloved* because it is channelled through rememory—a kind of vivid flashback that overwhelms Sethe at unpredictable moments, triggered by simple things such as chamomile sap sticking against her legs. Scenes of domination, subjection, and cruelty are all part of Sethe's rememory scenes that are too awful to be told. However, unless they are told, Sethe does not own the story and cannot master it. Therefore, past is shown not so much as repressed, but silenced and frozen in time.

Whereas Morrison uses her people's historical memories to unveil the past, Naipaul's *The Enigma of Arrival* is usually read as a fictional autobiography in which Naipaul interweaves and replays his own transatlantic memories of his childhood past in Trinidad and his living and writing in Britain. However, fictional autobiographies are simply one possible mode of self-representation. In *The Enigma of Arrival*, Naipaul reveals a thoughtful pending of reconstructing "a composite history and remaking the world for oneself at least in literary work because men need history; it helps them to have an idea of who they are" (*EA*, 386). Therefore, both Naipaul and Morrison use their own ways to unveil their past.

In their novels, Naipaul and Morrison have transformed the past into the hope for a meaningful future. Working on disrupted histories and broken memories, Naipaul and Morrison have revealed an intention to recast imaginatively the past to overcome and move beyond it. Motivated by the memory of the past alongside the present request, history always takes on new connotations and significance. Free from the concreteness of historical evidence, and free to take the wings of imagination to deliver history in fiction, Naipaul and Morrison have demonstrated different ways of fictionalizing history. Fiction and history are fertile grounds of experience where memory and imagination work together. Therefore, in short, Morrison turns to rememory, and Naipaul works on historical traces.

Morrison employs her ruse of memory to reconstruct the past. Only imagination can help her in the creative process of the invention. However, looking to the past is not an end in itself: Morrison overcomes her unwillingness to return to a fragmented past because the present amnesia is an obstacle to the psychological wholeness of an entire nation. Despite Morrison's reluctance to remember the history of slavery, she takes up, carefully yet resolutely, the task of restoring the very figures of that history to construct her and her people's cultural identity.

However, Naipaul's *The Enigma of Arrival* reflects his instability and the ambivalent enigmatic attitudes that arise from cultural dislocation. His hybrid text makes use of both postcolonial and postmodern elements. It demonstrates Fanon's postcolonial subjects' quest for personal history and the need for historicism as a basis for creating an identity. *The Enigma of Arrival* is complex and unsettling, full of ambivalence and contradiction. It is possible to explain the tension of the novel as a sense of "instability," flux and dislocation linked to the autobiography of postcolonial self on the one hand, and the desire to engage in the past, aesthetics, and illusion of stability associated with the romanticized country estate and country-house novel tradition on the other.

The Enigma of Arrival reflects on postcolonial identity, emerging as a consequence of British empire because the condition of Naipaul's migration is seen as a state of in-betweenness as Homi Bhabha would call it, and the immigrant is seen as the critical observer into their own condition. Therefore, the novel sheds light on distinctions between several assumed oppositions. These oppositions can be exemplified by history and fiction merging; the death of British empire and rebirthof a new postcolonial world; fantasies of England overlapping with fantasies of Trinidad; a "stranger" who builds his home in the heart of England and documents a "kinship" between himself and his seeming "opposite in every way" (*EA*, 191), and the English landlord of the country estate.

Naipaul's and Morrison's protagonists' problematic relationships with places and home can be traced back to their original displacement from their homelands. For Morrison, the Middle Passage left African people disoriented, displaced, and dispossessed of their African identity and knowledge of self. The Middle Passage is an in-between space—the movement from home to the hell of slavery—and as such marks the split of the self between one's old and new identities. Beloved's explanation of the Middle Passage as a founding event of American and African-American history defies representation within the bounds of a conventionally linear historical narrative. The girl's traumatic memory is mysterious and fragmented; like the bodies of the living and dead lying ambiguously on top of each other in the hull of the ship, her recollections are but fragments of memory lying around in shambles in her mind. By having Beloved narrate the Middle Passage in such a manner, Morrison wakes up the dead past, which is symbolized by Beloved, who unveils the truth behind the Middle Passage.

While Naipaul and his unnamed narrator are still torn between the enigmatic past, the chaotic present, and the unknown future, Morrison and her character Sethe struggle to reconcile their past so that they and all African-Americans may survive into the new future. Morrison, in this way, decides to take the responsibility to remember to make African-American people fully understand the haunting legacy of slavery. In contrast, Naipaul lives in an unsolved enigma and cannot arrive at or reach his past. The concept of Naipaul's mysterious past is evident in his unnamed narrator's in-betweenness. The narrator (Naipaul) hesitates between past and present. Naipaul's feeling of "in-betweenness" results from the fact that his relationship with his current environment and his incomplete view and understanding of place, so carefully examined in *The Enigma of Arrival*, cannot root him in that place nor justify his presence in it. Naipaul's views of home and exile correspond rather well to what Edward Said describes in "Reflections on Exile" as the distinctive features of a displaced person.

In contrast to the legitimate and rooted inhabitant, the exile is, as Said states, neither here nor there, but rather in-between things. Memories draw Naipaul back to his place of origin, while the new environment offers itself to full view but denies him emotional access. Unable to recall the loss of place, the exile then embraces the very notion of "in-betweenness," or being nowhere at all, thus turning this conceptual and experiential "nowhere" into a form of creative strength. In *Beloved*, Morrison brings the dead to life, only to bury them in the end. As a point of contrast to Morrison, who laments her ancestors' history, Naipaul laments the death of British empire and asserts the death of the Hindu rituals.

Past, Death, and Identity

While analyzing the two novels by Naipaul and Morrison, I notice that they both utilize the concept of death as connected with their past. However, they employ the concept of death differently according to each one's cultural background. As mentioned earlier in this chapter, Naipaul's and Morrison's *Beloved* and *The Enigma of Arrival*, respectively, can be related to Fanon's second phase of identity—the phase in which indigenous writers will recall their past to reconcile with their present and future. Therefore, Naipaul and Morrison recall their past using the concept of death but in different ways. Morrison uses the theme of waking the dead, but Naipaul prefers to lament his own dead past and the past of British empire.

In *Beloved,* Morrison is giving birth to her ancestors' past, which is considered a part of American history. The dead past, which represents black cultural identity, needs to be remembered. This past is conceived of as feminine; thus, the theme of what Morrison calls the dead girl is central. The dead girl clarifies all the themes of fragmentation, a haunting past, memory, resistance, bearing witness, and discarding, which are treated in the novel. Morrison imagines the space of the displaced self in *Beloved* through the projection into the earth of the ghostly figure, Beloved. She is an image of the dead girl that takes on flesh, raising with her all those questions about what makes a woman displace the self. The dead girl especially haunts women who have killed a part of themselves in the name of love with the best of intentions. There is something wrong in the act of remembering that can lead a woman to place, as Morrison argues, all the value of her life in something outside herself.

In *Beloved,* a living past has been cut off from the loving self, resulting in a deadened past and a divided self that demands to be remembered. Raising the dead is only one aspect of memory—just as important is the discarding aspect of reconstructing a narrative. Discarding takes on an element of exorcism when the figure Beloved mysteriously explodes before a community that confronts her. The purifying confrontation is a kind of burial. Since Morrison's reviving of the dead past cannot help but include memories, which must be discarded from present consciousness, those memories have the power to haunt unless laid to rest in some way. Indeed, Morrison sees it as part of her creative task of memory to release the present precisely from any haunting. Morrison's identification and discarding processes involve both putting an end to a haunting past and honoring the dead, some of whom are forgotten ancestors that should be remembered. Therefore, it is her responsibility to bury what has gone unceremoniously buried.

In comparison to Morrison's attempts to revive her ancestors' dead past, Naipaul's novelistic exploration of English pastoralism signals the former colonial's "arrival" as a significant literary figure in postimperial Britain as it simultaneously presents the author as an "intruder" upon an English scene now past its prime. Naipaul is burying his West-Indian past and history. In *The Enigma of Arrival*, Naipaul sheds light on a particular area of his background, England, where he has lived almost all his life. With the idea of flux dominating Naipaul and his narrator's minds in all matters, the narrator has gained a keen perception of Jack the gardener's life and death, which helps him re-envision Jack's past and the pastoral history of England. Feeling "a cycle has been completed," the narrator is ready to leave the rented cottage at the end of "Jack's Garden"—the first section of the novel (*EA*, 98). It seems that everything the narrator is viewing, from the gardens to the cows, is meditated through constant comparing and contrasting between England as the perfect pastoral idyll and Trinidad as an imperfect small island that enforces the sense of dislocation. So here, Naipaul is lamenting England's pastoral past, and at the same time, he mingles in his personal past with England's past to stress the relationship between himself and the old empire.

Throughout the narrator's journey in the novel, Naipaul attempts to connect his narrator with the places around him. Naipaul wants to create a relationship between his narrator and the place or the landscape so as not to feel like a stranger or alien. Often read as Naipaul's autobiography in disguise, "The Journey," the centerpiece and the second part of *The Enigma of Arrival*, describes another kind of cycle—a structural representation of the incorporation of the pre-Wiltshire existence into the rebirth at Wiltshire. "The Journey" starts with a description of de Chirico's surrealist painting, *The Enigma of Arrival and the Afternoon*, which I have mentioned earlier in the chapter. De Chirico's *Enigma* becomes an accurate representation of the troubled mind of Naipaul's narrator, his desperate quest for roots and a sense of belonging as the unnamed narrator states: "I felt that an indirect, poetical way the title referred to something in my own experience" (*EA*, 98).

Echoing the journey that Naipaul took at the age of eighteen from Trinidad to Oxford, the supposed journey that "had seeded all the others" would pave the way for the narrator's "second childhood of seeing and learning" at the Waldenshaw cottage in the English countryside (*EA*, 113, 93). As a writer-in-exile wandering among continents, the unnamed narrator of the *Enigma of Arrival* has a psychological need to attach himself in flux and mark himself in history. Memory and the past are for Naipaul a kind of lost sacred ground, which one has to leave behind and subsequently attempt to remake. *The Enigma of Arrival* recounts this process of remaking certainties and rituals in response to the migrant's uncertainties of migrant life. Naipaul's conclusion is that home is a fantasy one has to undo to remember its original meaning and its original "sanctity," as he puts it. Throughout the novel, this departure, not only from his native Trinidad but from the very notion of "home," is represented as the discovery of a relationship to a particular landscape, wherever it is and whatever national label it may carry. Hence, Naipaul's subject reflects extraterritoriality, which is neither here nor there, but rather in-between things.

Naipaul's sense of aversion for his colonial land and his interest in the world beyond India and Trinidad increased throughout his colonial education. Cultural figures and products like Shakespeare's dramas and Wordsworth's poetry, and the imagery of the English landscape, all generated in the young Naipaul senses of in-betweenness, fragmentation, and cultural displacement, which are explored in detail in his *The Enigma of Arrival*. His British colonial education in Trinidad on the one hand, and the isolation of his Indo-Trinidadian family on the other, generated a sense of dichotomy between the culture and place he belonged to and what he considered to be the civilized world: "I developed a fantasy of civilization as something existing away from this area of barbarity. The barbarity was double: the barbarity of my family and the barbarity outside" (Levine, 1977, 93). The word 'fantasy' shows that the dichotomy between colonizers and the colonized is more an assumption than one based on facts. Indeed, the representation of England in the colonial education system and books made him dream about a world free from the social and cultural issues of Naipaul's birthplace. In effect, Naipaul, as a young man, developed a sense of in-betweenness and cultural displacement, which is pervasively reflected in his fictional, nonfictional, and autobiographical writings.

While past and memory are lost and dead for Naipaul, they are Morrison's goals and treasures, although she does not experience any of those painful memories of slavery. Morrison's attempt to bury the painful past in *Beloved* releases the living from the underlying furies that, having been dishonored, seek revenge. However, before Morrison can bury the dead, she must first engage with the dangers of having raised them. There is a danger that disturbing the dead will further arouse them, as well as a danger that the past will become—to the characters charged to remember it—too attractive to bury. In other words, Morrison must confront precisely the desire to hold onto the past—a tenaciousness that springs from injury and resentment. The character of Beloved, who symbolizes the African past, in her very name, foregrounds a wish to remain loved; indeed, part of the epigraph to the novel states: "I will call her Beloved who was not beloved" (*B*, 20), suggesting the tendency to hold onto things that are not lovable in the name of love. Therefore, I would argue that although Beloved does hold the novel's characters in her thrall for a time, the final resistance to her power is not the same as the resistance to memory and the past itself.

Nonetheless, memory is configured as a kind of subconscious, underworld place of the psyche in which the dead and forgotten past dwells. Indeed, in *Beloved*, the past is dead, and consequently, the characters, disconnected from any source of life, are kinds of shades residing in a fruitless underworld. Morrison's excavation into memory and its attendant resistance evokes a whole underworld of images as an attempt to clarify and ritualize proper, fruitful relations to the past. For Morrison, memory is a kind of forgotten underworld containing the remains of all that has been lost to present consciousness: the identity, the feminine, the interior lives of black slaves, and the numerous partial selves.

The process of recovering the forgotten requires not just the confrontation of a painful past, but the resistance that is attendant upon any looking inward or looking back—a resistance that is both a condition of memory and offers support to assure the memory's continued existence. In other words, more than just a dilemma to be overcome, the resistance of memory is, in fact, an essential additive function. In Toni Morrison's *Beloved,* the forgotten is beginning to be remembered, having for some time been avoided. Nevertheless, in *The Enigma of Arrival,* there is always "some kind of exchange in the individual's life, he points out, and [the unnamed narrator] himself has had to pay for his sojourn in the woods with the sense of decay and loss that now dominates his thoughts and blocks his creativity" (*EA,* 88). After his sister's death, the narrator returns to Trinidad and is struck by the changes that have occurred there: the "sacred world" of the Indian villages of his childhood has vanished, and the island has been transformed, remade in an industrialized, late-twentieth-century image.

Naipaul is pained by both an intimate loss and the seeming death and loss of a past, but at the same time, he is released from an idea (about the former colony, about the metropolis, about his self, and his relationship to others) that has long held him in its grasp. His violent dreams cease, his melancholy dissipates. With a new dedication to life and man as the mystery, the true religion of men, the grief, and the glory, he becomes again a doer, faced with real death, and with this new wonder about men. The narrator concludes, "I laid aside my drafts and hesitations and began to write very fast about Jack and his garden" (*EA,* 354). While *The Enigma of Arrival* records the death of old ways of thinking and the change of old traditions and responses to change in a postcolonial world, *Beloved* records ways of reviving and remembering the death of the traumatic past of slavery. Therefore, Morrison's reviving of her ancestors' traumatic and dead past will be responsible for a change in the present and the future of African-American society.

NAIPAUL'S AND MORRISON'S
NARRATIVE TECHNIQUES

After exploring the relationship between cultural identity, memory, Naipaul's enigmatic past, and Morrison's ancestral past, it is essential to examine the connection of these themes and ideas to the actual narrative techniques used in the two novels. As stated earlier in this chapter, Morrison recalls her unseen past, whereas Naipaul traces his own colonial past. Morrison is supposed to have a mysterious past because she does not experience it directly herself but, surprisingly, she tries her best to go deep and dig into her roots to unveil her unspeakable past to the whole world. In contrast, Naipaul, who had an actual colonial experience, tends to neglect his past and traditions, even though he is the one with an enigmatic and vague past to explore.

Under the second phase of Fanon's theory, Naipaul and Morrison recall their past to search for their identities. In this sense, Naipaul stands in the position of in-betweenness. Morrison revives her ancestors' dead memories while Naipaul recalls England's past, and he interweaves it with his fragmented personal past. Thus, Morrison's appreciation of her past and Naipaul's in-betweenness appear in the narrative techniques used in their texts, which both of them utilize in their process of self-healing.

Naipaul uses a circular structure and metanarrative to arrive safely in any land to which he can belong. *The Enigma of Arrival*'s techniques disclose Naipaul's double distancing from Trinidad and England, which is his second home. Through his travels, which provide "spiritual nourishment," the narrator offers a link between two places and commands a double vision of home and abroad. Being a product of colonialism, like his Indian ancestors who were displaced to Trinidad under British rule, he is fit to explore the colonial encounter between Britain and one of her colonies, Trinidad. I agree that Naipaul's works represent as truthfully as possible the situation in the postcolonial world. From a comprehensive study of Naipaul's autobiography, his travel writings, and fiction, the central theme of his fiction work is a lifelong process of self-creation, an individual narrative of a search for truth that incorporates the historical and social framework it is enacted.

It is not difficult to understand Sethe's narrative in *Beloved* as Morrison's politically motivated rewriting of black history of slavery. In *Beloved*, Morrison uses her own techniques such as slave narrative, folklore, and nonlinear structure to amplify her authorial voice by rewriting the memory of a black slave mother who did not have sufficient language through which to tell the story of her infanticide. In other words, Morrison is determined to take back the authority and power of representation by giving the narrative voice to the black slave mother and rewriting the white master's narrative.

However, Morrison's authorial power in *Beloved* raises the question: can the authorized Morrison truly represent Sethe, who was a silenced slave mother?

Morrison in *Beloved* is politically determined to represent African-American history in America and to "find and expose a truth about the interior life of people who didn't write it" since "no slave society in the history of the world wrote more—more thoughtfully—about its own enslavement" (Morrison, 1987b, 109, 113). However, through Morrison's act of rewriting black history, it is not her representational power, but the mode of resistant black identity within the colonial space of slavery, that Morrison magnifies to contemporary readers. In other words, while Morrison rewrites the troubled memory of a black slave mother back into the historical context of slavery, more importantly, she configures resistant black identity right in the colonial space, and brings to light the history of African-Americans who resisted their harsh reality and maintained their self-authority.

As a point of similarity, Naipaul and Morrison disrupt the conventional structure of the novel. They use circular and nonlinear structures for the sake of recalling their past. However, they employ these structures differently. The primary tool of the nonlinear structure is using flashbacks to recall Naipaul's postcolonial past and Morrison's ancestral past. As stated earlier, while Morrison uses flashbacks to remind her readers of the past through fragmented and scattered images of black identity, ancestral culture, and black family unit, Naipaul's usage of flashbacks strengthens his senses of in-betweenness and fragmentation. Both Naipaul's and Morrison's usage of flashbacks creates circularity in both of their novels under study here.

The Enigma of Arrival's circular structure, mirroring a theme of the cycle of death and rebirth, begins with a dedication to Naipaul's brother, Shiva, who died suddenly in 1985, and ends with a description, in fictional mode, of the narrator's sister's death in Trinidad in 1984. This event parallels the actual death of Naipaul's sister, Sati, and signals the "birth" of *The Enigma of Arrival*. Naipaul and Morrison use flashbacks but for different purposes.

Naipaul's usage of flashbacks emphasizes his senses of in-betweenness and hesitation between his past and present, old and New England, and Trinidad and England. In contrast, Morrison's flashbacks are used continuously throughout the entire novel, forcing readers to stay engaged in both the story's past and present. All of the primary characters in *Beloved* are attached to their past in some way, and the past fuels many of the main events. Therefore, the flashback pulls the reader into the past and describes the events in much better detail.

On the other hand, written retrospectively and divided into five sections, *The Enigma of Arrival* takes place throughout Naipaul's ten-year residence in a cottage in the village of Waldenshaw in Wiltshire. Naipaul manages to frustrate the reader's expectations in his novel. The novel begins with a description of a landscape, which prompts an integral process of memory, thought, and feeling; and the end-point within the insight, recognition of loss and moral decision. *The Enigma of Arrival* is devoid of the traditional plot, characters, chronological order of events, and action.

A product of English colonialism, Naipaul was caught between an engraved desire for an English identity and a need for a national identity. Therefore, leitmotifs of flux, shipwreck, journey, void, and death enhance the paradox of creation and destruction, creativity and illusion, freedom and entanglement, as well as arrival and drifting. The metanarrative reflects the void at the heart of Naipaul's vision of life. In *The Enigma of Arrival*, the metanarrative, which means the story within a story, establishes the closeness between the fictional protagonist's development and the everyday world of publication, distribution, and reception. The novel consistently draws attention to its own strategies and techniques for world-making. At the same time, it remains a realistic work because of the fictional world that resembles our own. This resemblance is so close that, at times, the fictional world and our own world collapse into each other. This collapse relies partly on the tendency of the book toward autobiography: the worlds of the unnamed narrator of *The Enigma of Arrival* easily collapse into the everyday world inhabited by V.S. Naipaul because the narrator is to a large extent, Naipaul. His protagonist repeatedly attempts to write a novel called *The Enigma of Arrival*. The unnamed narrator says:

> I had thought for years about a book like *The Enigma of Arrival* . . . the story had become more personal: my journey, the writer's journey . . . the writer and the man are separating at the beginning of the journey and coming together again in a second life just before the end. (*EA*, 344)

In this sense, Naipaul reflects his fragmented and in-between cultural background. Using the metanarrative as his primary technique in writing his enigma, Naipaul is stressing his double consciousness by creating a character within the main character and a story within the main story of his novel. Naipaul is blurring his narrative by using a vague technique of metanarrative to describe his colonial past in the voice of his fragmented postcolonial unnamed narrator.

Where Naipaul reflects his lived experience of colonialism and postcolonialism using his technique of metanarrative, Morrison reflects her hidden past that she did not experience herself by using slave narrative. Naipaul employs his autobiography, but Morrison employs an autobiographical neoslave narrative to reach her goal of unveiling her ancestors' past. Morrison's *Beloved* is a modern version of the nineteenth-century genre of the slave narrative. The neoslave narrative is "a new body of historical studies of slavery that took seriously the agency and self-representation of the slaves, their community-and-culture-building energies, and the forms of resistance they exhibited" (Rushdy, 2004, 88–89). As stated previously in this chapter, Morrison came across the story of Margaret Garner, a fugitive slave from Kentucky who escaped with her husband and four children to Ohio in 1856. A gang caught up with Garner, and so she killed her youngest daughter and tried to do the same to her other children rather than let them suffer from slavery and oppression. Morrison claims in her foreword to *Beloved*:

> The historical Margret Garner is fascinating, but, to a novelist, confining. Too little imaginative space there for my purposes. (*B*, xi)

The narrative structure of *Beloved* is correlated with the characters' continuous struggles to delineate a path of self-discovery. The complex narrative of the novel is the symbol of the complicated lives of the characters. The overall fragmented state of African-Americans sets a constant dialogue between past scraps and present bits of their texts and selves in a collection, to sustain a loose textual and cultural continuity with a weak sense of belonging and self-identity. Morrison's storytelling characterizes mutability and shifting in perspectives, time and space, character, procedure, and composition. Her writing is characterized by constantly though unexpectedly shifting points of view, an unpredictable choir of narrative voices, and juxtaposed fragments of events and images that are in dialogue with one another but could hardly form a straightforward, linear, cause-and-effect plot monologue.

Within *Beloved*, this sense of fragmentation is evident not only in the prose-like structure of the novel but also in the narrative style. Mostly third-person omniscient, with an anonymous and subtle narrator symbolizing more the character in the limelight than a narrative persona, the focus shifts fast from one character to another and from past to present. As the story fragments into the complexity of viewpoints and narratives, it all the while alludes to and moves closer toward the crucial central trauma. Sethe's narrative always seems to be fragmented when remembering anything painful. While remembering another traumatic memory, Sethe thinks but is incapable of being coherent.

Naipaul's and Morrison's nonlinear structures cause events to be only gradually revealed to the reader. Naipaul and Morrison use the same structures, but their purposes differ. Morrison's use of a circular or nonlinear structure serves her primary goal of flashbacking her past and of always keeping her readers alert. She attempts to return to her roots and to honor her ancestors' past. Nevertheless, Naipaul's usage of a circular structure stresses his in-betweenness and his hesitation between his personal past and his present. However, Naipaul, in the first section, "Jack's Garden," presents a linear narrative that shadows Naipaul's presence at the cottage from arrival to departure, and as such introduces and focuses on the details of the seasonal experiences of the surrounding estate and his neighbors. "The Journey," section 2, enacts a reverse movement and turns the clock back from Naipaul's arrival at the cottage to his departure from Trinidad in the 1950s.

Therefore, in this section, Naipaul focuses more on his experiences and thoughts when he first set foot in England. He recalls being somewhat unaware of English culture. He indulges in a rather deep autobiography about how he reflects on English culture, which altered him in a way that required him to change his cultural background and beliefs. Sections 3 and 4, "Ivy" and "Rooks" respectively, exist within the same time frame as the first, and here the emphasis is placed on the landlord and his manor house to which Naipaul's cottage is attached. The final section, "The Ceremony of Farewell," reflects the purpose and importance of the narrative. Placing the closing emphasis on the central motif of death that pervades the novel, Naipaul returns to Trinidad for his sister's funeral. Just as at its beginning and its close, Naipaul's novel foretells the remaking of the world. Naipaul maintains: "Every generation was to take us further away from those sanctities. But, we remade the world for ourselves" (*EA*, 353).

The most crucial part of the discursive negotiation of *The Enigma of Arrival* is demonstrated in the emergence of a writer situated somewhere between the author, the unnamed narrator, and the characters. Although Naipaul's name is never actually mentioned in the narrative, the reader is aware that the writer corresponds to Naipaul, the man, because of their identical biographies. I maintain that it is Naipaul who is telling the tale for the same reasons. In this sense, perhaps as an indication of its general ambiguities, *The Enigma of Arrival* seems to fall somewhere between fiction, nonfiction, and fictional autobiography. In fact, in his review of the novel, John Thieme has categorized *The Enigma of Arrival* as "thinly-veiled autobiography":

> A personal meditation by a Trinidadian writer, whose origins replicate Naipaul's, who has written a series of books which (although never named) exactly match Naipaul's own and who, since around 1970, has, like Naipaul, been living on Salisbury Plain, the area which provides the novel with its main setting. (Thieme, 1987b, 200)

The unnamed narrator describes the story's plot, genre, and sources, which would be a release from the twinned pressures of the emotional and artistic challenges of writing and the business of writing. Although at first the story he will call *The Enigma of Arrival* seems like a release from these pressures, it eventually comes to be much closer to his own life. He first imagines that it will be "a free ride of the imagination" (*EA*, 99) about a traveler in a classical city, but he eventually finds "how much of his life, how many aspects of his life, that remote story (still the idea for a story) carried" (*EA*, 103). In this phrase, Naipaul evokes the novel that was eventually published as *The Enigma of Arrival*, which is all about "his life." The fictional world that Naipaul creates in the novel collapses into the material world in which the novel mingles as a material object. In my view, the collapse lies in hybridizing Naipaul's autobiography with the fictional world in *The Enigma of Arrival*. Therefore, there is confusion between Naipaul's personal life and his unnamed narrator, who symbolizes many postcolonial migrants.

In Morrison's case, the fictional world does not collapse with the everyday world because the narration moves only through the mind to interweave reality with memory and imagination. When the omniscient narrator takes on the very pattern and thought of the unspoken memories of Sethe and Denver, the narrator writes not for themself but for others, who in listening and relating the memories become the perfect receptor for their authentic, unspoken voices. As Sethe continues her quest for identity, she receives more memories about the past—memories that hurt her and all African-Americans. Thus, the colonizer's cultural strategy leads to black slaves' amnesia and forgetfulness concerning their native African language, traditional culture, and names. Morrison represents the kind of cultural devastation suffered by the slaves.

All through *Beloved*, a fragmented and a nonlinear structure is presented that keeps the reader at a distance from the narrative. In other words, the plot jumps between past and present as we follow Sethe's trauma side-by-side with that of Paul D, Baby Suggs (Sethe's mother-in-law), and Denver. Even though they portray many of the same events, their memories do not come together in a neat wholeness. It is significant for Morrison to tell her characters' perspectives of a shared past individually and equally, so the characters can collect the fragmented memories in order to struggle to build up a new identity.

Naipaul's various shadow-narratives, which pull critics into attempts at locating or fixing "the writer," are best exemplified and brought into question in the very title of the novel. The shifting sequence of arrivals enclosed in the text suggests the direct thematic relevance of the question or mystery posed in the enigmatic and symbolic title. Therefore, the narrative structure of this unwritten story's mysterious and blurring arrival, momentary crisis, and ambivalent ending work their way into Naipaul's psyche and texts. The assertion that "with me, everything started from writing" (*EA*, 154), in this sense, acts as a declaration of the narrative circuitry behind the book's title and structure. Hence, Naipaul and Morrison use circular and nonlinear structures to recall their memories of the past. However, Morrison's nonlinear structure, which shifts between past and present, succeeds in cherishing her ancestors' past and reflects her sense of belonging and rootedness. On the other hand, Naipaul uses a circular metanarrative that stresses his sense of in-betweenness and ambivalence, which arises from the colonial condition of cultural dislocation.

Repressing or Celebrating Indigenous Traditions

Naipaul's and Morrison's mentioning of their indigenous traditions explains Fanon's second phase, but differently. Naipaul tends to deny and criticize his rituals and traditions. From the beginning of Naipaul's literary life, he stresses the concepts of decay, isolation, flux, and death—the four leitmotifs intertwined with his Trinidadian traditions and society. However, Morrison's skillful manipulation of traditional African-American folklore attaches power and voice to many ordinary objects, such as ghosts, chokecherry trees, scars, quilting, and red ribbons.

Naipaul and his narrator's return to Trinidad involves dealing with the puzzles and discontinuities of the Hindu rituals and traditions which the family still feel to be appropriate for a funeral, out of "a wish to give sanctity to the occasion, a wish for old rites, for things that were felt specifically to represent us and our past" (*EA*, 316). However, the unnamed narrator, who symbolizes Naipaul and postcolonial migrants, discovers that wholeness resides not in those ancient sanctities themselves but in making anew, which is the only positive option left to the shipwrecked voyager.

Naipaul's search for his identity is closely related to Trinidad's responses that reach their most frantic level whenever he encounters his society. As he reaches further and further back into the psychological trauma of his origins to explain his present, what emerge are not facts but, as psychotherapists would describe, scenes in fantasy. Such scenes are activated through a creative process, and *The Enigma of Arrival* can be read as an attempt to explain the primal fantasy of Naipaul's indigenous culture. Nevertheless, Naipaul does not tend to accept his history and his West-Indian Indian background, and he tends to criticize his indigenous culture.

In this light, each of Naipaul's texts plays an irreplaceable role in obtaining knowledge of himself, of the different cultures he inherits, and of the diasporic worlds he inhabits. While reconstructing the historical past each time through reinterpretations of autobiographical or fictional material, Naipaul has realized that the present differs from the past and that it will not be repeated in the future. Therefore, Naipaul and his unnamed narrator, who represent most postcolonial West-Indian migrants, repress and criticize their past and culture for being combined with the metropolitan present and help construct a new future. Whereas Naipaul's narrator criticizes his rituals, Morrison crystallizes and revives her ancestors' culture.

Through the experiences of her characters, Morrison presents the folkloric image of her culture. Folkloric beliefs in the power of trees and the significance of ghosts represent a small portion of the many folkloric motifs that Morrison exercises. In Morrison's *Beloved*, folklore becomes a vehicle for the African-American characters' confrontation with unspeakable and disremembered experiences from their painful past. When using the term folklore, I refer to the customs, beliefs, traditions, tales, magical practices, proverbs and songs embraced by community sanctioning to reinforce a community's attitudes and beliefs. The purpose of folklore is generally perceived to be the preservation of cultural rituals and traditions. While, in general, folklore assures that a people's cultural history will not be lost, African-American folklore has a more urgent spiritual, social, cultural, and political imperative to maintain identity and pride despite a history of slavery. Morrison chooses to focus her novel on the ghost of Beloved and also states that most of her novels are based on African folklore. In so doing, Morrison expresses her attachment to her ancestors' traditions and culture.

The ghost of Beloved becomes a complicated part of the story's narrative, forcing Sethe and African-American characters to speak the unspeakable. In this way, Beloved points Sethe down the path of her evolution and healing, while enabling the text to voice the suppressed stories of slavery. Beloved represents the inescapable, fearful past of slavery returned to haunt the present. Morrison embodies her ancestors' past to revive her indigenous culture and to remind all African-Americans of their embodied and emerged past, which is forgotten and buried. However, Sethe's youngest daughter, Denver, who represents young African-American generations, claims: "I am Beloved, and she is mine" (*B*, 208).

Both Naipaul and Morrison speak about the new generations of their nations, and Denver here represents the new generation that will always remember the past—with this past becoming a significant part of their futuristic lives. Whereas Naipaul incites the young generation to change their rituals and rites, Morrison encourages the future generation to remember their past as they begin a new future and reconcile with their present.

Another example presented by Morrison in her novel is the tree. Trees are represented as symbols of protection and healing in African-American culture. However, through Sethe's "rememories," Morrison inverts the soothing quality of trees to reflect the physical violence of living as a slave. Morrison's revision allows her readers to perceive the duality of the trees at Sweet Home, with sycamores encompassing both incomparable beauty and unfathomable horror. Sethe recalls the rolling beauty of Sweet Home, and "although there was not a leaf on the farm that did not make her want to scream, it rolled itself out before her in shameless beauty" (*B*, 6). Rather than protectors, the beautiful trees of Sweet Home become synonymous with death and the brutality of slavery. These cruel associations with trees are imprinted in Sethe's mind as surely as the tree-like scars are imprinted on her back. Amy, the "white girl" who helps Sethe to escape across the Ohio River, first discovers the scars and declares: "It's a tree, Lu. A chokecherry tree. . . . Your back got a whole tree on it" (*B*, 79).

The chokecherry tree on Sethe's back is a painful and hurting reminder of Sweet Home and the cruelty of her white master, "school teacher," who "planted it" on Sethe's back while tying her up and whipping her as a slave. Thus, the sacred tree proves to be ambivalent, both protector and silent witness to the psychological and the physical destruction that happened to the slaves. Throughout Morrison's revision of the traditional folkloric significance of trees, the brutality and cruelty of slavery are brought to the forefront. As surely as the trees provide protection and refuge, they also serve as symbolic reminders of brutality and death. This revision is necessary for Morrison's purposes; the reader is allowed a glimpse into the terrible reality of slavery as Sethe begins her confrontation with that reality. The tree in African tradition serves primarily as a symbolic spiritual presence, whether it becomes a center for spiritual renewal or a protective friend.

NAIPAUL'S UNSAFE LANDING AND MORRISON'S HOPEFUL ARRIVAL

In the wake of the destruction of their identities, culture, traditions, and history in the Middle Passage, African-Americans have long tried to interrogate their forgotten and buried past. In *Beloved*, through remembering and interrogating their past, Sethe and other African-American characters develop a new understanding of the long, painful history of slavery's devastation. These understandings are vital for them to claim "ownership of that freed self" (*B*, 95). In their memories of the past, they have also developed their own discourse about what happened, enabling them to develop subjectivity.

In *Beloved*, the characters' memories of the past as slaves are so traumatic that no one wants to re-experience it. Even reimagining it mentally brings about pain. Every protagonist, not just Sethe, prefers to forget it entirely rather than expose it before others. They exist almost like dream walkers as they remain determined to keep the past buried. Morrison demonstrates the procedure of discovering and facing the past and combining the past with the present. Beloved and Sethe are portrayed as embodiments of the past to remember the colonial past, which causes the return of history. Beloved is the embodiment of Sethe's past, which she must confront. At the same time, Beloved is not merely a metaphor, but a real character who occupies a physical body. The character of Beloved, then, becomes the African-Americans' awakened past.

On the contrary, Naipaul's *The Enigma of Arrival* traces the withdrawal of its narrator into a space of safety and seclusion, a place of retirement from "the world" into the landscape of rural Wiltshire, as the novelist figure rents a cottage on the grounds of an old manor house in search of the "healing" of a "second life" (*EA*, 172). The narrator is like Naipaul: both of them prefer not to face their past and instead favor withdrawal. Therefore, arrival in itself remains an interrupted and repetitive act where emotional memories from an earlier past interact, and boundaries between the outsider and the insider constantly persist, stepping into every open space. Therefore, *The Enigma of Arrival* is a series of negotiations between the ontological self and the existential self—negotiations that make the act of living possible and stress the in-betweenness of Naipaul and his narrator.

At the core of their identities, Naipaul and his narrator are neither purely Indian nor English. Instead, they are a deformed combination of English and Hindu Indian Trinidadians—deformed in the sense that the latter has been historically repressed by the cultural superiority of the former during the colonial period. However, the narrator's travel into the global domain in 1950 brings to light his repressed ethnic and regional roots. At the same time, a multiplicity of global forces subjects his cultural identity to an unparalleled degree of change in motion, rendering it highly unspecified. Therefore, Naipaul and his narrator's fragmentation, ambivalence, and enigma must be positioned within postcolonialism.

For postcolonial communities, placelessness and the disconnection from habitat and habit are not a matter of rejection but choice out of a desire for moral autonomy. Therefore, the modern rationale works in opposition to any attempt at free will, and autonomy leads to the search for a place to serve as a common ground for ethical decisions and action. From the position of the oppressed and displaced minority, resistance works to establish a sense of place and group identity: laying claim to place, then, represents a rejection of the teleology underlying imperialism and its assertions about universal human progress.

In this sense, however, by finding a way of remembering and relating these memories together with her black women's communities, Morrison's Sethe becomes the communal healer and the catalyst for the revival of healing of her community. In *Beloved*, Morrison is undoubtedly interested in continued existence, but not only of the individual; instead, she is deeply committed to the existence of black communities. Morrison is a writer particularly interested in depicting, and thereby preserving and perpetuating, the cultural practices of black communities. Morrison's use and revision of African folklore illustrate her own preoccupation with cultural formation and preservation.

She highlights the importance of storytelling to gather the community and support its values, and her novel becomes cultural documentation.

Significantly, she locates women and their stories at the heart of her narrative to give voice to their long-overlooked contributions to community and culture. Morrison's cultural role is as a conservator in her belief in the epistemic powers of fiction and narrative. In so doing, her fragmented and nonlinear narratives act as methods of constructing the fragmented world of her characters. Where Morrison pays so much attention to her African-American community, which has an essential role in gaining and constructing her characters' identities, Naipaul's postcolonial community does not have the same importance to him and his protagonist. Trinidad offered him no continuity, India hung like a "loose end" (*EA*, 179) in his mind, and his past fell away into the chasm between England and Trinidad. He leaves Trinidad for good and returns to England, to a rented flat in London (where the talk of workmen beneath his window brings him into contact with a side of England he had never known, like 'an unknown country'), to a private house in Gloucester, and finally to the cottage in the Wiltshire valley. He decided to visit Trinidad and, finally, he has arrived in England. Naipaul and his narrator are in a circle that has no end, which reflects the circular structure of the novel. Trinidad might have antiquity, but it was broken by race and threatened by revolution. India had antiquity, even tradition, but it was a "loose end" (*EA*, 179). Even the decay he sees around him, he interprets as change, and change, which he once grieved over, he can now accept as a constant, stating that "I lived with the idea of change, of flux, and learned, profoundly, not to grieve for it. . . . Decay implied an ideal, perfection in the past" (*EA*, 300). The past, at last, can be laid to rest.

Although Naipaul and Morrison use nonlinear narrative structures, I would claim that Naipaul's narrative strategy is an enigmatic literary form—a style that merges fictional narrative, autobiography, feature story, and historical documentary. *The Enigma of Arrival* is a hybrid, and a liminal text full of tensions and conflicts frequently breaches traditional norms. In my view, it places the reader in a state of uncertainty as to whether the novel is fictional and/or autobiographical. Naipaul creates an enigmatic atmosphere by using this hybrid technique, which reflects his state of in-betweenness.

Naipaul withdraws from his past, but Morrison creates her own narrative to render her 'dearly beloved' past. Whereas Naipaul's in-between or hybrid text emphasizes his in-betweenness, Morrison's hybrid neoslave narrative emphasizes her rootedness. Morrison's *Beloved* offers a hybrid genre of a neoslave narrative, in which memory is an important phenomenon in oral tradition. Memories become a political and cultural statement in *Beloved*, evidenced by Morrison's combination of folktale and remembered history. Morrison utilizes folklore as a means of reviving her ancestors' past, and as a way of speaking the otherwise unspeakable. Folkloric beliefs in the power of trees and the significance of ghosts represent a small portion of the many folkloric motifs that Morrison exercises. Rather than merely beautifying the text with these traditional folkloric themes, however, Morrison revises them, infusing folklore with the ability to give voice to horrifying memories of slavery. Morrison creates fictional folklore, which pertains individually and collectively to the community in *Beloved*, which will be referred to in this text as community folklore. Like the traditional folklore that Morrison revises, the community folklore that she originates becomes an indispensable tool for confronting the past.

Morrison expands and recreates traditional forms of folklore to depict the consequences of slavery through these folkloric images. She intertwines folklore with the totality of her novel, continually blurring the lines between reality and otherworldliness until folklore becomes identical and inseparable from the lives of her characters. These unfamiliar images and perceptions may lead some readers to question the reality that Morrison represents. Indeed, readers know slaves who are beaten, slaves who run away, and slaves who are killed. These are the images that Morrison attempts to convey—images we will see more clearly if we can step outside our own cultural microcosm and into Morrison's enchanted world. Using African folklore represents black oral literature of African-American culture. It links African-Americans to their roots and expresses their cultural resistance against their sense of humiliation and fragmentation.

Whereas Naipaul and his unnamed narrator have a tendency to deny their traditions, customs, and Indian rituals, Morrison invents an utterly original body of folklore, referred to in this book as community folklore, specifically for her novel. For Naipaul, traditions, customs, rituals, and childhood memories are like something which [he] had missed, something [he] had never seen (*EA*, 105; brackets added). Back in Trinidad, the narrator sees the absurdity of the outdated practice of Hindu rituals by exploring a problematic relationship between the pundit who has style without substance, and a new generation who have no deep connection with the Hindu tradition. The narrator sees such people as dispossessed who, through clinging to what have become empty rituals, bar both themselves and their community from developing. A feeling of loss primarily guides the narrator's double exposure to England and Trinidad. In England, the narrator is seen as a writer-in-exile in limbo because of his crippling dislocation, first in the metropolis and later in the countryside. The migratory nature, which he has inherited from his Indian ancestors, leads him to a place without redemption.

Morrison and her characters somehow hesitate between celebrating and mystifying their ancestral traumatic past. Nonetheless, for Morrison, the only option to get out of the state of in-betweenness is connecting her past with her African folklore. Therefore, community folklore plays a significant role in the evolution and healing of Morrison's characters, simultaneously keeping painful experiences in a safe place, yet bringing them to the forefront. In each of these categories, the "enchantment" in Morrison's work is not present merely as a curiosity. However, it serves a purpose for characters who, along with Morrison's readers, are encouraged to confront their painful pasts and struggle to create an identity and community in a historically intolerant world.

Both Naipaul and Morrison are aware of their hybrid identities, but the difference is that Morrison does not physically travel to her own roots or land—she instead uses the American setting. While searching for their "primal place" the characters inform much of the conflict in Morrison's works. In other words, to lack a primal place is to be 'homeless' indeed, not only in the literal sense of having no permanent sheltering structure but also as being without any effective means of orientation in a complex and confusing world. Morrison revives and recalls her past and her black identity, while at the same time, she is aware that she is living in American society with her African identity. Morrison succeeds in preserving her African past, which is African-Americans' only way of surviving in white American society. Also, Naipaul is "always a stranger, a foreigner, a man who had left his island and community before maturity, before adult social experience" (*EA*, 226). Despite Naipaul's ceaseless effort to return or to arrive, the arrival is not done yet. Naipaul's themes and circular narrative structure in his *The Enigma of Arrival* reflect the vicious circle in which he and his unnamed narrator live.

According to Naipaul and his narrator, Trinidad's past offers nothing to them, so they prefer to be back in their chosen exile, England, as they cannot land safely after their numerous trials of arrival. For Morrison, who has arrived successfully at her goal of recalling her ancestors' past, the past is never dead. It lives on as the scars on all African-Americans' backs. It is the past growing like a tree on their bodies and minds, which usually symbolizes life and represents the haunting memory that can never be erased. The scars of the past are borne on Morrison's and her people's backs. They cannot see them because they did not pass through actual colonial experience, but they are conscious of their past existence. However, they are adapting to the white dominant society. Morrison implies that the traumatic impact of slavery can never be fully destroyed. Moreover, the past is "not a story to pass on" (*B*, 275), which means the pain of slavery will never pass on or away; that is, it will never die. Hence, she helps protect and record her ancestors' memories of the past as history passes from one generation to another.

In contrast, Naipaul and his characters have an "insecure past" (*EA*, 92) because their "past had been destroyed" (*EA*, 315). Therefore, Naipaul is satisfied with the concept of belonging to no land/culture, while at the same time belonging to everywhere and every culture to which he has been exposed.

Generally, Naipaul's transnational works articulate his characters' cross-cultural identities mainly through their uncomfortable experiences of unkind emotions. In *The Enigma of Arrival*, Naipaul accentuates the ethical value of the self by confronting his own alienation in a multicultural community. As I have analyzed, a transnational perspective allows readers to examine the difference in the protagonist's identity as embodying neither authenticity nor indignity, nor Englishness proper, but rather as a transitive and transformative dimension through which postcolonial migrants come to appreciate their past and the multiplicities of their identity as they cross various borders.

Conversely, Morrison's protagonists are displaced literally and metaphorically; they need a home and community as a result of a metaphysical dislocation that leaves them disconnected from personal and universal history. They have to master their relationship to place by narrating their past places, by remembering or constructing a history of trauma that is, despite its horror, the security of their existence. Through remembering, they find their roots, values, and ethics, and a sense of community, a place, and security in the world. In sharing memories of the past, people not only recall their places of origin but also create a collective defined by these individual memories.

In *Beloved,* Morrison attempts to alter the suffering and pain of slavery into a festive cause, commemorating and honoring the lives of the invisible, dishonored, and disremembered slaves. The purpose of making Beloved (the character) real is to make history possible—making memory real and forgetting possible. Bringing readers "to face the historical past as a living and vindictive presence," Beloved comes to represent the suppressed memories of slavery, both for the characters and for the readers. Therefore, the past is personified and re-enacted for the sake of confronting and going beyond it, as suggested by the double meaning of the phrase "pass on"—sharing and overlooking—in the concluding chapter of the novel. *Beloved* penetrates the dim and forgotten sources of history that continue to haunt African-American cultural imagination like a constant nightmare. Above all, the novel celebrates potential healing. As Beloved recedes once again into the land of the dead, a nightmare fades out when the hope of a bright future dawns on the people who suffered from and survived the nightmarish memories of a traumatic history.

Naipaul's hybrid prose style reveals the in-betweenness, the cultural plurality, and the complexity in his life and experience as an Indo-Trinidadian of English education and residence. Therefore, at the center of Naipaul's technique as a writer lies his mission to connect different aspects of himself and convey his diverse experiences. From the beginning, Naipaul's writing self is noticeably autobiographical. "I begin with myself," Naipaul remarks, "this man, this language, this island, this background, this school, this time. I begin from all that, and I try to investigate it, I try to understand it. I try to arrive at some degree of self-knowledge" (*EA*, 7). Intending to write his part of the story, Naipaul decided to remain in England after his graduation from Oxford and took up writing.

Unfortunately, in his initial years as a writer, he realized that he had neither a living literary tradition nor a highly organized society to fall back on and claim. His world of ancestral India is imagined, his Hindu extended family life is disordered, and his colonial society is disintegrated. Naipaul assumes responsibility for recreating the past and reconstructing the human story in his books, partly through creative interpretations of a historical document, and thus builds on the "traces" of the historical past. In order to do that, Naipaul, unlike Morrison, has traveled to the sites of the cultures themselves where traces of history are unrecorded or hidden from view. Morrison has never gone to the African continent, but she renders her ancestors' traumatic past through the creation of individual characters, permitting the narratives to record the psychological trauma vividly. She traces the existence of African-American traditions and customs from their early appearance in eighteenth-century personal narratives to their use in contemporary fictional narratives. Her fiction also echoes this critical-historical understanding. For example, in *Beloved*, she has used her research into African-American history to portray a complete image, from the time of slavery until its aftermath, which nonetheless still bears the traces and scars of slavery.

To conclude, I argue that both Naipaul and Morrison reach the second stage of Fanon's theory, in which indigenous writers recall the past as a way of celebrating a cultural identity. However, Naipaul and Morrison have different ways of recalling the past. Although Naipaul has actual colonial experience and physically travels to his original lands (Trinidad and India), his past is still enigmatic and vague. He is always hesitated, lost, fragmented, and dislocated because Naipaul himself denies his native characters past of any kind. As shown in *The Enigma of Arrival*, Naipaul has portrayed his unnamed narrator as a unique individual whose life or death, history or mysteries, comprise the enigma of never arriving.

Nevertheless, Morrison, who did not have an actual colonial experience and had never traveled to her African land of origin, can reach her roots and revive her ancestral folklore and culture. The past, in other words, is used to forge a communal space in the present because places serve as a guide for ethics because the memories they contain identify the inhabitants with the community and make them feel responsible for it. Nobody can change the past, but the idea is how we can relate to it—one can forget or reconcile. Morrison's characters always remember their traumatic past and arrive safely toward their identities. However, Naipaul and his characters are always in between their dead but inescapable past and their desire to change the present, which prevents them from landing safely at their identities.

Chapter Four

A Journey from Unhomeliness to Hybridity in V.S. Naipaul's *Half a Life* and *Magic Seeds* and Toni Morrison's *Home*

Hybridity: What and Why?

One of the most urgent difficulties of our time can be described in simple terms: how are we to live together in this global world? "We" and "together" are the critical sites of contestation here. In the last few years of the twentieth century, the growing global importance of what has come to be called identity politics has raised profound suspicion regarding any claims to global humanity. In this environment, the very idea of living together becomes immensely daunting. What are the promises of a sense of togetherness that can go beyond division and fragmentation, without returning to the old hegemony of colonization? How, in short, can people live together-in-difference?

This chapter can answer the above question while exploring the third phase of Frantz Fanon's theory regarding celebrating a cultural identity. I argue that Naipaul and Morrison achieve Fanon's third phase, and that they become their nations' awakeners while guiding their people to hybridity as a new way of becoming in the dominant societies in which they live. Furthermore, in my view, hybridity is tantamount to Fanon's fighting phase, in which indigenous writers create new revolutionary literatures. In these literatures, indigenous writers attempt to hybridize their folklore and culture with the dominant culture regarding the celebration of a new identity in an attempt to resist Western dominant discourses.

However, Homi Bhabha's usage of the concept of hybridity draws attention to its vital significance in postcolonial studies. He perceives hybridity as a necessary product of the colonial state. Bhabha asserts that postcolonial identities are always a matter of pain and suffering. Bhabha stresses the fact that the trauma occurs when colonized people realize that they can never perfectly mimic the colonizer's traditions, color, and language. Therefore, as mentioned earlier, hybridity is a means of resistance: colonized people hybridize colonizers' culture in order to undercut it. Furthermore, Ania Loomba in *Colonialism and Postcolonialism* supports Homi Bhabha's notion of hybridity as a form of resistance to marginalization in dominant Western societies.

> Colonial 'hybridity' in this particular sense, is a strategy premised on cultural purity, and aimed at stabilizing the *status quo*. In practice, it did not necessarily work in that way: anticolonial movements and individuals often drew upon Western ideas and vocabularies to challenge colonial rule. Indeed they often hybridized what they borrowed by juxtaposing it with indigenous ideas, reading it through their own interpretative lens, and even using it to assert cultural alterity or insist on an unbridgeable difference between colonizer and colonized. (Loomba, 1998, 174)

Therefore, hybridity exhibits the necessary displacement of all sites of oppression and supremacy. Thus, in my view, hybridity connects to Fanon's revolutionary or fighting literature as it meets his criteria of combat literature. Fanon states that this literature can be called combative literature, in the sense that it calls on indigenous people to fight for their existence as a nation, or as people, and to resist their marginalization. Later in this chapter, I argue that Naipaul and Morrison mold their national consciousness, "giving it a form and outline and flinging open before it, new boundless horizons" (Fanon, 1968, 240), which can be produced and aroused from hybridity, which is considered, by Homi Bhabha, as a form of resistance.

Hybridity helps describe an in-between space in which culture change may occur as the transcultural space where there is a repeated movement and exchange between different cultures. Therefore, Naipaul and Morrison, in their latest novels, create Fanon's new combative literature, in which they explore hybridity as a new way of belonging and resistance, rather than being caught up or lost in Homi Bhabha's in-between space. Besides, and in order to achieve Fanon's third phase, Naipaul and Morrison depict some parts of their indigenous cultures to be shown to the new generations of indigenous people, such as quilting in African culture and Casteism in Indian culture. However, Naipaul and Morrison have their reasons for presenting these traditions, which I will elaborate on later in the chapter.

Hybridity is considered a tool for resisting the relegation and marginalization of indigenous people in dominant societies as it disrupts the binary opposition between 'self and other'; it is an "in-between space, where hierarchies between cultures, colonizers, and colonized become destabilized" (Bhabha, 1994, 67). Hence, as mentioned by Fanon in his third phase, there will be a fighting literature in which indigenous writers address their people and resist the supremacy of dominant society by finding a new way of becoming, represented by hybridity. Hence, hybridity can allow postcolonial and African-American people to be heard and to have their own voices in the dominant societies in which they live.

I argue that hybridity highlights the impossibility of returning to any notion of an essential national or cultural identity after the colonial encounter, particularly in the present context of social, economic, and cultural globalization. Although the term is often used to signify a balanced and inoffensive mixing of cultures, the process of hybridization is never an even exchange, and is always necessarily lived deeply entwined with colonial violence and oppression as a painful, instinctual memory. Hybridity is the redefinition of the assumption of colonial identity through the repetition of discriminatory identity effects. It presents the necessary distortion and displacement of all sites of discrimination and domination.

Hybridity happens to people caught between two different cultures as they live a double life, sometimes among the colonizers with the images of their own culture and home, and sometimes among themselves with the images of the alien culture in which they have lived for some time. Consequently, indigenous people are ambivalent between two cultures, which brings about a fragmented and even lost identity. I mean that they are hesitant between their original culture and the culture of their former colonizers. In so doing, hybridity is critically important in that it can be a way of becoming in a world in which we no longer have the secure capacity to draw the line between 'us' and 'them' because nowadays, we live in a globalized world in which there is an ongoing variety of mixed-up differences.

However, in postcolonial discourse, hybridity is celebrated and privileged as a kind of superior cultural intelligence owing to the advantage of in-betweenness, the overlapping of two cultures, and the subsequent ability to negotiate the difference. In this sense, Naipaul's view of hybridity can be seen as a cross-cultural exchange. The in-between space carries the burden and meaning of culture. It stresses the intersectionality of cultures in the postcolonial process. Hybridity can also refer to the creation of new transcultural forms within the contact zone produced by colonialism.

Hybridity is the name for the strategic reversal of the process of domination or hegemony through refutation. Morrison's view of hybridity is that it disturbs the mimetic or narcissistic demands of colonial power, and replicates its identification in strategies of subversion that turn the look of the discriminated or the marginalized back upon the eye of the dominant power. Thus, I would argue that hybridity is considered a form of resistance to the hegemonic colonial pattern. Hybridity can be a distorting mirror which breaks the identity of the colonizing subject. Consequently, upon the failure of colonial ideology, indigenous people confront colonialism and dominant powers with more audacity. Thus, hybridity is regarded as an unwelcome aspect of colonialism.

In my view, hybridity in no way erases or puts an end to conflicts between dominant and marginalized nations and cultures. Instead, it places these conflicts in a different space—one that is more tolerant and where the autonomy of each culture is reconsidered. In my opinion, hybridity opens up a new space within which new identities can be constructed and new forms of resistance articulated. In this sense, hybridity provides a space of resistance, negotiation, and expression of new meanings in the face of ambivalence, fragmentation, and hegemony. Similarly, Robert Young supports Bhabha while stating that hybridity implies a disturbance and a forcing together of unlike things; furthermore, "it turns sameness into difference, and makes difference into sameness, but in such a way that what is considered the same is no longer the same just as the different is no longer merely different" (Young, 1995, 26).

Therefore, it becomes clear that cultural hybridization is meant to reconcile the conflict from which postcolonial and African-American people suffer because of their double status. Hybridity implies an integration process where postcolonial and African-American people have to preserve their indigenous culture alongside the dominant culture's way of living. From an idealized perspective, hybridization occurs on the level ground of equality, mutual respect, and open-mindedness. However, Naipaul and Morrison, in their novels—*Half a Life*, *Magic Seeds*, and *Home*—attempt to show hybridity as an anticolonial or resisting tool regarding identity, culture, and language, where hybridity breaks down the firm polarization created by the dominant societies and groups involved. Naipaul and Morrison regard hybridity as the mutual transculturation of the marginal and dominant culture, although the celebration of hybridity usually refers to the establishment of marginal cultures.

Bhabha's examination of colonizer/colonized relations and their interdependence and mutual structure of their subjectivities is based on hybridity. However, Bhabha contends that all cultural statements and systems are constructed in a space that he calls the "third space of enunciation" (Bhabha, 1994, 37). Cultural identity always emerges in this different and ambivalent space between cultures. Moreover, regarding this, I argue, no hierarchical purity of culture is possible. Hybridity is significant that the productive capacities of this third space have a colonial or postcolonial background

Hybridity is the process that begins when the leading dominant authority starts to translate the identity of the marginalized or minorities (the Other) within a single worldwide framework. Bhabha contends that a new hybrid identity or subject-position emerged from the intertwining of elements of the colonizers and the colonized, challenging the validity and authenticity of any essentialist cultural identity. At the very beginning of their literary lives, Naipaul's and Morrison's main characters are torn between assimilating into the dominant culture and celebrating their indigenous identities. They are caught in Dante's Limbo or Homi Bhabha's Third Space. Nonetheless, Bhabha's Third Space enables other positions to emerge to resist the hegemony and hierarchy created by any governing authority. Thus, the Third Space is a type of expression, a way of describing a creative, and not merely reactive, space that produces new opportunity. It is an "interruptive, interrogative, and enunciative" (Bhabha, 1994, 18) space of new forms of cultural meaning and construction, blurring the limitations of existing boundaries, and calling into question established categorizations of culture and identity.

Naipaul and Morrison once again depict the theme of the quest for home and belonging in *Half a Life*, *Magic Seeds*, and *Home*, but in a new way. In *Half a Life*, *Magic Seeds*, and *Home*, Naipaul's and Morrison's main characters try to build a hybrid identity to resist their marginal positions in dominant societies. Naipaul's young Indian protagonist in *Half a Life* and *Magic Seeds*, Willie Chandran, undertakes a journey through three different societies to find his place of belonging. Given that in *The Enigma of Arrival*, Naipaul acknowledges the need for new ways of seeing places, the question raised here is whether Naipaul sustains his transformative vision of place in his two latest novels. There is a clue to the response to the question in Chandran's concluding lines at the end of the quest when he says: "It is wrong to have an ideal view of the world" (Naipaul, V.S. [2004a] *Magic Seeds*, 294, hereafter cited as *MS*).

By contrast, in *Home*, Morrison continues with her project of imagining a new space of domestic and communal comfort which is physically and psychologically safe and, in the broad sense, a homeland for African-Americans. *Home* offers a place of refuge from the social, historical, and psychological dismemberment or traumas of racism, which results in experiences of fragmentation, amputation, and lack of coherence. Naipaul and his protagonist Willie Chandran finally choose to settle in England not because England appears homely to them but, rather, as this chapter argues, because he views England as moving toward a multicultural and global society with a hybrid culture where the cultural exchange has made society more active. *Magic Seeds* suggest that hybridity can be considered as an alternative way of belonging.

Nevertheless, Naipaul, in *Magic Seeds*, negotiates the notion of hybridity. I will argue that Naipaul refuses to view hybridity and the sense of unhomeliness as the empowering assets of migration. To a certain extent, acceptance of hybridity is shown by Naipaul to be the only feasible way of belonging and becoming for postcolonial migrants in an increasingly unhomely world.

The concepts of home and belonging appear in Morrison's fiction, but not as a physical or geographical locale. For Morrison, the concept of home bears emotional, psychological, political, and social connotations. Generally, Morrison associates the concept of home with a social place offering the possibility of co-existence—a place where one can "iterate difference" (Morrison, Toni [2012a] *Home*, 10, hereafter cited as *H*). Such a space does exist "outside established boundaries of the racial imaginary" (*H*, 9). Morrison's utopian concept of home exceeds racial and cultural boundaries and aspires to be a universal ideal—a place clear of racist detritus and where race both matters and is rendered impotent. Unlike Naipaul and his protagonist Willie, who does not belong to the places he has lived, Morrison and most of her characters celebrate their blackness and roots. However, they want to have the right to belong to the dominant American society in which they live but while sustaining their African culture and heritage. Naipaul and Morrison admit and are aware of their hybrid identities, and have their own way of negotiating hybridity.

NAIPAUL AND MORRISON: UNHOMELINESS AS A WAY TO HYBRIDITY

After decades-long writing careers bound up with the concepts of place and questions around belonging, Naipaul and Morrison depict the common theme of the quest for home in their recent novels, *Half a Life* (2001), *Magic Seeds* (2004a), and *Home* (2012a). In their earlier novels, Naipaul and Morrison present the concept of unhomeliness as an eternal dilemma. However, their later novels present the same concept of unhomeliness, but with a solution that might sort out this eternal dilemma. Unhomeliness is not quite the third stage of Fanon, but it is a precursory stage to Fanon's third phase. This chapter will examine whether Naipaul and Morrison sustain their divisional visions of place and home in their later novels. Moreover, this chapter will discuss the novels' questioning of the idea of home and highlighting the idea that home is nowhere for intensely unsettled postcolonial individuals; however, I will argue that Naipaul and Morrison address the possibility of hybridity as a new way of belonging in the dominant societies in which they live. Moreover, in order to achieve Fanon's combat literature, Naipaul and Morrison create their later novels to present hybridity as a means of resistance to marginalization and to the authority of dominant cultures.

Naipaul's *Half a Life* and *Magic Seeds* and Morrison's *Home* portray the theme of sociocultural displacement through unhomely houses. Such houses mark more profound historical dislocation, based on race, gender, or geographical origins. However, Bhabha suggests the possibility of moving beyond the binary opposition of the colonized and the colonizers. Living in an unhomely world is not a longing existence, but a hybrid one that is inherent in the costume of extraterritorial and cross-cultural initiation. In other words, unhomeliness disorients the border between home and the world and endows a person with a more dynamic marginal existence. I agree with Bhabha when he argues that colonial and postcolonial cultures and social structures are created in an in-between space, where the hierarchy between cultures is dissolved, and new forms are created. Such new hybrid forms enact the strategic reverse of the process of domination. Therefore, hybridity attempts to circumvent or negotiate states of authority and neocolonial realities.

Hybridity, the most discussed term in postcolonial studies in recent years, is as much a celebration of marginal identities as it refers to creating new linguistic, artistic, cultural forms, and transcultural forms to resist the marginalization of minorities in dominant societies. In this chapter, I will map out how *Half a Life* and *Magic Seeds* are full of literary echoes and references to Naipaul's own writings. Such an analysis functions as a form of arrival to the complexity of Naipaul's commitment to the issues which dominate his fictional writings. In *Half a Life* and *Magic Seeds*, Naipaul's same protagonist follows a journey from unbelongingness and unhomeliness to hybridity.

Half a Life and *Magic Seeds* can be read as responses to the ideas of hybridity. These novels explore and weigh up the relative merits of Africa, India, and England as places of belonging for an immigrant from a postcolonial country. These are the three places with which Naipaul is associated because of his Trinidadian background and via his wide-ranging travels. The two novels examine the possibility of establishing a comfortable life for an immigrant in these societies. Among them, Africa and India are shown to be missing the ability to change toward progressive and stable societies in the postindependent epoch; therefore, they are presented as unhomely. England, on the other hand, is shown to be establishing a multicultural society. Such viewpoints seem familiar in Naipaul's works; yet, what might be seen as new in these recent novels are, first, addressing the possibility of establishing a society based on dynamic cultural exchange and, second, accepting the idea that the reality of homelessness renders the longing for home useless. Whereas Naipaul's latest novels advocate cultural exchange, they refuse to approve the idea of accepting unhomeliness or hybridity unconditionally. At the beginning of *Magic Seeds*, Naipaul states: "I don't see what I can do. I do not know where I can go" (*MS*, 5); "I am always an outsider, now as well; I am in Berlin, but what can I do" (*MS*, 8), Naipaul stresses that postcolonial migrants are homeless and can do nothing about it. They want to amalgamate into the local society but are confused by their hybrid "roots." Willie's story and traveling experience reflect Naipaul's intention and thoughts around rebuilding a world without chaos and finding a "home" for his soul and to establish a new sense of belonging.

Similar to Naipaul, Morrison's *Home* makes the reader aware at the outset that its central theme, 'home,' is to be read in relation to Morrison's earlier fictional works. The lyrics of the epigraph at the start of this tenth novel highlight Morrison's permanent interest in the identity issues of home, belonging, autonomy, and freedom.

> Whose house is this? . . . Say, who owns this house? It is not mine. I dreamed another, sweeter, brighter . . . This house is strange. Its shadows lie. Say, tell me, why does its lock fit my key? (*H*, 1)

Furthermore, the novel's title indicates the possibility of closure. As the theme of acceptance, longing for stability, and togetherness, home has been central to Morrison's novelistic project from the start. In most of Morrison's fiction, cold and loveless homes are contrasted with warm and loving homes. The theme of home also provides significant motifs, most notably in Morrison's novel, *Beloved*. Such motifs, which are also projecting in *Home*, include the characters' return to a hometown and searching for a place of safety, while endeavoring to live with (literally) or come to terms with fragments of the past.

Also, a strong desire for independence and an identity crisis in Naipaul's writing is always noticeable. His fiction provides a sense of his biography of departure and exile from the colonial background of Trinidad to the cosmopolitan and multicultural atmosphere of England. He thinks that the colonizers have produced a mimic society, and the culture and knowledge of those societies have come from outside. In Naipaul's *Half a Life* and Morrison's *Home*, the protagonists, Willie Somerset Chandran and Frank Money, are the representatives of Naipaul's and Morrison's people, respectively. Unable to justify themselves within the dominant cultures, they are changed and turned into people who assimilate into the dominant societies in which they live. In their later novels, Naipaul and Morrison review their literary lives. They embody their three-stage journey while writing their *Half a Life*, *Magic Seeds,* and *Home*. These novels include Fanon's first stage of mimicry, the second stage of recalling past, and the final stage of revolution through hybridity as a new way of becoming.

The crises of unbelongingness and unhomeliness are always features, which one cannot ignore while reading V.S. Naipaul's writings. Willie Somerset Chandran, the protagonist of *Half a Life* and *Magic Seeds*, is born into and raised in an Indian family in a village in India. However, his Anglo-Indian name suggests that due to two centuries of colonization of India, Willie has a hybrid background rather than a purely Indian identity. His curiosity to know more about his hybrid identity and the cultures, which have formed it, drives him to commence a journey of self-discovery in relation to the places to which he assumes he belongs. There are two locations of India in the novel: India in which Willie is brought up, and India to which he comes back later with the belief that he might change it. Willie's understanding of India is shaped by these two encounters, which do not contradict but complement his idea of India.

Willie is like Naipaul, as both of them intend to search for self-identity and build their own subjectivity in the world via traveling. However, Naipaul portrays *Half a Life* as an example of a failed hybridity, rather than a successful one. In other words, *Half a Life* represents the hard effects of hybridity on postcolonial migrants. *Half a Life* starts with the words: "Willie Chandran asks his father one day, 'Why is my middle name Somerset? They at school have just found out, and they are mocking me'" (Naipaul, V.S. [2001] *Half a Life*, 1, hereafter cited as *HL*).

Thus, Willie possesses only half a name. The novel seems to disclose Willie's father's purpose that his son imitates British culture since he gave him half of a famous British writer's name, Somerset Maugham. In so doing, Naipaul can see the gap between postcolonial mimicry of former English colonizers and his desire to establish himself in a chaotic world. The name of the British writer attached to Willie's Indian name anticipates the 'half-life' that he is doomed to live for the rest of his life. Willie's half-life is incomplete, unrealized, and unfulfilled, because of his split or half identity. The idea of hybridity is not just how two cultures mix and blend to become one, since this mixture is not always a favorable one, as it can lead to a disturbing experience or result. Western names are hollowing because postcolonial migrants cannot possess Western identities only by possessing Western names. In contrast, identifying with the Western names and dismantling their Indian names symbolizes the loss and the failure of indigenous culture. Therefore, Naipaul uses Willie as a representative of postcolonial migrants, and he emphasizes that many of them are still excluded in and from the dominant culture, even though their fathers intended to prompt them by giving them a half-whitened name.

Willie's identity crisis takes place, early on, in his homeland, India. His inability to cope with his hybrid background alienates him from his own country and culture. Born in India to a Brahmin father and a low caste mother, Willie is bound to be disgraced by his mixed parentage. Feeling ashamed of his hybrid identity, he decides to forsake his family and country, "and that was how, when he was twenty, Willie Chandran, the mission-school student who had not completed his education, with no idea of what he wanted to do, except to get away from what he knew, and yet with very little idea of what lay outside what he knew" (*HL*, 124). Aspiring for a better life in another part of the world, Willie is willing to leave his indigenous country or what he already "knew" and ventures to explore a new life: the life of an immigrant.

In *Half a Life*, Naipaul presents characters that are products of racial and cultural amalgamation and shows how they resist finding their identities in the dominant multicultural society in which they live. Generally, these characters tend to deny one or more racial characteristics in order to become more respectable, in their estimation. However, they eventually determine that their identities cannot be fixed because they are the products of various cultures. All through the novel, Willie is drifting and fragmented without a stable and fixed identity. His identity is multiple, constructed across different and often intersecting discourses, practices, and positions. Naipaul and his protagonist cannot achieve one permanent identity because of their fragmented cultural backgrounds. *Half a Life* has three settings: first, there is postcolonial India, then London, and finally, preindependence Africa. All three are places with which Naipaul can identify.

However, these locations seem to indicate different connotations in *Half a Life* and *Magic Seeds*. India and Africa are vague, while the representation of London with street names and other markers is more explicit; thus, for Naipaul, England is situated with a different level of reality, firm and stable, while other regions can be relegated to haziness, but India and Africa are vague and blurred. Like Naipaul, Willie initially thinks of London as a stable place; however, he feels that he is still torn in limbo as a marginalized drifter in the big city. Such unhomely people as postcolonial, African-Americans, exiled, immigrants, marginal, and uprooted must defy their being in an indefinite state of suspension. Imprisoned between indigenous and dominant cultures, Willie and postcolonial immigrants lose their native cultural inheritance and sense of home. They identify neither with their homeland, an old world, nor with the new world that they desire.

In other words, Naipaul and his characters' identities are torn and fragmented. Thus, Naipaul may not create one identity, and "the identities of place are inevitably unfixed" (Massey, 1994, 169). Therefore, cultural identities focus on searching for a new route of belonging. Therefore, Willie and Frank are heading toward their identities to create new ways of becoming. In Morrison's *Home*, devastation occurs when Frank, his family, and the rest of the fictive community confront their forced exile from their homes and properties. Characters like Frank are faced with the existing paradigm of having nowhere to go and nowhere to call home. Frank equates such a state of homelessness to aimless loitering. However, in his mind, Frank, like Morrison and any other African-American, is haunted by the ancestral trauma of forced exile and being driven out of his home without any legal protection. The loss of home and property in Morrison's fiction, including *Home,* also represents the spirit from the author's own familial background. It is known from Morrison's numerous biographical accounts that her parents were forced to leave their home in the South in order to flee from violence, poverty, and racism.

Morrison gives expansive expression to the metaphor of home. For her, the concept of home does not merely signify the common understanding of domestic comfort and family life; rather, it encompasses the entire world and a deep-rooted sense of liability in our human relationships. I maintain that Morrison moves the idea of home from one contained within the house to an obviously gendered, open-borders communal space. From its ideal state of being an open-space raceless world, home also embodies a more realistic portrayal of "a failed or always failing dream" (Morrison, 1998, 3) grounded particularly in the notion of the American dream, which is one of the fundamental themes in American literature and cultural life. Morrison specifically questions "the failure of America as a national homeland to open up space for black citizens to be at home."

When Morrison talks about home as a failed or always failing dream, it is because historically, African-Americans were denied a home in the sense of both familial comfort and a broader sense of a homeland. Home has been, for African-Americans, an experience of alienation, displacement, and violent separation/dismemberment, basically dividing the consciousness of the self into a double or triple consciousness. Because African-Americans were violently separated from their parents, families, and homeland, the experience of life in the New World is one of meaningless existence, involuntary exile, homelessness, and the brutal experience of being slaves, as she depicts it in her characterization of life under slavery.

Home is not an exception to this general premise, for, despite the specificities of the historical period portrayed in the novel and the individualities of the main characters' experiences, there is no denying that the grief suffered by their ancestors still echoes in African-Americans' lives. Individual identity is supposed to be negotiated within the shared past. Consequently, while there is always a unique, biographical memory to explore, the past is described as being rooted in collective memory. Here, collective memory provides the individual with a cognitive map within which to orient present behavior.

Therefore, in the case of Frank Money, it soon becomes apparent that he has been the victim of some traumatic childhood experiences, war shocks, and racial disgraces that he has long suppressed and that produce a type of fissure in his mind. Morrison uses Frank as her main character and his sister Cee, as she wants to present an example of traumatic experiences for both black men and women. Frank and Cee signify the black nation. Both black men and women are fragmented, and they are always torn between their past and their present. In other words, recovering from the thoughtful damage caused by collective mental injuries is far more dangerous, since racial memory threatens to destroy that personal sense of identity by dissolving the individual within a collective experience of negation.

Similarly, Willie Chandran in *Half a Life* is also torn between his past and his present. His problem is like the problem of Morrison's Frank and Cee. The main character of *Home* is Frank Money, who has moved from Texas to Lotus. Bandera County, Texas, was his first home where he was forced to leave under threat by hooded men within twenty-four hours. Losing his home meant losing his future as his displaced sister, Cee, was born on the road with "no roof over her head," and his grandmother predicted this homeliness as a "worthless and sinful future" (*H*, 44). Morrison highlights the splitting, separation, and the fragmentation in African-American community itself. Leaving their home and land, Frank and Cee embody the African-American community's loss of their past, present, and future.

Longing for home and homesickness can be linked to the cultural mourning that results from cultural dislocation and loss of ways of life from which an individual feels historically severed or exiled. However, the experience of displacement is double as it entails migration/diaspora and a sense of exile. Thus, Naipaul's and Morrison's characters' search for home is the quest for an idealized home place, always already lost or missing in their lives. The majority of these characters feel and admit their inferiority in their direct contact with the dominant culture. Furthermore, indigenous people are colonized in their own country and wandering anywhere else to display their identity. Although some characters get along well with their circumstances in their postcolonial countries, for some others, like Willie in *Half a Life*, being exiled is better than staying. He drifted to experience a better life in London, but colonization had already shaped his personality, and he could not settle down. Since Willie symbolizes an intellectual being, copying or imitating the dominant culture was not easy for him. He wanted to resist mimicry and settle on a home, which was his identity.

Without a firm identity, Willie and Frank find that the dominant societies in which they live do not welcome them. Willie fails to find a home in either India or London. Frank also feels that he is an intruder in American society, but he cannot go back to his African homeland. So, Willie and Frank's failure to integrate into the dominant cultures in which they live signifies the failure of postcolonial migrants to integrate into the dominant colonial societies. Willie had rejected Indian history and culture from childhood, yet he does not find a place in British society either. This dislocation is the other feature of postcolonialism, which can be considered the main factor that leads to the mimicry of dominant powers.

Like most of Naipaul's fiction, *Half a Life* and *Magic Seeds* present Willie's situation as a shared experience among postcolonial people who imitate English culture. Like most postcolonial people, Willie is alienated from both cultures and experiences—an identity crisis that he never fully resolves, and its impact can be seen in his stories: "they are quite original. They are not like Hemingway at all. They are more like Kleist. One story on its own might not have an impact, but taken together, they do. The whole sinister thing builds up. I like the background. It is India and not India" (*HL*, 49). So, Willie's general sense of emotional hollowness is reflected in his writings.

Morrison, again in *Home,* stresses the concept of mimicking the dominant society as a cover to be accepted in it. Morrison's Frank also joined the American "integrated army" (*H*, 18) and performed many services for America; however, this community ignores his services and does not accept him as a citizen. Frank is like any African-American who tries to imitate and interweave with the dominant American society. Unfortunately, they are treated like "dogs" (*H*, 18) and "trash" (*H*, 122). This policy of ignoring African-Americans' existence influences their lives in such a way that they feel alienated, fragmented, and unhomely; as Bhabha argues, unhomely does not mean homeless. Bhabha notes that "this process is the relocation of home to another territory where the occupants cross to another culture; however, to be unhomed is not to be homeless" (Bhabha, 1994, 69). Therefore, postcolonial identities have no culture around which to center, and they become the double and hybrid characters that Homi Bhabha describes. Naipaul equates placelessness with loss and disorder.

This first experience in London serves to drive Willie into a descending twisting of emotional suffering, loss, and growing sense of helplessness and uselessness that shapes his adult experiences to follow in *Half a Life* and *Magic Seeds.* Therefore, Willie takes refuge in developing and imitating some of the colonizer's roles. Unsafe and without a clear identity, he drifts along, leading other people's lives. Through the narrative, Willie is presented as aware of his role-playing and that none of his roles ever fit. In a way, nobody is astonished at his inescapable failure. Willie's sense of disorder led to his role-playing; he finds himself in a cycle of action and reaction that repeatedly feeds on itself.

Morrison's Frank also fails to imitate the dominant American society when he volunteers in the Korean War. He tries to play the role of an American soldier, but he and the others like him have no acceptance and authenticity. Morrison, in *Home,* describes such a relationship as one in which the person is a receiver for the dominant society rather than for marginalized group. For instance, white society considers whites as the upper power and uses the dead bodies of African-Americans for medical research in order to find remedies to help sick white individuals. The following is a conversation between Frank Money and his friend Reverend Locke:

> Reverend Locke grunted. "Have a seat," he said, then, shaking his head, added, "You lucky, Mr Money. They sell many bodies out of there." "Bodies?" Frank sank down on the sofa, only vaguely caring or wondering what the man was talking about. "Uh-huh. To the medical school." "They sell dead bodies?" "What for?" "Well, you know, doctors need to work on the dead poor so they can help them live rich." (*H*, 12)

As far as Frank experiences these challenging times and recognizes the unfairness regarding himself and other African-Americans, Morrison focuses on African-Americans who live in a state of nonbelonging . She shows that African-Americans always live in a state of unhomeliness and that they are "not *totally homeless* but *close*" (*H*, 27; emphasis added). They do not know to which culture, country, or city they belong. Morrison shows this situation during Frank's conversation with Watson Billy:

> Frank Money. Where you from, Frank? Aw, man. Korea, Kentucky, San Diego, Seattle, Georgia. Name it I'm from it. You looking to be from here too? No. I'm headed on back to Georgia. (*H*, 28)

In general, by using the characters of Frank Money and Willie Somerset, Morrison and Naipaul want to say that most African-Americans and postcolonial migrants tend to reject one or more racial characteristics in order to become more appropriate, in their estimation. However, they eventually discover that their identities cannot be fixed because they are the fruits of multiple cultures. All through the novels, Frank and Willie are trying to fix a stable identity. Failing to obtain a place of his own in London, Willie does not know his way or his destination. He can "only go back to India, and he [does not] want that" (*HL*, 121; brackets added). The cultural identities focus on searching for a new path and creating new meanings in the flow; Willie and Frank must experience the journey of traveling toward their self-identities.

Willie and Frank genuinely realize that they must seize the time to construct their subjectivity because they have spent too much time leading a life of escapism. Willie and Frank are looking forward to starting anew with a new future. Naipaul and Morrison confront the sense of unhomeliness and discover that they have to call for a new way of becoming to create a new identity. Naipaul and Morrison, therefore, comprehend that identity is unstable but created in a process, just like the assertion of the postcolonial discourse. They learn to accept the cultural significance of "unhomely" asserted by Homi Bhabha:

To be unhomed is not be homeless, nor can the "unhomely" be easily accommodated in the familiar division of social life into private and the public spheres. . . . In the stirrings of the unhomely, another world becomes visible. (Bhabha, 1992, 141)

Naipaul and Morrison, like Homi Bhabha, believe that wandering in the world causes an uncertain status and a nonbelonging situation, in which the marginalized subject does not know to which culture they belong. This sense of loss is because they have been deprived of their true existence and identity. What Naipaul and Morrison declare in their latest novels is the remembrance of the past by their characters and their assiduity in terms of reconstructing their identities. Therefore, the unhomely moment relates the traumatic ambivalences of personal, psychic history to the wider disjunction of political existence. It is evident that the wandering of Naipaul's and Morrison's characters in the world of nonbelonging and unhomeliness reflects these inner worlds, which are unstable and unpredictable.

The term unhomeliness proposes that what is involved in the creation of hybrid identities of characters like Frank in *Home* and Willie in *Half a Life* is an alienating sense of the repositioning of home and the world—the unhomeliness—that is the condition of being extraterritorial whereby indigenous people encounter two different worlds—that of the colonizer or dominant power and that of his or her original culture. These two different worlds conflict with each other, and consequently, indigenous people feel a sense of unhomeliness, so they start their journeys toward a new way of becoming.

HYBRIDITY, INDIGENOUS CULTURE, AND FANON'S THIRD PHASE

As mentioned above, and according to Fanon's third phase of revolutionary literature, hybridizing indigenous cultures with dominant cultures in Naipaul's and Morrison's later novels is considered a tool for resisting the abrasion of indigenous history and traditions. Meanwhile, Fanon's third phase stresses that indigenous writers shed light on their cultures and traditions to be presented to the new generations so as not to forget their original homelands and cultures. In order for the revolutionary effects that Fanon envisions in his third phase to occur, new generations must struggle to find a space between the dominant Western cultures and their indigenous cultures; the negotiation of the space between is a potential sight of hybridity.

In my view, Naipaul's *Half a Life* and *Magic Seeds* and Morrison's *Home* authorize the notion of hybridity as a new way of becoming, through which an individual can relate to the world, but the imperatives of location condition the efficiency of hybridity. More to the point, it is a way of resisting any form of binary opposition created by colonial powers or dominant groups. By referring to their indigenous cultures, Naipaul and Morrison clarify their different notions about hybridity.

Therefore, recalling indigenous culture will help postcolonial people and African-Americans to build new cultural identities that reconcile and hybridize with dominant societies and resist any form of hierarchy and domination. Naipaul and Morrison believe in hybridity as a new way of belonging; however, they negotiate it differently. While Morrison stresses the concept of community and African folklore as a way to help heal and resist racial practices, Naipaul criticizes his Indian culture when he refers to Casteism as a way of deconstructing his nation. Whereas Morrison hybridizes and quilts her indigenous culture with that of American society to build a new identity, Naipaul criticizes his indigenous culture's defects to increase the fragmentation of his people's identities. To Naipaul, the problems and fragmentation caused by Casteism could destroy his Indian traditions and culture. Therefore, Naipaul believes that cultural exchange is a condition of building a hybrid identity in the global world, but Morrison believes that quilting her African culture with dominant American culture can create a new hybrid identity that resists the supremacy inherent in white American society.

By stressing the idea of quilting as a central aspect of African traditions, Morrison emphasizes the interconnectedness of women from one generation to the other, and the interconnectedness of African-Americans to their past and their present. This interconnectedness will heal trauma and help in reconciling the two identities of being African and American. The quilt is not just a historical hybrid document of a mortal past but rather a bridge of memories between African-Americans, their ancestors, and their coming descendants. Quilting symbolizes many things that are connected with identity, cultural legacy, and mythical aspects of African-American life. The most metaphorically booming quality of quilt making is a trait shared by European and African-American traditions—the promise of creating unity among disparate elements, of establishing connections in the midst of fragmentation. In so doing, Morrison emphasizes the concept of hybridity as a way of healing and connecting the two parts of African-Americans.

Morrison's Frank had saved Cee, his sister, but "she neither missed nor wanted his fingers at the nape of her neck telling her not to cry, that everything would be all right" (*H*, 131). It is African-American community or the new home that saved Cee and reconstructed her physically and psychologically. By the end of *Home*, Cee is presented as having acquired a "newly steady self, confident, cheerful and occupied" (*H*, 135), and the fact that she spends most of her time piecing together quilts may also be an appropriate symbol signifying that she is also succeeding in finally putting together all those fragments of her identity. By sewing the quilt, she is quilting her own new identity, and she is reviving her native folklore, which is going to be hybridized with the dominant American society.

Quilting is a creative art form that is considered an integral part of African-American folklore. There are four steps in patchwork quilting. First, colors and fabrics are selected from material found mostly from the old clothes of ancestors. Then these scrap materials are cut into small shapes. After that, these shapes are joined together into a patch. These patches are then sewn together into a larger pattern, forming a quilt, which is stitched together with padding and durable backing. This patch is also a vestige of wholeness that signifies loss and creative design challenge. It may symbolize rupture and impoverishment: it may be the faded glory of the already gone. However, as a fragment, it is also rife with the explosive potential of the yet to be discovered.

The use of the quilt episode plays a vital role in the structure of Morrison's novel as she quilts her literary archaeology by combining her ancestors' past and her own present. For Morrison, "quilting is life" (*H*, 122). Just as the quilt is made of scraps and fabric from outgrown clothing, Morrison's narrative is also composed of a wide variety of elements that make a unique community, which is an embodiment of the firm and unified African-American culture. The community of women of Lotus is greatly influenced by African folklore, family, history, interrelations among generations, and slavery. These elements are skillfully woven together to form a distinct unified pattern that represents the female community of Lotus.

The community as the primary healing mechanism that the novel presents is Morrison's new way of belonging. When Frank rescues Cee from Dr Beau's medical experiments, he travels with her unconscious body to their hometown of Lotus, Georgia, where he immediately relinquishes the care of Cee to the women of the Lotus community. Morrison depicts these women as nearly supernatural in their ability to heal Cee's horrifying physical wounds, which symbolize the emotional and mental wounds that Cee does not have words to express and does not have the strength to confront alone. Just as Cee's mental trauma is symbolized in her physical unresponsiveness, the physical healing that the women mediate symbolizes Cee's simultaneous mental healing. Cee's recovery process is dominated by some of the traditional healing elements present in Morrison's narrative and African-American literature written by women, namely, the ideas of community, natural and traditional remedies, quilting, singing, storytelling, and love. Working on her self-esteem and self-love proves vital to her recovery: "Who told you, you was trash?" (*H*, 122) Cee is asked. Miss Ethel's words of wisdom empower a previously helpless Cee:

> Look to yourself. You free. Nothing and nobody is obliged to save you but you. Seed your own land. You young and a woman and there's a serious limitation in both but you a person too. (*H*, 126)

At a certain point in Cee's healing, Cee becomes involved in her new community's "embroidery, crocheting, quilting, talk and songs" (*H*, 122). For the first time, she has positive role models and belongs to a group that is capable of helping and healing each other (*H*, 123). Her constructive contribution to the women's crafts can be understood as a reflection of the healing—or internal construction—that is occurring when Cee is empowered to build self-worth and self-love. The fragmentation of Morrison's characters endures—like fragmented pieces of quilting material—but they are metaphorically restored to unity and harmony at the end of the healing process, thus resembling the implied meaning of quilting as African folklore. Thus, Morrison states that the main reason for the healing process is cherishing African folklore. Therefore, the handcraft of quilting entails an opportunity to rework the outmoded, whether it is in clothing, novel structures, or conceptions of the self. The quilt that Cee makes at the end provides her with a sense of autonomy and self-empowerment, which she did not have before: "Cee refused to give up the quilt. . . . The quilt was the first one she had made by herself" (*H*, 141). This sense of empowerment creates a new, healed identity that can hybridize with the dominant American society. Morrison wants to say that in order to reconcile and hybridize with the dominant power, African-American people have to be healed and cured of their past traumatic memories caused by white masters since the Middle Passage.

While Morrison is proud of her traditions and revives her ancestors' folklore and culture, Naipaul criticizes his Hindu traditions and culture, which, according to him, hinder India's progress He criticizes one of the most important Hindu values and traditions, which is Casteism. Casteism is "an endogamous and hereditary subdivision of an ethnic unit occupying a position of the superior or inferior rank of social esteem in comparison with other such subdivisions" (Velassery, 2005, 2).

The idea presented in *Half a Life*—that Casteism delays the unity of India against subjugation and corruption—is not new in Naipaul's writing. Indeed, Naipaul envisions India as a society with several fields of complexities: class, caste, religion, and colonial history. Each of these complexities has, in one way or another, created an unbridgeable gap in the social sphere that hinders progress in the country, according to Naipaul. Naipaul sees India as an area of darkness and a wounded civilization that needs to be healed. In my view, Naipaul does not criticize his traditions and customs to despise them, but he diagnoses the sickness to help in the healing process of his nation, so he has to stress the problems. Also, it is clear in *Magic Seeds* after Willie joins the revolutionaries that he realizes the root of the problem lies in the Hindu tradition of Casteism, and so fighting against this is far more complicated than an anti-imperialist war.

For Naipaul, there is the prospect of a comfortable life in multicultural England, but not in postcolonial societies that lack the capacity for social growth. Naipaul describes "India as one of the saddest places in the world" (*MS*, 37) because, to him, the difficulties of caste and the lack of prospects for change are reason enough to make India an uncomfortable and unlikely home for Willie Chandran. Therefore, Casteism is in diametric opposition to quilting because the former is a way of splitting up rather than connectedness, but quilting connects the fragments of the past. However, according to Fanon's third phase, Naipaul and Morrison can share the same task of healing the fragments of their nations, but differently. Naipaul exposes the reader and his nation to the facts that hinder their progress and unity. However, Morrison highlights her ancestral traditions because she believes that the past will lead her people to cherish the present and will construct a new future. Naipaul and Morrison guide their nations to be exposed to their indigenous cultures, and they stress hybridity as a new way of belonging and a product of the healing process.

NAIPAUL'S AND MORRISON'S VIEWS ON HYBRIDITY

Resisting a sense of displacement begins with questioning the cultural disparagement and boundaries that regulate marginalization and sustain unequal power relations, as displacement can indeed be a platform from which resistance begins. The wedding scene in *Magic Seeds* and the burial scene in *Home* clarify Naipaul's and Morrison's different views of hybridity as a way of resistance to marginalization. For Fanon, Naipaul and Morrison are now the awakeners and guides of their own nations because they help their indigenous nations to find a new way of belonging, asserting their existence, and resisting the dominant societies' dichotomies in which they live.

Establishing a connection between postcolonial and metropolitan identities and cultures is presented in Naipaul's *Magic Seeds* regarding the marriage between an English aristocratic girl and a West-African diplomat, whose dream is "to have a white grandchild" (*MS*, 240). However, the postcolonial conflict in the novel ends with a revolutionary conclusion. Here, I interpret the wedding scene by the end of the novel as confirming that Britain now recognizes cultural exchange. It is essential that cultural exchange is conditioned by time and place, meaning that it could happen only in stable societies like English society at the time of the dominance of late capitalist culture.

In my view, *Magic Seeds* neither reduces the idea of hybridity in Britain to a festival of difference, nor ignores the dominance of the late capitalist culture that overshadows the efficacy of the discourse of hybridity. Indeed, the novel renegotiates the way hybridity has worked in England, as hybridity resists any form of hierarchy and distinction. In *Magic Seeds*, hybridity is not shown as a celebratory dominant cultural force that levels the hierarchies. Instead, in *Magic Seeds*, firstly, hybridity is shown in the creation of new art forms (such as new music) and new ways in which people of different cultural backgrounds can live together. Secondly, while there is melancholy over the loss of home, hybridity is shown as a predictable cultural form in postcolonial era when the idea of home and belonging is no longer suitable.

Moreover, hybridity in *Magic Seeds* suggests that living through a hybrid cultural exchange would be predictable in postcolonial era when the ideas of home and belonging, for Naipaul, are no longer acceptable. The image of a rotting grand country house in which the wedding is taking place brings to attention the timing of the beginning of hybridity. The roofless country house figuratively suggests that it is only at this point in history (after the breakup of the empire) that the symbolic marriage between postcolonial and urban cultures is possible. The noble family of the bride, just like the house, "is past its leading member." We are told that the founder of the girl's family was a great man, early in the nineteenth century. Some years ago, they decided to "let their house" decay (*MS*, 286). In a sarcastic tone, Naipaul moderates the background of the English family and what remains from their past glory. The deterioration of the English family's grand past parallels the deterioration of the state of their roofless house.

Such imagery suggestively emphasizes that the marriage between an English girl and the son of a West-African diplomat marks a moment in the history of the relationship between the former colonies and the metropolis, which was only conceivable in the aftermath of the decline of British empire. The wedding is presented as being as strange as the house in which it takes place. The estrangement is displayed in the music of the ceremony and black and white couple among the guests. Although the manner and outfit of the stylish couple seem to defy the holiness of the occasion, together they portray the new image of a hybrid society in which globalization and cultural exchange prevail. Moreover, when the bride and groom have two children out of wedlock, it is another signifier of transformation in the conventional and cultural values of both metropolitan and postcolonial cultures.

However, the peak of the wedding is the music with which the novel ends. A Dutch-Antillean band plays African-Caribbean music after parts of *Othello*, and some of the Shakespearean sonnets are read to the guests. The amalgamation of English literature and Caribbean music in the wedding signifies the metaphorical marriage of two cultures. What is extraordinary about the music is not the performance but that the guests try to pick out the beat and, regardless of the fact that the music sounds unfamiliar, try to follow the melody: the noise "was fearful, but some of the fair women in new frocks were swinging their slender shanks, as if they were picking out a beat, and it was too much to resist" (*MS*, 294).

The English guests' appreciation of folkloric and black music as a fluid cultural practice proposes that they are trying to cope with the cultural exchange ongoing in their country. Black music is a creative expression and commitment to a better life whose goal is to bring Africa, Europe, and the Caribbean together. The melody and the music in the final scene provide a romanticized view of cultural exchange. The Caribbean music incites people of colonial and imperial cultures to be in tune with hybrid forms of art and foster harmony. The music stays in Willie's ears until the end of the novel, and it fetches memories of the plantation system and slavery, through to the migration of the offspring of laborers of the colonial societies, to the metropolis. The scene suggests that the imperatives of migration and the new dynamics of postmodernism have rendered cultural exchange foreseeable in England. Naipaul ends *Magic Seeds* with the hybrid-wedding scene that negotiates hybridity as a new way of belonging in multicultural England. In so doing, Naipaul guides postcolonial people to a new way of becoming in multicultural societies. He places cultural exchange as a condition of his new way of belonging. Naipaul leads his people to self-recognition and a new sense of belonging; he no longer misses his homeland because he has a spiritual home in his imagination.

However, Morrison also sets out her black heritage and her people's confession as primary conditions for self-healing and belonging. Morrison's reference to quilting represents her people's recalling of their past and old heritage and mingling it with their current situation. By the very end of *Home*, Morrison employs a burial scene, using Frank and his sister Cee to emphasize the healing process that both of them have undergone. Finally, home is a matter of finding a proper place to which one can belong. For Frank, the memory of home is a site of childhood epiphany. He has to bury the memory of his own idyll to complete the trajectory of his homecoming. This idyll is attached to the memory of the "burial of a stranger" (*H*, 134) that he witnessed in the company of his sister when they were just children. Frank's revisiting of the scene and of "the slaughter that went on in the world" (*H*, 143) in the company of Cee not only introduces his past but also asserts his sense of belonging through the proper burial of the dead person whom he had witnessed being deserted unceremoniously in the ground.

Frank's performing of the burial expresses his solidarity with the community to which he belongs. In a final gesture to assert his sense of belonging/ solidarity, he goes to uncover with Cee the remains of the unidentified dead body, an unknown black man, who had been forced to fight his son in mortal combat. He places the remains of the dead body on the quilt embroidered by Cee, which becomes "a shroud of lilac, crimson, yellow and dark navy blue" (*H*, 143). This ritual burial by Frank shows his respect toward the dead black man, who symbolizes the sixty million slaves who lost their souls in the Middle Passage. To mark the dead man's grave, Frank nails a wooden epitaph on the tree painted with the words: "Here Stands A Man" (*H*, 145). In my view, the epitaph indicates a monument and memorial for the unburied victim of oppression and suggests a new relationship between African-Americans and the American land. Since their coming in the Middle Passage, many slaves died and were buried without any sense of being named or remembered; however, Morrison wants to say that they will be buried properly and that they will have the right to live and die with pride.

When she uses the colorful quilt for a shroud, Morrison stresses the idea that I have discussed in the previous chapter of the book—the idea of reviving her ancestors' past. Meanwhile, Morrison prefers to bury the dead black man in the quilt, which is a hybrid document of the interconnectedness of past fragments. She accentuates that African-Americans have hybrid identities and that they will sustain their ancestral past while living on American land. However, their past lives inside them like the scars on their backs.

Naipaul, in effect, chooses to end his *Magic Seeds* in England where multiculturalism and hybridization of identities appear to him to allow the possibility of a hopeful integration for immigrants, and allow them to live in a progressive and ordered society. Naipaul and Morrison share hybridity as a common theme, and that is clearly apparent in the final scenes of their novels, *Magic Seeds* and *Home.* However, whereas Naipaul creates a hybrid scene in which there are many cultures together, Morrison's final burial scene emphasizes both her African culture and American culture. In so doing, Morrison, as usual, stresses her unity with her ancestral African culture and community, whereas Naipaul stresses his global view of home. I mean that Naipaul and Morrison achieve Fanon's third phase differently. Morrison leads and guides her African-American people to remember their ancestral past while living in American society. However, Naipaul guides postcolonial people to cultural exchange in dominant multicultural societies such as English society.

Once again, Morrison in her final scene resorts to paradox and inversion; physical death is not the end—it is not falling but standing, soaring up on to the spiritual dimension and a different kind of life. Morrison gives her readers hope of a new hybrid relationship between African-Americans and dominant white society by erecting the epitaph "Here Stands A Man" (*H*, 145).

Lotus symbolizes home to Frank and his sister when they return to it; they complete their journey of growth from alienation and self-loathing to personal enlightenment and a renewed self at the end of the novel. Apart from the idea of place, the name Lotus evokes the traditional symbolism of the lotus flower, which represents rebirth and enlightenment. In Ancient Egyptian culture, the lotus flower "symbolizes the sun, creation, and rebirth" because of its life cycle: "The lotus starts as a seed in a muddy environment at the bottom of a water source. As the flower grows, it moves toward the sun until it floats to the top of the water and blooms . . . moving toward the sun is the process of gaining clarity" (Brown, 2009, 27).

Consequently, for Morrison, the lotus flower is a metaphor for the soul's journey from the primeval mud of suffering, through the waters of spiritual practice, into the bright sunshine of enlightenment. While reading these descriptions of the lotus flower, it is inevitable to find clear associations with Frank Money's journey of growth from alienation and self-loathing to personal enlightenment and a renewed self at the end of the novel, back in Lotus. In my view, the concept of home for Naipaul and Morrison transcends physical location, as Morrison argues in one of her interviews: "home is an idea rather than a place. It's where you feel safe. Where you're among people who are kind to you—they're not after you; they don't have to like you. And if you're in trouble, they'll help you. . . . It's community" (Morrison, 2012b).

Half a Life and *Magic Seeds* sum up Naipaul's approach to how individuals relate to places. These two novels show that an individual's quest for home and a place of belonging is complicated by the reality of unhomeliness and the sociocultural complexities peculiar to every place. In other words, the reality of unhomeliness renders the desire for home elusive. Naipaul and Morrison represent a revolutionary concept of belonging. This concept lies in being aware of their hybridity and in trying to find a new way of belonging after failing to belong to a specific place.

NAIPAUL'S AND MORRISON'S NARRATIVE HYBRIDITY

As Fanon says, indigenous writers are their people's awakeners, supporters, guides, and advisors. Consequently, Naipaul's and Morrison's styles of writing illustrate their roles in helping marginalized groups find a new way of belonging. Naipaul and Morrison portray the concept of home in a hybrid revolutionary way by mingling the Western fairy tale technique with their indigenous narratives; therefore, there is *narrative* hybridity happening on the level of their textual forms as well. In order to achieve Fanon's combat literature, in which indigenous writers try to resist and subvert the authority of dominant Western societies, Naipaul and Morrison employ hybridity in their styles of writing. Thus, hybridity is not only what Naipaul and Morrison write, but it is how they write and deliver their literary messages to their nations. Therefore,

> hybridity is used deliberately to disrupt the flow of the novel, which is generally written in standard metropolitan language but includes . . . elements contesting the authority of that colonial norm. (Bandia, 2010, 185)

In their later novels, Naipaul and Morrison revisit the Western fairy tale genre, mainly to depict the journey of self-definition and self-acceptance, engaging in a social and cultural critique of the patriarchal postcolonial society of the time. However, Naipaul and Morrison go much further than they did in their earlier fiction. They not only use fairy tales to underpin their narratives, connecting them with many of the significant motifs of the novels, but also, a fairy tale develops the basic structure in which the characters' identity struggles take place. Therefore, according to Fanon's third phase, in their later texts, Naipaul and Morrison use hybridity as their central theme, and as the primary technique when framing *Half a Life*, *Magic Seeds*, and *Home* within the Western fairy tale technique, as a way of hybridizing Western literary traditions with their indigenous cultures.

However, the question here could be: are Naipaul and Morrison still mimicking the dominant Western cultures, while adopting the Western technique of fairy tale to frame their later novels? The answer is, they are not mimicking, but they are resisting the supremacy of Western discourse. Naipaul and Morrison transgress the limits of colonial discourse and subvert its authority.

Fairy tales sometimes occur only as a metaphor, or as an intertextual reference, but they can also appear as the central theme of a literary work. They frequently occur in postmodern texts, and particularly in novels that incorporate biographical elements narrated by their protagonists in the form of storytelling. V.S. Naipaul's *Magic Seeds,* which is a sequel to his *Half a Life*, and Morrison's *Home* are significant examples of fairy tale structures. Fairy tales are structurally organized as a quest, a journey, or as a series of trials or sacrifices. *Magic Seeds, Half a Life,* and *Home* are considered journeys from unhomeliness to hybridity. Naipaul's and Morrison's characters are simplified archetypes that usually represent binary oppositions: self/other, male/female, good/evil, hero/villain, strong/weak, and colonizer/colonized. Naipaul's and Morrison's usage of fairy tale frameworks gives readers the impression of a happy ending. Through their use of fairy tale structures, Naipaul and Morrison dramatize nation-building and collapsing in postcolonial work: in-between beings' engagement in the process of construction identity, knowledge, and 'home' is, in itself, mythic.

Naipaul's and Morrison's later texts are culturally hybrid texts, which combine the colonizer and colonized literary traditions. In *Magic Seeds* and

Home, Naipaul and Morrison write from what Bhabha would call a "liminal" space: their "texts exist in the web of tradition; they are enmeshed in its intersecting lines" (Wall, 2005, 11). While they choose storytelling as a way of narrating their history, they decide on a traditional Western tale as a frame for their novels. Thus, through textual hybridity, they have produced fictional structures of personal and national identity.

Home depicts the story of two siblings, Frank and Cee, Morrison's true American Hansel and Gretel, on their journey to self-definition. Both narratives revolve around an intimate sibling relationship, show striking parallels in their plots in which the protagonists have to face and eventually overcome enormous obstacles. Also, Naipaul's *Half a Life* and *Magic Seeds* discuss the story of Willie Chandran's journey toward self-definition. Naipaul's *Magic Seeds* includes three chapters entitled: "The London Beanstalk," "The Giant at the Top," and "'An Axe to the Root"; each title refers directly to the English fairy tale *Jack and the Beanstalk*. Naipaul and Morrison deal with one of the leitmotifs of their fiction, the quest to find their way home, which is the fairy tale's true quest. Willie, Frank, and his sister Cee are born into a world that does not give them true self-consciousness but only allows them to see themselves through the eyes of others. Theirs is the history of indigenous people's strife to attain their self-consciousness, merge their double self into a better and truer self, and overcome their paradigmatic unhomely condition. Analogous to the *Hansel and Gretel* fairy tale protagonists, the Money siblings encounter difficulties outside their parental home. Hansel and Gretel, for instance, have to face almost challenging obstacles in a hostile outer world such as a deep forest and a cannibalistic witch. Similarly, Frank and his sister face the cannibalism of racism and marginalization in dominant American society.

Why, then, do Naipaul and Morrison use the fairy tale framework? The story of the fairy tales can be interpreted from different perspectives, and Naipaul and Morrison read these stories from a different point of view by entirely deconstructing the characters' roles and revisiting events in the fairy tale to subvert both the narrative of imperial storytellers and to mock the discriminatory attitudes of Western ideology. I argue that subversion is reflected mainly in the unspoken and understated within texts. It emerges in ironies, double meanings, unlikely juxtapositions, and disjunctures.

In *Magic Seeds,* the fairy tale is revisited both stylistically and thematically. Willie, in *Magic Seeds*, moves to London, and there he finds himself to be upper-middle-class, and at this point there begins the story of *Jack and the Beanstalk* with the chapters' titles already mentioned: "The London Beanstalk," "Giant at the Top," and "An Axe to the Root." In so doing, Naipaul subverts the stylistic patterns of the fairy tale by omitting ogres, gigantic plants, and dream-like lands, and instead, inserting contemporary elements as the first phase of his deconstruction. Naipaul hides thematically-subverted ironies behind stylistic changes. He ironizes each chapter; at the end of the chapters, he achieves a satirical version of the fairy tale with a different happy ending.

Naipaul creates a world in which all roles and characters of the fairy tale are matched. Willie Chandran is in the role of Jack, Perdita acts as the wife of the giant or ogre, while Peter the banker is associated with the ogre and lastly, Marcus is shown as a fairy tale character who lives happily ever after. Nevertheless, Naipaul satirizes the perception of Western narratives, especially fairy tales, by associating Jack with an outsider and by matching the happy ending with a dream-like wish that subverts the egocentric European white race with a combination of an African-oriented man and a white woman. He creates the characters Willie, Roger, Perdita, Peter, and Marcus as the ones who are morally and ethically deformed. Willie sleeps with his friend's wife, who is also a lover of Peter, while Marcus is obsessed with the thought of having sex with whites. However, in fairy tales, sex and violence take the perverse form of incest and child abuse, for the nuclear family furnishes the fairy tale's main cast of characters just as family conflict constitutes its most common subject. Naipaul mocks and severely satirizes the moral division of good/bad by terminating the roots of Western family relations. By this means, he portrays a deconstructed panorama of the fairy tales by highlighting the idea that "the mischief starts" and "everything starts unraveling" (*MS,* 280).

Naipaul challenges the dominant culture on its own ground and on its own terms as he changes and mocks the process of the Western fairy tale by altering all the patterned roles and by addressing the conclusion of the fairy tale. The fairy tale–like ending of Naipaul's version of *Jack and the Beanstalk* consists in the triumph of Marcus, a West-African, who has devoted himself to "inter-racial sex and wanted to have a white grandchild" (*MS*, 230). Marcus achieves his goal and he lives happily ever after like Jack, who succeeds in achieving his goal of being rich and marrying a great princess, and he lives happily ever after.

Naipaul with such a reversed ending compares the importance of the discursive power of Western narratives with the happy ending scenes. In the fairy tale *Jack and the Beanstalk*, as a representative of Western fairy tales, goods—Jack and his mother—are rewarded while the wicked ogre is penalized; however, Naipaul subverts this thematically moral lesson. For example, Willie is neither rewarded nor punished though, in the novel, he is in the role of Jack, instead of him, Marcus is rewarded with a happy ending and his wishes come true. Naipaul satirizes that Jack and the ogre in the fairy tale are not rewarded or punished because of their vices and virtue. For Naipaul,

Jack is rewarded because he is the representative of the West, capitalism, and the colonial attitude while the ogre is punished because he is an outsider. By this way, Naipaul shows that moral judgment is ideological. Naipaul disrupts the general stylistics of fairy tales and their Western ideological outlook and mocks with the thematic concern of fairy tales constructed on moral lessons. Thus, Naipaul's usage of fairy tales enables him to achieve Fanon's third phase of creating a fighting literature that deconstructs and resists the discursive power of the dominant Western narratives.

Morrison's *Home* is mainly about the trauma of war and the inability to return home. *Home* is an exploration of what it means to be at home or not at home on American soil. It dramatizes the senses of alienation, dispossession, and lack of belonging in the context of the Korean War, which broke the pattern that armies go home at the end of the war. Morrison unveils the truth of a war that America has forgotten. Also, through her fairy tale intertexts, Morrison powerfully critiques U.S. colonialism of both past and present, the system of patriarchal racism, sexism, and classism that has not only denied the freedom, self-determination, and even humanity of African-Americans. Morrison poses that same interconnectedness by making her protagonist in *Home* a veteran in the Korean War and a bearer of collective memory of racial violence and persecution. America's political actions in Korea and its racial discrimination at home are intertwined in Frank's memories, reinforced by further parallels made in the novel between 1950s racism and nineteenth-century slavery.

Anti–fairy tales are possibly healing in their search of society's transformation. In *Home*, Morrison's reinterpretation of one of the most famous Western stories, *Hansel and Gretel*, allows her to create her own tale of the African-American self's struggle for self-realization. Morrison's anti–fairy tale focuses on the process of individuation of those politically and culturally disempowered. Also, the anti–fairy tale structure allows Morrison to unveil the horrors of racist, damaging gynecological experimentation on African-American women. In so doing, Morrison resists and protests against American hegemonic racist practices against African-American women. Through the character of Dr Beau, Morrison delves into medical experimentation on African-Americans, which was a common practice in American science history until and throughout the twentieth century.

Moreover, Morrison deconstructs the Western stereotypes of black men as barbaric and wild beasts. The moment Frank walks in the door to save his sister, Cee, Dr Beau, who feels "threatened," shouts: "There's nothing to steal here!" (*H*, 86). The villain's (Dr Beau's) cowardly behavior contrasts with the hero's (Frank's) humane and manly one. The wicked physician epitomizes African-Americans' deep Western cultural fear, questioning and subverting the so-called white supremacy and civility. Morrison fractures the myth of the ideal white beauty, which is represented and symbolized by Dr Beau. Morrison criticizes Western sciences, which she sets against her black ancestors' healing powers. She contrasts the wicked scientist's hideous patriarchal medical procedures without healing objectives to curing the self and body provided by black women's communities.

She uses a fairy tale frame to narrate their journey from trauma to empowerment because meta fairy tales generally convey the characters' transformation from alienation and symbolic amputation to greater consciousness, community, and wholeness. Morrison stresses how the black self cannot achieve self-definition without coming to terms with their traumatic memories. Like her other novels, Frank and Cee's story is one of reconciliation with the history of racial prejudice and oppression. African-Americans must confront the ghosts of the past through the healing powers of memory.

Morrison hints at the connection between traumatic memories and the present and suggests the need to lay the haunting ghosts of the past to rest before you can build a hopeful future. As in nearly all fairy tales, Morrison encodes an important spiritual and moral lesson: the best defense against the destructiveness of racism is the formation of a cultural identity derived from an understanding of history and the reconciliation with the ominous past. That is why Cee's quilt, which symbolizes her newly reconstructed identity, is used as the burial shroud. Cee and Frank represent African-Americans who can redeem themselves and begin their psychological and emotional healing, moving from fragmentation to wholeness.

Morrison uses fairy tale motifs to depict African-Americans' typical quests of self-definition in a patriarchal hegemonic society full of social and economic hardships for those suffering racial discrimination and oppression. In the fairy tale of *Hansel and Gretel*, the children return to their father's home. However, in *Home*, Morrison's metafiction embeds and sometimes reverses or subverts the plot, structure, themes, characterization, motifs, and images of its fairy tale intertexts, mainly *Hansel and Gretel*. By deconstructing fairy stories, she engages in a racial and cultural critique of dominant cultures, creating a revolutionary narrative that meets Fanon's fighting phase, in which "the crystallization of the national consciousness will both disrupt literary styles and themes" (Fanon, 1968, 238) of dominant Western cultures and discourses. For example, in *Home*, and while reversing the conventional end of fairy tales, in which heterosexual love usually triumphs, Morrison contrasts the unsuccessful man–woman relations, Cee with her boyfriend Prince and Frank with his lover Lily. Hence, Morrison deconstructs the gendered white, heterosexual, romantic myth of the traditional fairy tale. In *Home*, the brother–sister relationship ends in the marriage-like family they create at the end of the story and the patriarchal system is questioned in their plans for sharing a common life on equal terms. Thus, instead of heterosexual romance and offspring (Cee is sterile), the two siblings, who have been engaged in constructing personal identity, succeed in creating a family, community, and a true home, on their own terms.

Naipaul and Morrison use a fairy tale frame to narrate their journeys from trauma and alienation to empowerment and hybridity. In my view, the power of hybridity can be seen in its ability to question what appears natural and complete, to problematize naturalized boundaries and binaries created by any dominant groups. Naipaul's and Morrison's usage of the fairy tale technique has helped them to a great extent to unsettle the hegemony of the colonial ideology while highlighting themes which are substantial in postcolonial and in African-American societies, such as the construction of reality, struggle for survival, power, body, racism, dehumanization, gender, postcolonialism, self-image, the quest for identity, home, and a new way of belonging.

While using fairy tale intertexts, Naipaul and Morrison powerfully interweave Western fairy tales as primary frames for their novels in order to interweave Western culture into indigenous people's cultures. Thus, in *Magic Seeds* and *Home*, Naipaul's and Morrison's reinterpretations of Western tales, *Jack and the Beanstalk* and *Hansel and Gretel*, allow them to create their own tales of marginalized nations' journeys from self-denial to self-realization. Thus, Naipaul and Morrison create their own combat literature, in which indigenous writers incite "the whole people to fight for their existence as a nation" (Fanon, 1968, 240).

NAIPAUL'S AND MORRISON'S NARRATIVE VOICES AND FANON'S THIRD PHASE

Naipaul's and Morrison's hybrid narrations and their use of multiple narrative voices enable their novels to stage individual points of view and outlooks for different fictional agents. Naipaul's *Half a Life* and *Magic Seeds* are novels about incompleteness. Willie, as an example of postcolonial migrants, has no firm objectives, no clear ambitions, and is always leaning on people around him. Somehow, Naipaul's narrative style mirrors his and Willie's unstable and unhomely character. The narrator's presentation of the damaged characters—mostly in the third person—makes it hard for the reader to sympathize with them. Much of the narrative is presented in monologues and letters and, primarily, through the characters' thoughts. Naipaul here affirms the alienation and unhomeliness of postcolonial migrants. However, nothing is elaborated on in detail; there are few descriptive excursions. For example, there is no description of the protagonist's physical features. This feature keeps the reader at a distance.

In several episodes, the narrator seems like a fabulist. The scenes are set pieces that always end with Willie spelling out the moral, featuring characters who deliver speeches instead of conversation, and who seem less like real people than mouthpieces for the narrator's opinions about everything from colonialism to multiculturalism. Despite its severe style and ungenerous vision—characteristics shared with *Half a Life*—the sequel *Magic Seeds* is well-paced. Besides, differently from *Half a Life* with its substantial first chapter, *Magic Seeds'* twelve chapters are told in sequence. Most of the novel runs like a philosophical dialogue between characters. Willie's thoughts punctuate many of the small episodes. There is a kind of a dissatisfied clarity of analysis of the characters' lives. The novel's language is associated with Willie's unsteady and fragmented character.

The flat narration with coordinated and short sentences is suitable for someone like Willie as a narrator. Having lived eighteen years in a Portuguese colony, then in Germany, then in India's countryside, he seems to forget his command of the English language. The way that the story moves through events and diverse settings follow Willie's broken language. Even before going to Africa with Ana, Willie's mind is occupied with the confusion that such frequent changes in location and language would lead to, and he senses the loss of language:

> He thought about the new language he would have to learn. He wondered whether he would be able to hold on to his own language. He wondered whether he would forget his English, the language of his stories. . . . Willie was trying to deal with the knowledge that had come to him on the ship that his home language had almost gone, that his English was going, that he had no proper language left, no gift of expression. (*HL*, 124)

The narration is made up of extensive dialogues that are small monologues, which tell the past and backgrounds of characters through solid tales. Almost all the characters—people that pass through Willie's life have their lives told in this kind of inset tale, in both *Half a Life* and *Magic Seeds*. The novels consist of stories within stories in which the protagonist—frequently in the third person—tells the reader of stories that other people told him, or which he told other people

Similarly, in *Home*, Toni Morrison alternates the narration of her novel between her omniscient narrative voice, and that of her protagonist Frank Money, through which most of the story is told. The narration of *Home* is divided in parallel between two narrative voices—one where the narrator is far away and absent from the story she tells, and the other where it is a character in the story. In other words, Frank's narrative voice is different from Morrison's; he uses colloquial language and shorter sentences most of the time, and also uses contracted forms. Frank's chapters are also smaller and shorter than Morrison's. He also keeps interfering with the third-person voice narration and criticizes Morrison herself that she cannot capture his experience. This draws the reader's attention and, in some way, characterizes him as an irritating, angry, and perhaps cruel figure.

According to Fanon's third phase, Morrison is an awakener, an observer, and the main narrator of *Home*, who is outside the world of the story she narrates. She is an objective, omniscient narrator that knows not only every aspect of the story but also what is going on inside her characters' minds. Her narrative style is different from Frank's; she uses longer complex phrases, dialogues, free direct and indirect speech, and her chapters are more extended than Frank's. Frank is a subjective narrator. He tries to convince the reader of his own views, though he tends to lie on multiple occasions in order to hide his disgrace and guilt, which are the main reasons for his trauma. The alternation and combination between the two narrative voices in *Home* permit the continual dialogue between Morrison herself and Frank, which creates a sort of personal dialogue between them "since you are set on telling my story" (*H*, 13). The fact that Frank's first-person point of view makes him an unreliable narrator builds a negative image in the reader's mind, but with the presence of Morrison's narration, she explains to the reader why Frank acts in this way. This amalgamation and alternation raise the reader's empathy.

In my opinion, there is some distance between Morrison's two narrators in *Home*, that is, through the structure of the novel. In this sense, Morrison succeeds in presenting Fanon's words of being the awakener of her people as she keeps a distance between herself and her characters. Morrison tries to stress her role of being her people's advisor and awakener by using different fonts, where the first-person narrator uses italics while the third person uses the standard straight font. In other words, the reader of the novel can notice the physical division of the narration, in which each narrative voice occupies specific chapters in the novel's structure. This is despite the narrators being separated through the structure, as Morrison interweaves them in a frequent interaction, and the reader can notice this throughout Frank's direct interaction. The presence of a hybrid weaving between the first- and third-person narrative voices helps Frank to come to terms with his traumatic memories.

Frank keeps repeating 'I' through his confession, which seems to sink into his mind as he speaks. With each sentence, the burden he kept carrying inside for so long is vanishing, and he is finally able to see his self-denial and accept his feelings: "A little child. A wee little girl, I didn't have to, better should die . . . she took me to a place I didn't know was in me?" (*H*, 226). Frank's confession represents African-Americans' confession, as he represents most of them. Morrison emphasizes that remembering past traumatic memories is the only way toward self-healing and self-recognition in most of her novels.

When Morrison creates a dialogue between her and her protagonist, she approaches her nation. She is now their advisor who helps them to heal. She gives them clues to remember their past and to face it. Morrison achieves Fanon's words and becomes her nation's "awakener," helping them to overcome their feelings of unhomeliness and fragmentation through her writing. She isolates her narrator's narrative from hers to stress that she is healed from her trauma and that she will be her people's support in their process of self-recognition.

Likewise, Naipaul has used mainly realistic narratives in his novels because he is persuaded that there is always a truth to be unveiled, and a reality with which to be coped. Naipaul allows the voices of many characters to be heard and expresses their fragmented feelings. Naipaul's narrative shifts, and Willie's effect guiding the storyline is dropped in favor of interventions from an omniscient narrator. Naipaul also has a role in waking his nation. He too achieves Fanon's third phase of being an observer and advisor to his nation, but the difference between him and Morrison is that he identifies himself with his characters. Naipaul's shifting narrative style from the first person to the third emphasizes his in-betweenness and his occupancy of Homi Bhabha's third space.

However, Naipaul believes in supporting and awakening his people by exposing them to their truth. He makes them face the defeats of their culture to change for the better. Naipaul is aware of his hybrid identity, and he succeeds in finding a new way of belonging. His earlier novels give an insight into how postcolonial people develop a sense of cultural inferiority and/or a sense of unhomeliness. In his latest novels, he views places as changing, notions of home and belonging as unstable, and the geographical order—the difference between primitive and civilized societies—as a production.

Morrison's traumatic memories are not simple African-American histories. They are unresolved, uncontained, and they insinuate themselves into the present like the eponymous ghost child in *Beloved*, who haunts the living with such force that she becomes flesh and blood. Frank and Cee, who signify African-Americans, are finally able to "reclaim Lotus as their literal, physical home. Through their willingness to confront their past, they find their true home within them in the memories they share" (*H*, 135). Thus, Morrison accentuates the concept of unity as a final step in the healing process.

Finally, Naipaul and Morrison choose their main characters, males or females, to be the representatives of their people. These characters are always on a quest. They represent the status of all subaltern people who live in an in-between position as a result of their fragmented backgrounds. Naipaul and Morrison summarize their literary lives in their latest novels, which include Fanon's three phases of identity. These stages are crystallized in the lives of Naipaul's and Morrison's main characters: mimicry, recalling the past, and finally hybridity as a new way of belonging. They want to expose their nations to the truth of their quest. Naipaul and Morrison state facts about their people and, at the same time, guide them to new ways of resolving the psychological conflicts that result from their double and fragmented identities.

Naipaul and Morrison renegotiate their hybrid identities but in a different way. As mentioned before, Naipaul's new home is in a multicultural society, in which there are cross-cultural exchange and mutual experiences and knowledge, regardless of one's origins and roots. Nevertheless, Morrison is still sustaining her ancestors' traditions and culture. Ancestral African culture for her is like an infinite scar on her back and all her people's backs. Morrison's home is any safe place with her community, which will help in the healing process. Therefore, Naipaul and Morrison do exceptionally well in presenting the three phases of Frantz Fanon's theory of indigenous writers, but each of them does so in their own unique way. They succeed in being their people's 'awakeners' who help, guide, support, and surprise them with revolutionary literature, which will help in understanding the revolutionary meaning of the concept of home. The concluding point here is that postcolonial writers and critics might have different approaches, but they are more or less unified in addressing the need to establish a decentralized geographical consciousness as a prerequisite for ending the imperially created sense of dislocation.

The ambiguous state of indigenous people within but outside the mainstream of the colonizer's dominant cultures creates a double-consciousness. This duality is not always a curse, but it can be a blessing. It leads to hybridity and a specific perspective, which allows for openness, the embrace of contradiction and paradox, and full completeness, even incorporating one's deepest fears. The concept of hybridity as a product of the feeling of double-consciousness is undertaken to present how cultural hybridity is considered a means to reconcile the identity conflict of postcolonial people. Hybridity turns out to be a possible solution rather than a dilemma for the hybrid characters who try to resist their marginalization in the dominant societies in which they live.

Morrison does her utmost to revive her ancestors' past and to celebrate her African culture in the dominant American society. As Fanon asserts in his third phase, she also succeeds in being her people's awakener because she represents an image of American society that can be a home for her and her nation while maintaining and celebrating their ancestors' past, culture, and traditions. As a postcolonial writer, Naipaul also succeeds in guiding his people to a new solution to belong and to land safely. He sheds light on his traditions and rituals, not to belittle them, but to help develop postcolonial societies.

Naipaul and Morrison present a possible solution to their people's eternal dilemma of home in their latest novels in which they summarize their literary journeys: *Half a Life*, *Magic Seeds*, and *Home*. Naipaul wants indigenous people to live like magic seeds that can be cultivated anywhere. These magic seeds can adapt to any soil and any land. Also, Morrison finds home when she finds her past, which she hybridizes and quilts with any land that she and her nation live in together as one community. Naipaul and Morrison guide their nations to a new way of belonging through which marginalized groups can resist hegemonic power. However, the question here may be: is hybridity considered the end of the struggle for postcolonial or indigenous people?

I think through hybridity, postcolonial and indigenous people will start living their lives while trying to fight against their relegation in the dominant societies, in which they live. In other words, the Middle Passage and history of colonialism have left ineradicable scars on the social, cultural, and symbolic worlds of postcolonial and African-American people, which no formal process of decolonization can ever entirely erase. Hybridity is a way by which postcolonial or subaltern people have challenged established codes of identity. They have embraced hybridity in terms of language, culture, and identity. The ambivalence, ambiguity, and contradiction that they have experienced in these hybrid positions have opened up a third space, in which they have reconsidered, negotiated, and extended their positions. The negotiation of their identities in the third space has resulted in new ways of defining themselves, which have enabled them to embrace and express their ways of being in the various worlds to which they belong. For Naipaul and Morrison, the politics of their undertakings may vary, but the artistic intent is constant: hybridity is the alternative to mimicry; it is a force against hegemonic powers. It is not the end of the struggle of postcolonial and African-American people, but, as mentioned earlier, at least it can operate as a site of resistance to forms of categories, or essentialism, imposed by colonialism and dominant social groups that like to read the so-called 'other' as the binary opposite of the imperial/white self.

Chapter Five

Gender in Naipaul and Morrison

For literary research today to preserve a sense of cultural and social relevance, it must recognize the importance of gender roles and the images of gender within literary texts. Also, literature, being a tool for social change, must shed light on women's issues in postcolonial patriarchal societies. In order to enrich the comparison between Naipaul and Morrison, this chapter will address gender issues in selected novels by both of them. In the previous three chapters of this book, I have related Fanon's three stages of identity to both writers. However, I will also highlight gender issues in Naipaul's and Morrison's selected novels.

Traditionally, the terms 'sex' and 'gender' have been used interchangeably, but it is significant to understand the distinction between both of them. Generally, 'sex' denotes the biological differences between males and females, such as genetic differences, hormones, and genitalia. In other words, the sex of a person is associated with the anatomical features of male, female, and intersex. Nevertheless, gender refers to the cultural and social roles of each sex within a given society and culture. Instead of being purely allocated by genetics, as sex differences usually are, people often change their gender roles according to the environment, including family relations, media, and education. Therefore, the difference between sex and gender makes a separation between the sexed body on the one hand, and the gendered behavior of people on the other hand.

The prevailing opinion that asserts biological sex as binary (male vs. female), natural, and essential, creates the basis for binary gender, which is regarded as the cultural interpretation of sexual desire and sex. However, Judith Butler, a gender theorist, is critical of this distinction between sex and gender and suggests that sex and gender could be the same. Butler suggests and argues, "sex is as culturally constructed as gender," and she concludes that if that is the case, then sex and gender are the same (Butler, 1990, 10–11). She calls sex a cultural norm because "sex is no longer treated as something determined by the body" (Butler, 1993, xii). In other words, there is a traditional faith that a male baby will grow up to perform and identify as a man and, as part of this gender role, be sexually attracted to women. Likewise, there is another belief that a female baby will grow up to behave and identify as a woman and, as part of this gender role, be sexually attracted to men. Butler argues that these configurations of sexual desire, sex, and gender are the only understandable genders in our culture. Therefore, Butler argues that the distinction between sex and gender is meaningless, and that "perhaps . . . sex is as culturally constructed as gender; indeed, perhaps it was always already gendered with the consequence that the distinction between sex and gender turns out to be no distinction at all" (Butler, 1990, 9).

This chapter does not debate or argue that biological processes do not exist or do not affect differences in anatomy or hormones. However, I argue that bodies do not exist outside of cultural interpretation and that this explanation brings about oversimplified, binary viewpoints of sex. By way of explanation, biological processes do not themselves produce two meaningful, distinct, and natural categories of people. The two main sexes only seem apparent, natural, and essential to us because of the gendered world in which we live. More specifically, the repeated performance of two opposite, polar genders makes the existence of two natural, inherent, prediscursive sexes appear reasonable, creating the illusion of binary sex. Therefore, according to Butler, there is no natural or objective sex, but it is performatively constructed.

While describing gender as performative, I mean that gender creates a series of effects. For example, we speak, act, and walk in ways associated with the impression of being a man or a woman. Therefore, gender is "an act, or, a sequence of acts; a verb rather than a noun; a doing rather than a being" (Butler, 1990, 25). In parts of this chapter, I will explore the issues of representation and identity politics that depend on these "performances" that construct what it means to be male or female.

In general, gender denotes the social and cultural attributes and opportunities connected with being male and female, the relationships between men and women and boys and girls, and the relationship between women, for example, and broader society. These traditional attributes, "opportunities and relationships are socially constructed and read through the acculturation processes" (Collins, 2002, 201). Through acculturation—the process of adopting another group's cultural traits or social patterns—gender roles have become vague over time and are not as specific now as the evolutionized traits that previously defined these strict roles.

Therefore, within a dominant hegemonic culture, new conceptions of gender emerge, and these conceptions resist and defy the traditional dichotomies of self/other, male/female, or heterosexual/homosexual. Similarly, Judith Butler has called into question the very definition of what constitutes "male" and "female," undermining the notion of proper gender roles. In my opinion,

Butler calls for a gender revolution or gender trouble, as she entitles her book, by unsettling the gender binary to deconstruct and dismantle patriarchy's domineering and oppressive system.

In this chapter, I argue that Naipaul and Morrison address gender in their novels, but differently. Also, in parts of this chapter, I argue that Morrison suggests that traditionally prescribed norms of gender have to be replaced and resisted. Moreover, Morrison emphasizes the concept of black women's communities as a means of safety, security, and resistance to white patriarchy and black male phallic power. It is not solely about gender inequalities; instead, "it is a mixture of several elements that assist in oppressing . . . women" (Mohanty et al., 1991, 322). These several elements can be exemplified by race, class, and sexuality. Therefore, for Morrison, black women's communities can become the place for resistance to arise and take shape and, more importantly, the sense of community can work as a form of resistance in itself. Besides, Morrison exhibits a rejecting image to a traditionally feminine representation for some of her characters, such as Sula, who decides that she "really would act like what you call a man" (Morrison, Toni [1973] *Sula*, 143, hereafter cited as *S*). Morrison instead circumvents and resists the establishment of phallic and patriarchal domination, the latter of which is powerfully supported by Naipaul in most of his novels.

In my opinion, Naipaul might oppose resistances to normative gender as normative gender ensures phallic masculinity, male power/privilege, and heteronormativity—but this also comes from social norms, which are perhaps inherited from colonialism since the colonial encounter reproduced phallic masculinity.

> Colonial custom and practice stemmed from a world view, which believes in the absolute superiority of the human over the nonhuman and the subhuman, the masculine over the feminine. . . , the colonial process was sex-differentiated in so far as the colonizers were male and used gendered identity to determine policy. (Oyewumi, 2005, 339–340)

By subjugating colonized people, the Western world deprives all indigenous people of their cultural identity and double colonizes indigenous women. The presumed masculinity of colonization coupled with the hypermasculine image of the Western world further subjugates women in colonized societies. Consequently, most of Naipaul's female characters are submissive, flat, and dominated by phallic masculinity produced by colonialism.

However, Naipaul emphasizes patriarchal power to oppress colonial power, which white women embodied in his fiction. Naipaul and his male characters try to resist and oppose colonial power as he depicts a symbolic image of sexual relationships between white women and postcolonial phallic men.

In these relationships, white women, who represent the dominant colonial culture, are humiliated and oppressed by postcolonial men who perform normative gender masculinity as a way of resistance to the hegemonic colonial power. Furthermore, Naipaul resists the hegemonic power, but he resists and defies the traditions of developing countries in Africa, Asia, and the Middle East that ban bisexuality and queerness while depicting an African Muslim bisexual leader.

In postcolonial and African-American societies, the acculturation process is that identity is linked to behaviors, which translate into learned gender roles. Therefore "gender identities act as cognitive filtering devices guiding people to attend to and learn gender role behaviors appropriate to their status" (Devor, 2010, 388). In this way, the construction of gender (and thereby the establishment of the norms of sexual difference) is achieved through the continual repetition and 'performance' of particular discourses.

Gender is important in constructing self and identity as it denotes socially approved roles, behaviors, actions, and features considered to be fit for men and/or women. These specific roles bring about gender inequalities that intentionally give favor to one group by oppressing and dominating the other. For example, "women have been left out of history, not because of the evil conspiracies of men in general, but because we have considered history only in male-centered terms" (Lerner, 1979, 39).

In other words, women's oppression refers to women's inferior position and the patriarchal domination that women are subjected to in most societies. In this chapter, I will shed light on the feelings of weakness, discrimination, and experience of limited self-confidence and self-esteem that contribute to the subordination of women in selected texts by Naipaul and Morrison. I will also present how women's subordination in a power relationship creates a kind of empowerment and resistance to the prescribed gender norms, which are asserted by a specific culture.

Therefore, Naipaul is complicit in the power of the masculine standard and believe that it is the only means of progress. Naipaul's works emphasize society's firm structure that stresses women's inferiority and weakness. However, Morrison asserts feminine power in both private and public spheres. In most of Morrison's fiction, "the pressure of the past that wants to erupt into the historical narrative is embodied by female figures" (Seward and Tally, 2014, 105). History in Morrison's novels is always celebrated, and using female figures to embody and symbolize the African past is one of Morrison's techniques to appreciate and elevate women's status and resist black patriarchy. Besides, Morrison's works argue that despite what society believes to be appropriate now, cultural variability will soon break and confront the patriarchal traditions and perceptions that inferiorize women and nonbinary genders, such as bigender and transgender.

On the contrary, oppressed and fragile women inhabit most of Naipaul's fictional works from the beginning, and one must search hard in his more recent fiction to find a woman who has not been denied the reader's sympathy. Naipaul's female characters are either harshly restricted by traditions or made to use men for personal ends; thus, Naipaul does not challenge the traditional norms of gender roles. Morrison's novels represent a wide variety of female figures whose behaviors and actions describe African-American women's ironic position and existence in American society. Furthermore, Morrison's work perhaps tries to undermine dominant gender norms.

Therefore, the dominant relations between sex, gender, and sexuality, are not natural relations, but inventions (by masculine power) and can be resisted. Morrison creates defiant characters who challenge any racial oppression in American society by changing and deconstructing the traditional norms of gender. In her works, Morrison explores the dilemmas of women in a male-dominated and white racist society. She documents the lives of African-American women who are struggling hard to quilt their fragmented identities and lives back together again, and to claim a sense of self that they have lost or never even had. Morrison presents the unique heritage of African-American culture at the center of her intricate and multidimensional narrative. Gender is a significant issue in Naipaul's and Morrison's fiction, but each of them has their own perspective on portraying and presenting it.

MIMICRY AND GENDER OPPRESSION

At the very beginning of their literary lives, Naipaul and Morrison presented the traditional pattern of typically prescribed gender roles in patriarchal societies. In so doing, Naipaul's and Morrison's earlier characters imitate conventional gender. Naipaul and Morrison illustrate normative and traditional gender roles in their earlier novels. Morrison represents the character of a frustrated African-American father who practices his masculine power to rape his weak daughter. While depicting this pattern of sexual oppression, Morrison describes the traditional image of gender dichotomy, which will be challenged later in most of her novels. Meanwhile, while presenting the character of Ralph, who tries to oppress and dominate white women sexually, Naipaul gives the readers a preliminary idea of all his novels in advance. Naipaul is against any change in his traditional phallic beliefs, as in most of his novels, he depends on normative masculinity as a tool of oppression.

In other words, in most of Naipaul's fiction, (post)colonized Indo-Trinidadian men collectively found themselves subjected to hegemonic white British masculinity, with the prevailing social institution of colonialism allowing white English masculinity to present itself as the authentic controlling form of masculinity. Indo-Trinidadian men, who came to represent ideal masculinity, were always inadequate and inferior to English men and were culturally positioned as subordinate and/or marginalized. Therefore, Indo-Trinidadian men came to rely upon and to imitate highly stylized forms of masculinity as a means of asserting their cultural and individual agency, at once affirming and challenging how the (post)colonial subject becomes viewed as a copy or mimic of the original British subject through his compromised position.

On the contrary, Morrison stresses her resistance to the patriarchal oppression later in her novels. Therefore, in her first novels, Morrison expresses that gender oppression leads her to undermine and deconstruct the traditionally prescribed norms of gender roles. However, Morrison is similar to Naipaul when using gender oppression as a tool to mimic the dominant power as the dominant or "colonial rule itself is described as a manly or husbandry or lordly prerogative" (Oyewumi, 2005, 339). For instance, Naipaul's Ralph in *The Mimic Men* and Morrison's Cholly in *The Bluest Eye* use their physical strength to overpower and oppress women. Ralph in *The Mimic Men* has many sexual relationships with white women to feel superior and to mimic English society in dealing with the idea of practicing sex. Ralph's failure in his role as a husband or even as a man of affairs is considered a symbolic defeat in his attempt to play the part of the superior. He fails in assimilating into English culture. These sexual issues are adopted by the Third World immigrants who move from their local society, which imposes sexual taboos on a liberal Western world, which is not subject to such inhibitions. Ralph is a man fated to live in the shadow of a Western lifestyle, not his own.

Ralph hopes that living in London will help transform his thinking and self-image. He wishes to achieve a better social standing by residing within high-class society. His housekeeper, Lieni, inspires him with her goal of becoming a "smart London girl." Her attempts at assimilating were more "like a duty owed more to the city than herself" (*MM*, 14). As a postcolonial migrant, Ralph attempts to become an excellent British citizen and believes that relationships with various white European women will lead him to achieve this ideal Westernized life that so many European men have achieved. When he is unable to be intimate with these women, he feels disconnected from them and his claim on London. Naipaul establishes a relationship between Ralph's sexual escapades and imperial conquest. Naipaul directly compares his protagonist's desire for the city with his passion for sexual affairs:

> It is so whenever, moving out of ourselves, we look for extensions of ourselves. It is with cities as it is with sex. We seek the physical city and find only a conglomeration of private cells. In the city, as nowhere else, we are reminded that

we are individuals, units. Yet the idea of the city remains; it is the god of the city that we pursue, in vain. (*MM*, 22)

Naipaul tries to introduce the reader to the postcolonial world, and so does Fanon. One of Fanon's central themes was that "for the black man there is only one destiny. And it is white" (Fanon, 1952, 10). His logic is that white slave-owners took away their slaves' own identities, and as a consequence, the slaves could only see their identities in mimicking the whites and "being" white. However, how could they become white? There were some ways. They could strive for the objects that whites had: housing or languages. However, one crucial way was by having sex with a white woman. Fanon explains: "I found that the dominant concern with those arriving in France was to go to bed with a white woman. . . . It is, in fact, customary in Martinique to dream of a form of the salvation of magically turning white" (Fanon, 1952, 44). Therefore, for postcolonial men, the venting of their inner annoyance toward the dominant society turns savage, and their female accomplices suffer as a result. Naipaul imposes his political views, which resist the hegemonic English society when creating troubled sexual relationships between postcolonial migrants and white females. Therefore, Naipaul reflects his defiance of the dominant culture and the oppression of English society, symbolized by white women.

In *The Bluest Eye*, Morrison presents the mimicking of white cultural domination when Cholly (the father) feels humiliated and suppressed by the whites. He projects his anger on to the only beings he knows to be lower on the social scale. He mimics and practices white domination to regain his self-image, once damaged by whites. So his abnormal behaviors with Pecola are nothing but unloading his own painful experience of the dominant white society. He tries to feel superior while mimicking white oppression over his sick daughter, Pecola. In other words, "colonized native male . . . has the only kind of power left—his greater physical strength as a male to overpower the female" (Wirth-Nesher, 1984, 542). Thus, patriarchy is seen in the violence perpetrated on Pecola as her own father colonizes her. Pecola's rape is the depiction of the destruction of the cultural identity of black women's communities. Consequently, Pecola's growth is increasingly stunted as "she draws nearer her personal abyss" (Lee, 1984, 349). Pecola's father (Cholly) violates her body like her society, which breaks her soul. When he penetrates her body, he stabs her soul, which will lead her to a total withdrawal from life. Being a child whose position is hugely assailable, Pecola becomes an easy victim.

In *The Mimic Men*, Ralph's sexual frustrations are not his own but are the failures of society, of race, of culture. Ralph is attracted to the English Sandra (his wife) because she is English and belongs to British culture. His marriage is simply another strategy for assimilating into and mimicking English culture. She is the symbol of English culture with which Ralph feels secured and protected: "To attach myself to [Sandra] was to acquire that protection which she offered, to share some of her quality of being marked, a quality which once was mine but which I had lost" (*MM*, 56; brackets added). Ralph's gradual deracination into cosmopolitanism is played out in the sexual territory of his encounters with his neighbors, prostitutes, and Sandra, his English wife. In this way, he shows the fetishistic and anxious nature of his sexual relationships. This sexual myth—the quest for white flesh—is perpetuated by Fanonian alienated psyches:

> By loving me, she proves that I am worthy of white love. I am loved as a white man. I am a white man. Her love takes me onto the noble road that leads to total realization. . . . I marry white culture, white beauty, white whiteness. When my restless hands caress those white breasts, they grasp white civilization and dignity and make them mine. (Fanon, 1952, 63)

Meanwhile, through a symbolic association between the colonizers and the colonized, the subjugated will practice his superiority as a male with his English wife. Ralph wants to prove to others that he is powerful and their equal; he tries to whiten himself in a sense by marrying an English woman in London. Thus, he hopes to become more completely a part of English society. Cholly also wishes to obtain a white woman's love and respect to gain his place and to convince himself that he is superior, but he rapes his weak black daughter. Still, Ralph cannot be an authentic English person through whitening himself in a sense, and mimicry, and these acts only serve to bring him greater anxiety and restlessness. As Memmi asserts: "a product manufactured by the colonizer is accepted with confidence. His habits, clothing, food, architecture are closely copied, even if inappropriate. A mixed marriage is the extreme expression of this audacious leap" (Memmi, 1965, 121). Ralph is also attracted to Stella for similar reasons. Stella's manner "was a way of looking at the city and being in it, a way of appearing to manage it and organize it for a series of separate, perfect pleasures" (*MM*, 231).

Ralph's fascination for the colonizer's culture and lifestyle prompts him to form relationships with white women (Sandra and Stella), but he has no emotional attachment to them. The relationships lead to frustration and disappointment and alienate him from his family and society. His mother does not accept Sandra warmly as she is English. By entering a relationship with her, he has rejected the cultural tradition of his people, and his only chance for survival is to withdraw into emptiness.

Likewise, Morrison employs gender oppression to show that black men practice sex to vent their internal humiliating feelings over women who are considered double victims. African-American women are victims of the dominant white society and an object of oppression by African-American men. Pecola is oppressed and rejected by the dominant white culture, her fellows, classmates, and teachers: "The ugliness that made [Pecola] ignored or despised at school by teachers and classmates alike. She was the only member of her class who sat alone at a double desk" (*BE*, 39; brackets added). Besides, she is brutally oppressed by her father, who turns to misogyny, substance abuse, and crime as ways to express his own masculinity.

Oppression and rejection drive Pecola to insanity. She views herself always as a detested girl, and the inherent feeling of ugliness heightens her desire for further separation. However, she finds solace in her separation despite her marginalization. In a patriarchal system, the victimization of women, or even young girls, is seen in how people accuse them of the sexual abuse they receive, while they fail to condemn the actual perpetrators. In the story, one woman incriminates Pecola for her father's statutory rape: "She carries some of the blame" (*BE*, 149), implying that Pecola did not fight him, even though she was only eleven. African-American community's disdain toward Pecola is severely transferred to her baby, whom they think will "be the ugliest thing walking" (*BE*, 149). Her identity dissociation is complete and irreversible. Even through the 'bestowed' blue eyes, Pecola does not get the reward, but she remains trapped in a schizophrenic state, which stops her from achieving the flight she thought would come with the blue eyes. Sexual abuse triggers Pecola's total identity fragmentation. Her self becomes so crazed, so fragmented, that it conducts a conversation with itself—and with no one else. Therefore, her feeling of inferiority, internalized oppression, and shame inhabit her life, as well as the hurt of racial discrimination.

While Cholly mimics white culture by raping and oppressing African-American women, Naipaul's Ralph mimics English society by having sexual affairs with white women. Naipaul also pursues the city as he pursues white women, only to end up isolated. He hopes for a relationship with these women and pictures its magnificence just as he sketches his relationship with the city. However, he is left in his private cell—a prison that falsely presents itself as a safe haven of order and stability. Ralph is disappointed by this order and lack of intimacy with the city. He hopes that London can offer him status and make him feel important and influential. For him, London is "the great city, the center of the world, in which, fleeing disorder, I had hoped to find the beginning of order" (*MM*, 22).

The oppression and frustration of colonized people during the colonial period led them to believe that the Europeans were superior and they were inferior. The oppression and failure of postcolonial people are similar to the abuse and subjugation of African-Americans in general and African-American women in particular. Oppression creates fantasies of superiority and makes

African-Americans believe that they are always "ugly." A blind imitation or mimicry of the dominant powers would lead indigenous people to fantasies of superiority to access the powers of the dominant culture. Mimicry becomes a hopeless attempt to be a copy of the dominant power. Mimicry and performing masculine colonialism lead to gender oppression and to humiliating women as indigenous men try to impose their masculine power and vent their humiliation over the female because she is seen as unequal to them. Therefore, the question is how can a society that is profoundly mimetic produce anything that is not in itself mimicry; or "how can a man, who is not sure what he is, produce anything that is genuinely his own" (Boxill, 1976, 13). Mimicry of the husbandry role of dominant cultures will create copies but not an original white person because "mimicry repeats rather than represents" (Bhabha, 1994, 125); mimicry imprisons but does not elevate roles.

SEXUALITY AND GENDER OPPRESSION

Naipaul's and Morrison's use of sexual behavior portrays their characters and their social struggles and conflicts. My investigation, therefore, focuses on how Naipaul and Morrison use sexuality to demonstrate the problems of marginalized and indigenous societies. In postcolonial and African-American societies, there are "different forms of oppression based on gender, sexuality, race, ethnicity, class and so forth [that] intersect, connect and reinforce each other" (Harcourt, 2016, 7; brackets added). I believe that it is interesting to observe how Naipaul's and Morrison's characters' attitudes and backgrounds are revealed through their sexual behaviors, which demonstrate how sexuality is a result of social and cultural production. As Judith Butler maintains in *Bodies That Matter*, "sexuality is regulated" in culture "through the policing and the shaming of gender" (Butler, 1993, 182). This shaming creates a form of oppression of those who do not fit into the traditional model and degrades them.

However, at the very beginning of this chapter, I have shed light on the prevailing conceptualization of women of color in dominant patriarchal societies as being doubly oppressed. Therefore, women are undeniably in a risk of sexual assault, even women of higher social status. Meanwhile, oppression and shame produce resistance, which is "a response to power from below" (Johansson and Lilja, 2013, 269)—a subaltern practice that can challenge, negotiate, and destabilize the dominant power.

For example, Morrison's Sula is punished and accused of all her illicit sexual encounters and her nihilism regarding the norms of her society. Sula's male-dominated society ignores the fact that the men who visited her were equally guilty. These men fulfill their sexual appetite by utilizing her body, and later accuse her of being a whore and a witch who has to be burned because she does not fit into the traditional model. Men in Sula's society should have been accused and socially degraded by the community that alienated and oppressed her. Such an invalid society, which is static regarding individual growth, oppresses and devastates Sula because she defies and resists the traditional and social norms imposed by patriarchal cultures. Morrison's characters, especially her black female characters, resist gender norms in various degrees. In *Sula*, "[African-American women] were neither white nor male, and that all freedom and triumph was forbidden to them, they had to set about creating something else" (*S*, 52; brackets added). Nevertheless, Morrison sheds light on female sexual abuse to emphasize women's double victimization.

Naipaul also highlights sexual affairs in his novel, but he wants to celebrate his and his characters' masculine power as he and his male characters always sustain normative gender views. Focusing on the subtleties of normative masculine performances between differently positioned men within a single, yet multitudinous, culture, readers notice Naipaul's careful consideration of the pitfalls of masculinity to comment directly on the emasculating effects of colonial rule and postcolonial consciousness between more and less hegemonic men.

Morrison uses historical facts and details concerning the past to make her reader aware of the rich and complex heritage of African-American culture and the place of women within it. She reminds her readers of the past by presenting fragmented images of ancestral culture, black identity, and the African family unit. While not allowing the reader to forget the horror and humiliation of slavery, Morrison's focused descriptions often relapse back to an earlier time of identity, closeness, and order. She combines the psychological and cultural aspects of African-American communities. She explores the issues of identity, family, and self-possession in a world where slavery has apparently become a tragic issue of the past, but emerges, throughout, as a haunting presence. For example, in the Middle Passage, women's bodies "were offered as evidence to support racist notions that black people were more akin to animals than other humans" (hooks, 1992, 62). As indicated earlier, Morrison stresses the inferiority of black women since the beginning of the Middle Passage to gain readers' sympathy and to highlight black women's double oppression.

However, in most of his works, Naipaul's female characters are either severely constrained by traditions and customs or made to be semiwhores turned to use men for their own personal ends. Naipaul's female characters are submissive and oppressed as they are performing hegemonic masculinity and femininity, respectively. However, Naipaul's male characters get embarrassed in horror at the modern women's ability to control their reproductive functions. Taken together, such remarks make up an approach toward women and sexuality, which Naipaul has imposed on his fiction—an approach amplified by the violence inflicted on women generally in his works. In general, Naipaul gives the reader of his fiction a hideous portrayal of women: "There are no successful love affairs, no successful marriages. . . . Women appear repulsive, and [sexuality] becomes boring, violent, or abhorrent" (Hemenway, 1982, 193; brackets added). For little apparent reason, Linda, in *In a Free State*, is deemed by her companion to be "nothing but a *rotten* cunt" (Naipaul, V.S. [1971] *In a Free State*, 220, hereafter cited as *FS*; emphasis added). The target of apparently illogical anger, Yvette, in *A Bend in the River*, is beaten liberally around the face and between the legs; Jane in *Guerrillas* suffers the indignity of anal rape before she is cutlassed to death. In Naipaul's *A Bend in the River*, Salim and his lover, Yvette, have an upsetting encounter. Salim beats Yvette, but instead of escaping or objecting, she undresses and prepares to make love with him.

> Much agitated, Salim goes to her, I went and sat on the bed beside her. Her body had a softness, pliability, and a great warmth . . . At this moment! I held her legs apart. She raised them slightly? Smooth con? Cavities of flesh on either side of the inner ridge? And then I spat on her between her legs until I had no more spit. (Naipaul, V.S. [1979] *A Bend in The River*, 215, hereafter cited as *BR*)

Here Naipaul stresses the masculine ability to enslave and humiliate white women. In so doing, Naipaul emphasizes his conventional patriarchal views of gender. Naipaul despises women's bodies, and his male characters use their sexual power to oppress white women who symbolize the white culture. On the other hand, Morrison wants to draw her readers' empathy with her female characters. Similarly, *Beloved* is an example of Morrison's text that suggests that "a fictional account of the interior" life of an enslaved person might be more historically "real" than actual documents, which were often written from the viewpoint of the dominant culture (Davis, 1998, 248). In addition to the complicated and hard work that exceeded the physical aptitude of enslaved women, black women were also slaves to the whims and desires of their masters. Their bodies did not belong to themselves; they were forced to offer their bodies to their masters whenever they wanted. Black women's bodies were regarded as the property of their masters, which indicates female slaves' powerlessness. I would argue that they were viewed and treated as sexual objects by their white masters and, even sometimes, by their own family members. Besides, a black female's body "was relegated to the lowest position on the scale of the human development" (Hammonds, 1997, 172).

In an interview with Bonnie Angelo in *Time* magazine, Toni Morrison states that the American nation tries not to remember the painful history of slavery. In her novels, especially *Beloved* and *The Bluest Eye*, Morrison stresses the history of slavery and its horrifying issues and effects—something that she thinks has been avoided and forgotten in traditional slave narratives. Besides, in her earlier novels, Morrison depicts the normative and conventional gender to initiate women's resistance to the prescribed gender norms in hegemonic societies. Also, she mentions that even black characters in *Beloved* do not want to remember the history of enslavement in America. Furthermore, Morrison notes: "I do not want to remember, black people, do not want to remember, white people, do not want to remember" (Morrison, 1989, 122).

Morrison's novels, however, remind readers of the crime of slavery, which some prefer to forget. During slavery, "African-American women were defined as property, and their social, political, and legal rights barely exceeded those of farm animals. They were subjected to the same form of control and abuse as animals" (Hammonds, 1997, 173). For Morrison, gender oppression is not a noticeable problem that exists between black men and black women, but I would argue that it survives inside the context of the unbalanced relationship between master and slave. Race alone is considered enough justification for the subjugation of all African people.

Naipaul also presents different sexual affairs in which women are humiliated and forced into sex. He shows indigenous men with indigenous women and indigenous men with white women. In both cases, women are humiliated and despised. Naipaul's *Guerrillas* presents parallel scenes, even more violent and aggressive than Morrison's scenes. One particular scene involves an African bisexual Muslim revolutionary leader, Jimmy, forcing Jane, the white bourgeoisie, to have a sexual relationship. After the act, the narration is exceptionally unsympathetic, ending with an insult to the female, who is treated as "rotten meat" (Naipaul, V.S. [1975] *Guerrillas*, 18, hereafter cited as *G*).

The question is: why does Naipaul create such scenes? The answer lies not so much in his revulsions, whatever they may be, as in the vision he feels compelled to impose. Naipaul's sexual politics may be suspect, but they are part of a more significant political matter—his concern about the social contract. Naipaul's novels are meant to exemplify how the sexual contract between white women and black men reflects political associations in the Third World, degrades Naipaul's politics in *Guerrillas*, or attributes them entirely to sexual confusion about his manhood. Naipaul places the symbol of the white woman at the center of Jimmy's bisexual personality and, by connotation, at the center of Black Power ideology. Jimmy's identification with the poor and the downtrodden becomes secondary to his irrational response to white women—the representatives of the colonizers he wishes to defeat.

White women have been a somewhat consistent concern of Naipaul, perhaps revealing more about his art than his politics. If the sexual contract is to serve the political vision, white women become useful symbols. Also, white women embody much that Third World people must react against in developing an independent political status. However, Jane's role threatens to become a racist cliché; Naipaul's need to destroy Jane, to make her politically and morally revolting so that her sexual contracts will seem perverse, cripples the characterization of the novel.

In most of Naipaul's novels, such as *A Bend in the River*, *In a Free State*, *A House for Mr Biswas*, *The Mimic Men*, and *The Enigma of Arrival*, Naipaul's characters are always confined by their self-deception, and their romantic refusal to acknowledge reality. As in these novels, *Guerrillas* raises serious questions about whether or not Naipaul's technique, so much in the service of his vision, will not always cause him to deny his characters the kind of growth that might lead to self-revelation, and therefore a valid politics. Naipaul apparently cannot control his vision; he cannot transfer the capacity to see "that which is obvious" from himself to his characters. An African bisexual Muslim leader, Jimmy Ahmed, serves as an example of what Naipaul withholds from his creations. Jimmy's bisexual behavior reflects Naipaul's political confusion. Therefore, Jimmy's bisexuality can be interpreted, first, as identification with the poor and oppressed and, second, his anxious response to white women—the representatives of the system he wishes to overthrow or resist.

Jimmy's fantasies of sexual conquest and domination awkwardly evoke the psychoanalytical discourse of Frantz Fanon's allegories of racial empowerment through the symbolic subjection of white women's bodies and other "black radical autobiographies . . . with their ideological defense of raping white women" (King, 1993, 109). The problem with this fantasy is that its satisfactions are double-edged. Taking or raping white women becomes a kind of political resistance to the whole system of phylogenetic interrelationships, no matter whether the woman is willing or not. Like many postcolonial migrants, Jimmy accepts the white woman as a substitute for real political power, finding refuge from guilt over his impotence in the myth of the black race's sexual superiority. In my view, rape for him was a revolutionary act against the dominant colonial power.

Jane, who represents English culture, is sexually assaulted and oppressed by postcolonial Jimmy. The battle of passion becomes the battle of pride and prejudices. This ugly murder scene has been described as one of the "harshest scenes of sexual violation in modern literature" (Thrope, 1976, 40). Thus, in this novel, Naipaul portrays sexuality combined with horror. As a white woman, Jane becomes powerless in the male-dominated society. Her whole life symbolizes the essence of emptiness or nothingness. The ritual murder of

Jane is "the ultimate perversity engendered by colonialism" (Wirth-Nesher, 1984, 543). Naipaul's Jane is considered an "apt metaphor for European imperialist colonization of Africa and North America" (hooks, 1990, 57).

Rape has been used as a weapon by which indigenous men attempt to reverse their circumstances and gain control over white culture. Therefore, Naipaul creates rape scenes to allow indigenous males to take revenge and to declare their power over the dominant white society. Similarly, Naipaul must make Jimmy bisexual—another transformation because sexual confusion is intended to reflect political chaos. The relationship between Jane and Jimmy becomes an allegory of the way a Third World nation conceives its former colonial masters. The relationship, Naipaul implies, represents the political situation in the Third World; without a contract between individuals, the idea of the state careers toward chaos. The price for Jimmy's complication is the reader's pity toward his politics.

However, the question here is, why does Naipaul create the character of Jimmy as an African *bisexual Muslim*, although he opposes any resistance to the conventional normativity of gender? When Naipaul creates Jimmy Ahmed, an African bisexual Muslim revolutionary leader, Naipaul is not critiquing the normativity of gender. However, he is reversing Islamic religion rules and the traditions and customs of developing countries in Africa, Asia, and the Middle East that do not tolerate the concept of bisexuality and queerness. Naipaul resists and challenges Islamic religion, which is, for him, "a complicated religion" (Naipaul, 1981, 10), as it prohibits bisexuality as well. In his *Beyond Belief,* Naipaul expresses his attitude toward Islam.

> Converted peoples have to strip themselves of their past; of converted peoples, nothing is required but the purest faith (if such a thing can be arrived at), Islam, submission. It is *the most uncompromising kind of imperialism*. (Naipaul, 1997, 72; emphasis added)

Therefore, Naipaul's complex formation of Jimmy Ahmed's character subverts "the imperial demands" (Naipaul, 1997, xi) created by Islamic religion, which Naipaul criticizes in some of his texts such as *Among the Believers* and *Beyond Belief.* Furthermore, Naipaul further complicates the web of multicultural sexual transgressions by exploiting the racial significance of Jimmy's homosexual scenes with Bryant. In my opinion, through his sexual use of Bryant, Jimmy enacts "his own love-hate relationship with blackness, seeing in [him] that deformed part of himself" (King, 1993, 107; brackets added). Bryant attracts and repels Jimmy, and, as a reminder of his inauthentic, corrupted racial identity, Bryant helps him discharge his secret hatred and desire for authentic blackness, which parallels the white woman's transgression of the taboo of black sexuality. The significance of Bryant's role is that he "serves simultaneously as the sexual body upon which Jimmy realizes his domination as well as the politically disenfranchised body whom he manipulates for his cause" (Mustafa, 1995, 127).

As I have mentioned earlier, Naipaul uses rape as a weapon by which indigenous men attempt to resist and control white culture, which white women symbolize. However, Morrison discusses rape, but she explains different types of abuse. She stresses that both African-African men and women were exposed to sexual oppression. However, Morrison focuses on the wretched condition of slaves, especially female ones, of whom Sethe is a perfect representative since she is raped, mistreated, and violated. In *Beloved*, Sethe mentions:

> After I left you, those boys came in there and took my milk. That's what they came in there for. Held me down and took it. I told Mrs. Garner on em. She had that lump and couldn't speak, but her eyes rolled out tears. The boys found out I told on em. Schoolteacher made one open up my back, and when it closed, it made a tree. It grows there still. (*B*, 16)

Sethe's milk symbolizes her need to mother and feed her children—a need, which was denied to her mother but one which she refuses to have rejected. This is why she is so adamant about having Paul D understand the significance of her having her milk "taken" by the schoolteacher's pupils. In Morrison's novels, African-American women are the most oppressed as white men and black men double victimize them. Morrison also stresses that sex and rape are used to oppress not only black women but black men as well. For example, life as a prisoner also oppresses and humiliates Paul D. When Paul D and his fellow prisoners are forced to perform oral sex with the guards, they are trapped in a "ritual of white male bonding intended to humiliate its victims by feminizing them, parodying while rehearsing the primal act of nurturance" (Moglen, 1993, 27).

Paul D's experience is an inversion of Sethe's; whereas Sethe had to endure having her milk taken away from her, Paul D is forced to "take" the "milk" (semen) of the white guards. Morrison portrays similar reactions of black women and men to the rapes. Sethe remembers being overcome with revulsion at the thought of the young boy's "mossy teeth" and, Paul D, "convinced he was next . . . retched" and still can remember "smelling the guard, listening to his soft grunts" (*B*, 108).

Morrison paints a portrait of Paul D in contrasting masculine/feminine characteristics. While rape can usually be asserted to a male executor and a female victim, that is not the case in *Beloved*. In other words, Morrison decides to employ multiple forms of rape, including homosexual rape, to deconstruct and resist the traditional views of gender. Her African-American characters were raped on numerous occasions. Morrison chooses to show this aspect to maintain that women were not the only victims of rape or sexual abuse. Besides, she wants to stress the victimization of the black race in general, whether male or female. The entire experience with the chain gang in the South made Paul D traumatized since it was something that he refused—he was forced into it under threat of death. Paul D did not choose death over this behavior as Sethe did when she killed her children. It shows us that both male and female characters have different perspectives on life based on what happened in their lives. The sexual oppression of black women is not only an end in itself; it is also an instrument in the oppression of the entire black race. I mean that when black men are also raped and sexually abused, they are "symbolically castrated and assaulted in their essential dignity" (Lerner, 1972, 172).

In Naipaul's and Morrison's novels, sexuality indicates how oppressive and pathological and patriarchal society can be. At the same time, sexual oppression is shown to be the most devastating and cruel kind of oppression. Naipaul's image of sexual oppression is to stress his and his male characters' masculine power, but Morrison sheds light on sexual oppression to highlight, first, the suffering of black women who are victimized by both white society and black patriarchy, and second, the suffering of black men as well by dominant white culture. Morrison uses narration to make a statement about the cruelty and hopelessness of her African-American characters to describe the traumatic effect of violence and abuse. Morrison here "portrays victims rendered voiceless . . . a victim of incest and violence" (Holloway and Demetrakopoulos, 1987, 163).

In Morrison's novels, black women not only defy the limitations of gender norms, but through their complex characters, she shows how these images blend as the boundaries between them blur. For example, in *Beloved*, Sethe, on the surface, and especially at the onset of her mothering performance, resembles the ideal black mother, self-sacrificing and absorbed in the interests of their children.

This need for the reconstruction of the social order arises as a result of an oppressive social hierarchy, which ranks black women at the bottom of social stratification, after white men, white women, and black men. Patriarchy further tries to justify its order by maintaining that black women are socially inferior. However, black motherhood, as mentioned earlier, is doubly restricted by gender and racial factors. Black women have, since slavery, attempted to struggle against the social forces, which condemned them to silent suffering. The reality of the experience of black motherhood reveals the nature and patience of black mothers' active and articulate resistance to the imposition of the passive image of idealized motherhood. Black women's use of every expression of racism launches multiple assaults against the entire framework of inequality, which has been a threat to the status quo. To contribute to black women's struggle against imposed stereotypes, contemporary Toni Morrison has tried to expose patriarchal society's oppression of black women through the literary and social treatment of women's issues.

Toni Morrison's novels are women-centered and revolve around women's lives, problems, and search for identity. Thus, a dominant concern of many contemporary African-American writers, motherhood is a recurrent theme in Morrison's fiction. I am suggesting that Morrison has chosen an alternative avenue for investigating the definition of womanhood and motherhood—an interpretation that revises, reconsiders, and reassesses the image of the mother as the biological medium of producing babies. Morrison wants her readers to discern the complexities concealed by the ideology of black motherhood, which attempts to bring artificial coherence and order to the different aspects of the lives of mothers. The importance of this exposure lies in creating an active space of articulation for mothers and the potential for the expression of the experience of black motherhood from women's points of view.

Morrison, who is concerned with the revision of history and illumination of the neglected areas of African-American culture, takes up the task of rescuing black mothers from this historical silence. Morrison's novels create a space of representation for mothers by enabling them to break their silence and talk in their own right. Morrison's mothers defy the "object" position they are placed in, and as "subjects," speak and act on their own behalf. bell hooks's definition of identity in terms of subject and object successfully describes the cultural and historical significance of resisting stereotypes and the social imposition of controlling images: "as subjects, people have the right to define their reality, establish their own identities, name their history" (hooks, 1989, 4). However, as objects, she contends, "others define one's reality, one's identity created by others, one's history named only in ways that define one's relationship to those who are subject" (hooks, 1989, 24). By emphasizing the distinction between "self-reliance" and "dominance or power," I would assert that many of the misconceptions about African-American women's powerful presence in their families "comes from the fact that women in American society are held to be the passive sex, but the majority of black women have, perhaps, never fit this model" (Ladner, 1971, 53). The dynamics of sex and class oppression are considered instrumental in forming damaged images of African-American women in American society.

In exploring Morrison's novels, I have attempted to investigate how "structures of dominance" work regarding Morrison's female characters' attempts at growth as she develops critical thinking and critical consciousness, as she invents new, alternate habits of being, and resists from that marginal space of difference inwardly defined. Morrison's *Beloved* presents the cumulative trauma of slavery and the Middle Passage in prose sympathetic yet persistent. Her description of rape, which epitomizes the many kinds of aggression and violence enacted upon women and men during slavery and the Middle Passage, exemplifies how traumatic experience may be represented while remaining fundamentally incomprehensible. Morrison chooses rape to symbolize the trauma of slavery and the Middle Passage because it is the most aggressive action that can happen for both black males and females. Nevertheless, Naipaul's use of sexual relationships in his novels indicates that he wants to celebrate his masculinity. In his novels, Naipaul always creates sexual relationships between a white woman and a man of color. He builds these relationships to celebrate his and his male characters' power over white women. Likening the colonizers to women shows that Naipaul wants to put the colonizer's culture in an inferior state. Hence, women in Naipaul's earlier novels are always inferior, whether white or persons of color.

From Morrison's point of view, mothers, biological or otherwise, are individuals who are suitable to act, as the existing circumstances require. Although mothers are usually sacrificing, loving, and caring in ideal situations, they are, above all, unique individuals, capable of making choices, which their communities might not endorse, but are opportunities for self-determination. Furthermore, they are or grow to become aware of the value of their selves and identities, distinct and independent from their children. On the other hand, in Naipaul's world, the sexual contact in the bond, which symbolizes the social contract, brings no mutual benefit. There are no flourishing love affairs or successful marriages in his works. Women appear repulsive, and sexuality becomes annoying, violent, or offensive. Naipaul seems fundamentally incapable of declining his or his male characters' normative views of gender. Therefore, Naipaul cannot create an admirable woman character for fear she might offer hope to the politically powerless and frustrated men who serve as his protagonists. He intentionally denies his readers the belief that modern men and women, confronted by earth slowly going back to the bush, by nation-states self-destructing in genocide and guerrilla warfare, can find solace in the personal bonds of love, sex, or marriage. The failure of the sexual relationship reflects Naipaul's personal and philosophical belief that modern individuals cannot enter into any contract, including the idea of the state, which will provide mutual benefit. Naipaul's women are marginalized and humiliated because Naipaul celebrates patriarchal power in his fiction.

EMASCULATION AND WOMEN EMPOWERMENT

In the earlier parts of this chapter, I discussed female oppression and male celebration of masculinity. I have also stressed that men can oppress women while mimicking the dominant colonial power or celebrating masculine sexual power. Now I will argue that both Naipaul and Morrison, in their novels, present the two concepts of emasculation and female empowerment. Also, I argue that in some of Morrison's novels, emasculation will bring about women's empowerment, leading to a form of resistance to the patriarchal hegemonic societies. In short, "when femininity changes—generally when women try to redefine their identity—masculinity is destabilized" (Lewis, 2003, 97). Since the beginning of their writing, Naipaul and Morrison have exposed their readers to the oppressed images of women.

In most of her novels, Morrison presents emasculated black men who are deprived of their identity and the doubly victimized black women who are oppressed both by black patriarchy and white dominant power. However, Morrison's women try to empower themselves by resorting to their own black women's communities and by deconstructing their traditional gender roles as ways of resisting the hegemonic power. For example, in *Beloved, Sula, Paradise,* and *Home*, Morrison presents a powerful image of women connecting to their community and emasculated black men who try to restore their identities. In contrast, Naipaul creates his drifting male characters who are always searching for their own identities but without referring to any powerful woman trying to celebrate her identity.

One can understand the sociohistorical contexts of most of Naipaul's novels—and in particular, the power relationships that constrained the performances of masculinity for both white, hegemonic, British bourgeoisie and their brown-skinned, marginalized, East Indian counterparts—as central to understanding how gender norms both "constrain and enable life, how they designate in advance what will and will not be a livable existence" (Butler, 2004, 206). An exploration of masculinity within a single culture is complex enough, yet the effect is infinitely multiplied once creolization and colonialism are taken into consideration and examined through Naipaul's male protagonists. As individuals disempowered by their race and class in their representative colonial and postcolonial societies, their masculinity is frequently emasculated and destabilized through competing for cultural representations of manhood.

Therefore, Naipaul indirectly presents the revolutionary image of women who fight for their people's issues in his *Half a Life* and *Magic Seeds*. Naipaul gives examples of powerful women who drive his male protagonist to restore his fragmented and emasculated identity. While presenting the characters of Ana and Sarojini, who are going to be discussed later in the chapter, Naipaul presents Sarojini (the sister), who can hardly be categorized as a traditional Indian woman, and the Portuguese Ana, who has enriching and not emasculating power to help her husband in "undoing of fear, the granting to [him] of full manhood" (*MS*, 145; brackets added). So, in most of Naipaul's literature, women are the "catalyst who is only there to prompt the man's actions" (Boyne, 2017).

On the other hand, Morrison's unified female community works to support women in regaining their fragmented identities, and it also works as a way of resistance to white patriarchal society and black male power. Morrison, through a complex interweaving of peopled spaces, displays how communities and home serve as places to gather strength, invent strategy, and rest, even if they are insufficient for the task of solving institutional and social problems. Naipaul's return to his home and community reflects his society's fragmentation and loss. Therefore, Naipaul's and Morrison's male characters' senses of emasculation and fragmentation lead them to oppress women and to perform conventional masculine power on them. In other words, mimicry, sexual abuse, and female oppression are linked to the sense of psychological emasculation and identity loss for men.

Morrison presents black women's communities as the only shelter to help women empower themselves and gain their identities. In so doing, Morrison "confounds binary oppositions" (Smith, 2012, 32) created by dominant white society and by black patriarchy. This image of the community as a place of shelter is continuously foregrounded in Morrison's novels as related, firstly, to their enslaved past. In *Beloved*, the community provides women with support and their only joy because they care about each other. It would serve the function of a family because familiar unity was under extreme and constant threat. The women always had somebody to turn to, despite their apparent solitude. This idea determines Beloved's role in the novel because it is only through her actions that the characters allow themselves to feel once more, trust and love each other, and come to terms with their community and the world around them. The development of the characters can then be seen as following different stages: from searching in the inside part of their history to the outside flow of their feelings and, afterwards, from the inside of their family life to the outside of their community—a community that claims them back.

> For Sethe, it was as though the Clearing had come to her with all its heat and simmering leaves, where the voices of women searched for the right combination, the key, the code, the sound that broke the back of words. Building voice upon voice until they found it, and when they did, it was a wave of sound wide enough to sound deep water and knock the pods off chestnut trees. It broke over Sethe, and she trembled like the baptized in its wash. (*B*, 261)

In this scene, black women's communities are "the key," "the code," and the "sound" (*B*, 261), which defeat the evil that has trapped them—their past, which they are unable to deal with or forget. African-American women were stuck in a present that had witnessed the loss of their ancestral values based on loving and caring and had not been replaced. Slavery is not to be forgotten, but analyzed and claimed back the way it was: the roots of a community way of life, of understanding human existence as the presence of individuality supported on a strong sense of belonging, real caring, and sharing. The legacy from the past can be reactivated to illuminate the present reality and to help work out its various changes. Feeling whole can only be achieved through constantly reworking and revising the traditional value system based on the ideals of love and trust.

In my view, black women's communities in Morrison's novels go through the same "consolidation of identities," or Othering, through experiences of "exclusion and domination" (Butler, 1993, 182). While Morrison's characters are subjugated by a discourse that defines both racial and gender norms, their marginal position creates a space where they have the opportunity to explore and construct their own identities. This space, which is represented by black women's communities, can potentially encourage self-expression, self-definition, and ultimately healing as they can live in "a new world . . . a world where [they] never get to the bottom of things, a world that demands a shift from an either/or orientation to one that is both/and, full of shifts" (MacDowell, 1988, 80; brackets added).

Therefore, some women in Morrison's novels get to initiate themselves and other characters into the value of self and individuality. Mrs MacTeer, Claudia, Sula, Sethe, and Cee, all in their unique ways, celebrate their identities and reject the images imposed on them by the patriarchal society on the larger scale, and African-American community in particular, as it is presented in the world of Morrison's novels. Morrison's exposure of these harmful stereotypes implies that unless women can demystify motherhood and thus empower themselves, social and gender oppression will continue. Furthermore, Morrison's women are empowered because of their association with black women's communities and because of black men's emasculation. In so doing, Morrison challenges and resists the familiar constructions of gender to be replaced by the more fluid concepts of masculine/feminine. Morrison plays with gender to create a new character that interrupts the hegemonic discourse by exchanging the traditional gender roles. So, Morrison calls for resisting patriarchal domination.

For example, in *Beloved*, slavery has emasculated black men by stealing their manhood and preventing them from existing. Therefore, while motherly sensibilities and femininity are taken away from Sethe, she has to adopt and perform the masculine construction of gender roles to ensure her family's survival. Hence, black women "effectively take on the stereotypical characteristics of the opposite gender as a result of their former servitude" (Dueker, 2007, 1).

By creating a space in which mothers might articulate their stories of pain and anger, power and vulnerability, mothers can stop becoming victimized by the ideology of motherhood and assert the uniqueness of their identities. However, self-realization is the starting point for African-American women's true liberation from socially coded stereotyping: identity is not the goal but rather the point of departure in the process of self-definition. In this process, African-American women's journeys "toward an understanding of how their lives have been fundamentally shaped by interlocking systems of race, gender, and class oppression. . . . This journey toward self-definition offers a powerful challenge to the externally defined, controlling images of African-American women" (Collins, 2002, 106). The achievement of identity, then, becomes the impetus for moving women toward self-expression, the realization of the importance of self-value, the necessity of self-reliance and independence, and, finally, a belief in black women's empowerment to withstand constant social oppression.

Sula is another critical example in Morrison's novels. As mentioned earlier in this chapter, she is an empowered woman who rebels against patriarchal and social norms. *Sula* is considered "a fine cry—loud and long—but it had no bottom and it had no top" (*S*, 149). Through the character of Sula, Morrison represents an oppressed category of gender. Sula is a rebel against her society's traditional gender normativity. As a result, her people accuse her of being a devil. Sula demonstrates her nihilism through her rebelliousness against all morals, norms, and social mores, and with her firm declaration of sexual autonomy/anarchy. Morrison calls for the binary gender model to be demolished, and manages to undermine dichotomous thinking by suggesting that the issue cannot be viewed merely as an either/or proposition; factors such as race, class, heterosexism, and even age impact our culture's perceptions of gender roles. Sula creates the pretext for her patriarchal society to victimize and oppress her. As a result, Sula is deemed "the bearer of pleasure and desire" (Foucault, 2003, 192) and is thus identified as evil and a witch. Morrison's remark in her interview with Robert Stepto exemplifies how gender politics define Sula's unfortunate fate:

> She is a masculine character in that sense. She will do the kind of things that normally only men do, which is why she's so strange. She really behaves like a man. She picks up a man, drops a man, the same way a man picks up a woman, drops a woman. . . . She's masculine in that sense. She trusts herself; she's not scared; she really ain't scared. So that quality of masculinity—and I mean this in the pure sense—in a woman at that time is outrage, total outrage. (Morrison, 1977, 474–475)

It seems that the sexist gender ideology is complicit with assigning different lives and identities to Sula, a symbol of liberated women, and the privileged men. Sula's presence as a pariah cannot be accepted "because of her community's rigid norms for women" (MacDowell, 1988, 83). For her patriarchal society, Sula is evil and dangerous because she rebels against the demands of morality and conformity. In this sense, the body is an arena for power contestation between an individual who struggles for self-definition and a society, which demands discipline and compliance.

In contrast, women are marginal figures in V.S. Naipaul's latest novels like *Half a Life* and *Magic Seeds*. Naipaul's narrative space is a paradox where female characters, despite being marginal voices, are the pillars on which the men are leaning, and without their presence, assistance, and approval, no fulfillment is possible for men. Men are the dominant characters but have limited significance in private spaces. Women are the directional forces of the narrative in that they lead the male characters in their quest for destiny. Without women's existence, Naipaul's men would be in a state of limbo. Their push forces the men into action and occupies a silent yet forceful place that gives direction to the narrative. Many critics of Naipaul consider him to be a misogynist, and I have explained his misogyny in the previous part of this chapter. This perception arises from the gender-based violence depicted in Naipaul's books. As Bruce King states: "because Naipaul has scenes of sexual violence in his fiction, he sometimes has been regarded as antiwomen" (King, 1993, 13).

However, and despite the limited narrative space granted by Naipaul to the female characters, I argue that women in Naipaul's fiction are not often central but can often be significant. Here lies the difference between Naipaul and Morrison. For Morrison, women are the fundamental and pivotal characters, but for Naipaul, men are always the central characters, but women characters have their own space by assisting men to fulfill their purposeful roles. I draw on Naipaul's *Half a Life* and *Magic Seeds* in this chapter. The two novels have one point in common—an Indian male protagonist. In *Half a Life* and *Magic Seeds*, Naipaul's two most recent novels, the action takes place across three continents—Asia, Europe, and Africa—and Naipaul does not confine himself to one community or people. In these two novels, Naipaul depicts immigrants, local migrants, and locals, who come from varied ancestries.

A closer examination of these novels discloses that the physical space that the female characters occupy bears no correlation to their influence on the direction of the narrative and the progress of the plot. The physical space that the female characters have in Naipaul's novels is deceptive. One common point in all three of these novels by Naipaul is the depiction of the powerless female as a myth on which the male ego feeds to find relevance and strength. Naipaul portrays how the male resorts to physical and emotional violence to find meaning and significance but feels emasculated on a more profound level. In trying to fight this feeling of being crippled, Naipaul's male characters realize their weakness and the strength of the females. At some stage in Naipaul's *Half a Life*, the male protagonist is struck with the realization that he derives his power from the women in his life. He realizes that he has depended on women and that they are the stronger in this equation while appearing to be the weaker and subservient of the two. Willie, in *Half a Life,* tells Sarojini, his sister, "I drew comfort from Ana, her strength and her authority. Moreover, just as now, as you may have noticed, Sarojini, I lean on you" (*HL*, 141). Unlike being a member of the suppressed feminine space, Sarojini chooses to escape patriarchal domination. She is very straightforward in making her observation and does not wait for freedom to be given to her by the male. Female existence, often described as emasculating in Naipaul's earlier novels, is now a liberating force. Here, Naipaul depicts the advent of the realization of the empowering female presence whose acceptance by the male protagonist leads to a more mature and accepting attitude that was earlier lacking.

Although the narrators and the main characters in Naipaul's fiction are men, the women are the directional forces that lead the male characters to pursue their destiny. The women's push forces the men into action and provides silent yet strong direction to the narrative. In the patriarchal, mainly Indian world that Naipaul showcases in his novels, females who break this norm are most evident in his latest novels, *Half a Life* and *Magic Seeds*. These novels stand out in their portrayal of female characters who may not occupy a massive narrative space but whose usually silent existence is the dominant force that develops the narrative. When reading Naipaul, what needs to be kept in perspective is the social reality of the society and time that Naipaul is presenting in his novels. Naipaul's desire to present the complex relations that manage the personal spaces that his characters have, brings forth the hidden power of his women "whose assistance of men discharge their purposeful roles" (Saradhambal, 2017, 15). This partial physical space is not central to defining their arena of influence. The nature of Naipaul's absent female narrative voice is paradoxical in terms of the significance and strength of these silent voices, which murmur across the narrative or the plot.

The importance of the female characters is evident not so much in the physical space they occupy, but in the influence that they exert in the limited area granted to them. Whereas Naipaul gives his female characters minimal space in his novels, Morrison expands her narratives through her female characters. Morrison's female characters have independent and influential voices in most of her novels. In *Home,* Morrison draws attention to the psychological damage and enslavement that black women endured as a result of their gender and race. She also emphasizes the positive characteristics of the female communities surrounding her female characters, which sharply contrasts with the emasculation, isolation, and violence behind her male characters, such as Frank Money. This theme of female empowerment by black women's communities becomes most apparent in the dialogue between Ethel Fordham, the African-American woman who nursed Cee back to health, and Cee.

> See what I mean? Look to yourself. You are *free*. Moreover, nothing and nobody obliged to you but you. Seed your own land. You young and a woman and there's serious limitation in both, but you a person too. Don't let Lenore or some trifling boyfriend and *certainly no devil doctor decide who you are. That's slavery. Somewhere inside you is that free person.* . . . Locate her and let her do some good in the world. Cee put her finger in the blackberry jam. She licked it. I ain't going nowhere, Miss Ethel. *This is where I belong.* (*H*, 126; emphasis added)

Morrison strategically utilizes the word "free" in this passage to refer to Cee's newfound opportunity for growth and development. Cee is limited as a young woman, but foremost she is a "person" and should not let the limits of her gender determine her strength and ability. Morrison clearly distinguishes between her positive, community-oriented, and supportive female characters and her emasculated, isolated, and destructive male characters. Most of Morrison's male characters are always in quest of their selves because "white men effectively emasculated them, reducing them to an effeminate state" (hooks, 1982, 20). Frank Money suffers alone with the mental oppression of his gender and race. Often feeling secluded, helpless, and socially rejected, he is forced to endure his oppression with a little comfort from the other male characters in the novel. All the while, Cee is nurtured, encouraged, healed, and protected by the other women in her community. In most of her novels, Morrison portrays the female communities as a paradise that provides women with the power to confront patriarchal domination amongst blacks and in white society. For Morrison, black women communities are "the most peaceful place in the world" (Morrison, Toni [1997] *Paradise*, 182, hereafter cited as *P*).

In *Paradise,* the convent, which also depicts black women's communities, is a safe refuge for women seeking shelter and understanding without judgment. The convent is strictly for women who can come and go after recovering from their suffering, and it is a place where they can be free and loved and protected. In the convent, women seek no conflict and escape patriarchal oppression and violence. However, the convent, which symbolizes women's community, represents a little paradise—a place filled with love and religion and understanding, rather than rigid morality. Morrison asserts: "the Convent women were no longer haunted" (*P*, 266). The women in the convent seek this place to heal themselves and to try to start a new life. In contrast with the emasculated men in Morrison's fiction, many of her female characters seem to share a sense of unity, which helps them feel empowered.

Naipaul's and Morrison's concepts of emasculation and female empowerment, therefore, provide an insightful contrast that ultimately draws attention to the natural conclusion that gender and racial integrity are essential for a healthy person as well as a healthy community. Nowhere does Naipaul's representation of female characters gain the importance of mutual bonding between male-female relationships. Now, I can assert that Naipaul's conventional views of gender roles appear in his representation of the relationships between men and women. Most of Naipaul's female characters are flat and lack development, yet they contribute to the narrative's development. However, they do not develop their status, and their only means of survival is to adapt to the male-oriented world and remain stereotypes forever, with minimal scope for individualistic feminine space. Although Naipaul's female characters have evolved from age-old customs and codes of living to the present mode of living, their scope for a temporary feminine space remains mostly unrealized. In Toni Morrison's novels, the concept of black women's communities helps African-American women to discard their former selves—a self they need to bury to become a reclaimed self for their future.

> We Black women are the single group in the West intact. So anybody can see we're pretty shaky. We are ... the only group that derives its identity from itself. I think it's been rather unconscious, but we measure ourselves by ourselves, and I think that's a practice we can ill afford to lose. (Giovanni, 1971, 144)

By the end of each of Morrison's novels, women have gained the right to claim themselves for themselves by resorting to their own African-American communities, which represent safety and security. Morrison wants to show the living conditions of her female characters, who are suppressed and oppressed by dominant white power and black male power. She wants to state that they are searching for their true being or identity and that, for them, home is resorting to their community. Most of her female characters are homeless, with this homelessness depicted from birth. In the patriarchal and colonized society, they belong to nowhere with "no culture, no identity and no history" (Spivak, 1988, 271).

Toni Morrison shows the "vicious genocidal effects of racism on the black race" (Bhardwaj, 2017, 340) as dominant American power depriving blacks of their actual being through violence against them. In this way, African-American women are double colonized entities in this process and have to tolerate all kinds of subjugation and violence, not only from society but also from their own families. They do not have good relationships with their husbands based on love; in this way, they are surrounded by a thick fog of displeasure. Through Lily and Frank's life, Morrison states: "their bed work . . . became a duty" (*H*, 79), showing victimization and the double colonization of black women and women of color, physically and mentally, in colonized and masculinized societies. These female characters struggle to search for their identity and find a position in masculinized society to announce their being. In this way, Toni Morrison "deconstructs male-centered power regarding the identity of women and particularly black women. She hopes that Western patriarchal society will "learn to read the words of talk" (Spivak, 1988, 276); consequently, there might not be subjugation and objectification of women so that all women can be free.

Unlike Naipaul and Fanon, who take masculinity as the norm as they sustain the normativity of gender, Morrison defends her female characters and supports them by fighting for their independent identities. Morrison resists binary structures in male-dominated societies by deconstructing the conventional views of gender. Naipaul depicts symbolic violent sexual relationships between English women and postcolonial men to oppress white culture that he fails to mimic symbolically. Morrison also presents black women's communities to resist oppression in a phallic, patriarchal American society.

NAIPAUL AND MORRISON: GENDER AND CONCLUDING THOUGHTS

In the previous sections of this chapter, I have presented different examples from Naipaul's and Morrison's novels that discuss gender and its relation to sex, mimicry, emasculation, and female empowerment. In this part, I argue that Morrison focuses on female emotions to gain the reader's empathy, but that Naipaul imposes his masculine language to show off his and his male characters' masculine power. The examples that I have presented from Naipaul's novels demonstrate Naipaul having a kind of misogynist attitude toward women, but Morrison's novels show empathy and pity for women's struggle for identity. Morrison shows her constant persistence to resist phallic patriarchal power while converting women's position in the prescribed gender dichotomy as she always feminizes her ancestral history as to stress the importance of women's role.

On the contrary, Naipaul has claimed, "I read a piece of writing, and within a paragraph or two, I know whether it is by a woman or not. I think it is unequal to me." He has criticized female authors for their "sentimentality" and "narrow view of the world," going on to reject Jane Austen for her "sentimental ambitions" (Flood, 2011). Naipaul still emphasizes the normativity of gender as masculinity is his norm. Whereas Morrison treats black males' and black females' struggles more or less equally in her novels, Naipaul describes women as less equal to him and portrays women in his novels as being incomplete and inferior.

Morrison focuses on the roles of black mothers, daughters, and wives that are doubly victimized by their societies. As a result, Morrison's style is different from Naipaul's. As mentioned above, Naipaul's style reflects his masculine power in the patriarchal society and his continuous opposition to any challenge of normative gender views, whereas Morrison's style reflects her empathy for black women. She leans toward a complete description of her characters, male or female. She focuses on their psyches before their physical appearances, but Naipaul does not care much about the psyches of his female characters. He does not give a complete description of his female characters as, according to him, they are incomplete and are not equal to men. In *Half a Life* and *Magic Seeds*, he does not provide a detailed description of Ana and Sarojini—the two female characters considered the protagonist's motif toward his identity. On the contrary, in *Beloved* and *Home*, Morrison describes her females in detail, and she sheds light on their feelings and personalities to join the past with the present.

While analyzing their novels, I have found that most of the titles of Morrison's novels express feelings such as *The Bluest Eye*, which means the saddest eye, *Beloved*, *Paradise*, *Love*, *A Mercy*, and *Home*. Morrison also feminizes her ancestors' past and history in *Beloved* by likening her ancestors' past to the character of Beloved to praise women's roles in African culture. Morrison wants to say that women are as important as the African past, which has to be remembered and appreciated.

Alternatively, Naipaul's resistance to any change in the conventional views of gender normativity is apparent while choosing the titles of his novels. For example, Naipaul uses sexist language in his titles, such as *The Mimic Men* and *A House for Mr Biswas*. His other titles refer to facts rather than feelings, as Naipaul cares less about feelings. Morrison has been successful in her writings to express and record "the thoughts, words, feelings, and deeds of black women, experiences that make the realities of being black in America look very different from what men have written. In this tradition, women talk to women, and their relationships with women are vital to their growth and well-being" (Washington, 1987, xxi).

Morrison praises and glorifies women's image by representing her ancestors' past in feminine images, whereas Naipaul feminizes the colonizers and colonialism to inferiorize, weaken, and degrade the image of the colonial power. In most of his novels, Naipaul presents the colonizers as a white woman who is raped and sexually assaulted by an indigenous man. In this sense, he tries to impose his power over the dominant colonial power. Therefore, both use the same technique and style of feminizing some figures, but each of them uses it differently.

Unlike Morrison, Naipaul portrays contemporary males as too possessed by their egos to look after females' feelings. Naipaul and his male characters look at women as instruments of fantasies and ideals. Naipaul's negligence of women's feelings appears in most of his novels. In *The Mimic Men*, the submissive Ralph is shown to take out his frustration on the female he knows. He asks a girl whom he had been talking to for some time one evening, "Do you dance?" When the girl complies with his wish, "the impulse of *cruelty*" comes to him out of nowhere: "I said I don't, and I left" (*MM*, 17; emphasis added). In his novels, Naipaul legitimizes the humiliation of women, which is obvious in the rape and sexual scenes. I believe that the worst humiliation of all is reserved for the young black prostitute near the end of *The Mimic Men* who has her body intimately described:

> Her *breasts* cascaded heavily down. They were enormous; they were *grotesque*, empty *starved* sacks, which yet contained some substance at their tips, where alone they had some shape . . . *flesh* hung in *liquid* folds about her legs, which quivered like risen dough. She was ghastly, tragic, a figure from hell with a smiling girl's face, the thin, starved face of the slimmer. (*MM*, 281–282; emphasis added)

Naipaul's use of words that describe a woman's sexual parts affirms his patriarchal attitude; for Naipaul, women are just "breasts," "flesh," and "starved." He deals with women as sex objects, but Morrison stresses the feelings of the female, not her body. He describes the female body from a male point of view, so he is not like Morrison, who cares about women's needs, behaviors, and minds more than their physical traits. In an interview with Stephen Schiff, Naipaul's attitude toward women is revealed clearly as he resists any change in his conventional views of gender performance:

> I was an extremely passionate *man*, and *utterly heterosexual*—an adorer of women, all my life . . . women have sunk in my esteem quite a bit. I'm no longer blinded by this way of looking at them. So in a way that's a kind of loss. One has lost this excitement about women. . . . I adored women . . . thought they were wonderful. I loved their *voices*. I loved the quality of their *skin*. (Schiff, 1997, 145-146; emphasis added)

Naipaul and his male characters deal with women as just physical objects, so they refuse and resist any change that can deconstruct their masculine power and superiority. In *Guerrillas*, Naipaul shows rape to be a form of endorsement of the male ego, and anal rape becomes a way to express his contemptuous mastery. In this scene, he focuses on a man's feelings of victory and superiority after deflowering a woman without even caring about the woman's reaction to being raped. Naipaul portrays the woman's pain and submission in the scene and how the man does not care about the woman's "wail," "suppressed scream," and "cry" (*G*, 81). He states that the only action the man (Jimmy) in this scene cares about is to feel his masculine power over the woman (Jane) by taking out "her virginity" (*G*, 81).

Naipaul always expresses masculinist feelings. For example, in Jane's slaughter scene, Jimmy holds Jane by the neck, like a chicken or a weak animal, to facilitate the attack: "He scarcely felt Jane's neck; *he felt only his muscles*. He concentrated on that smoothness and tension until she began to fail" (*G*, 238; emphasis added). Naipaul claims that he writes "from the deepest sympathy" (Eyre, 1982, 115) for all his characters. His treatment of female sexuality in his novels may well have a point. The apparent emotional freezing out of the female during the act of sex suggests that Naipaul's sensibilities influence his narration style; he cannot empathize with the idea of women as warm, responsive lovers. Furthermore, the slaughter scene proves what I have mentioned above about the concept of revenge. In creating the slaughter scene, Naipaul symbolizes the relationship between the colonizers and the colonized to end the unprecedented colonial era by murdering the white woman representing white colonizers or dominant white culture.

In a similar rape scene, but from a different perspective, Morrison sheds light on the girl's feelings after and during the rape. The difference between Naipaul and Morrison in portraying their rape scenes is that Pecola is psychologically slaughtered, but the white Jane is physically slaughtered. Morrison's Pecola and Naipaul's Jane are victims of a man's hatred and fury. Cholly in *The Bluest Eye* and Jimmy in *Guerrillas* hate being psychologically emasculated by the dominant societies in which they live to celebrate normative masculinity to vent and impose their fury on the females. Pecola's rape in *The Bluest Eye* leads to her ultimate demise and loss, and Pecola "turns away from reality" (hooks, 1992, 6). Through this devastating experience, Morrison embodies the devastating effect of sexual violence and the oppressive force of sex in these women's lives. In this scene, Morrison states that the male's "failure in his life made him devoid of feelings" (Bloom, 2010, 80). Morrison explains, "the most masculine act of aggression becomes feminized in my language, passive, and I think more accurately repellent when deprived of the male glamour of shame, rape is or once was routinely given" (*BE*, 215).

In other words, rape is also written and described by Morrison's language since she does not want to tell the story of male shame, which is only romanticized by patriarchal culture. By portraying Cholly's horrific deed sympathetically, "Morrison makes his aggressive actions all the more violent and insidious" (Page, 1996, 180). In the rape scene, Morrison mutes Pecola by telling the scene from Cholly's point of view. Morrison writes Pecola's experience into literature since Pecola's muted scream lied beyond the pages. Pecola becomes the maimed grotesque, flailing without words. The only sound she can make is "the hollow suck of air in the back of her throat" (*BE*, 155). Morrison even goes so far as to use words such as "friendly," "innocent," and "tenderness" (*BE*, 126) to reduce the damage while the rape is in progress. Although Morrison uses a masculine point of view to describe the rape, she gains readers' sympathy through her raped female. Morrison silences Pecola, but her hidden scream appears when she loses her mind by the novel's end.

Morrison softens the action of rape but magnifies its consequences and its influence over black women. Morrison stresses women's feelings and victimization as a result of men's aggressive phallic performance, but Naipaul highlights men's masculine power and women's inferiority. While Morrison tries to soften the scene of rape by using words like "tender" and "friendly," Naipaul describes women aggressively. Jane and Jimmy's sexual encounters are described with a tinge of a racial consciousness as their sexual scenes represent the relationship between the colonized and the colonizers. Naipaul describes the white woman, in referring to the colonial culture, as being a *"starved woman"* and a *"prostitute"* (*G*, 81; emphasis added) who wants to take the lead and dominate colonized man. Meanwhile, Naipaul states the true feelings of colonized and postcolonized people toward the dominant colonial power as they are "full of *hate* of her" (*G*, 81; emphasis added). Therefore, Naipaul states that these senses of inferiority and emasculation lead Jimmy, who represents postcolonial people, to expel his hatred of Jane, who represents dominant culture, while raping and violating her virginity brutally and murdering her by the end of the novel.

In Toni Morrison's *The Bluest Eye*, the rape of Pecola by Cholly, her father dramatizes violence and aggression that neither begin nor end with the fragmented and broken body of the young girl. While the narrative forcefully expresses the horror of the rape, its trauma emerges from a more extensive web of negative experiences and horrendous losses that grasp both father and daughter. The description of the "perpetrator—the one who is responsible for destroying the spirit of this African-American girl—never settles on the shoulders of the defeated father but shifts in turns in a broader drama of racist brutality" (Haaken, 1996, 1073). Morrison writes about victimized women to make black women visible, voices heard, and identities acknowledged. She works to invert and dispel many negative stereotypes exposed in writing by and about black women. Morrison claims that one of her motivations for writing is to allow black women to redefine their identities by creating characters who go against typical white American stereotypes of African-American females and exemplify many of black womanhood's hidden strengths and characteristics. Also, in his latest novels, *Half a Life* and *Magic Seeds*, Naipaul's women have their own beliefs and ideas to which they cling and which they realize. However, these women appear as a man's catalyst to find himself and restore his identity. So, Naipaul's women are either submissive or empowered, but in both cases act like catalysts for men to restore their fragmented identities.

Such negative images and stereotypical normative gender roles help declare female inferiority, and on another level, legitimize patriarchal dominance. It is also noted that most of Naipaul's texts do not have role models that female readers can emulate. This portrayal of gender images and roles has the danger of condemning women to a state of continuous smugness in the face of a male-constructed culture that mistreats them. This chapter seeks in no way to attack Naipaul for his portrayals of women. On the contrary, I wish to present the inherent gender bias in the existing literature. Besides, it argues for a revisionist mentality in creativity, as it aptly recognizes that negative female images in literary phenomena legitimize and achieve male dominance.

Unlike Naipaul, Morrison's novels illustrate the history of enslavement and the condition of slaves. Morrison uses black female characters as the protagonists in her novels. This attention to black women in general and to African-American women in particular, their problems in dominant white society, racial discrimination, and issues of sex and gender has made Morrison's novels great sources for cultural studies. Taking advantage of the issues mentioned above in her fiction, Morrison has made readers aware of African-Americans' tragedies in their lives. Moreover, Morrison has pierced into the minds of her characters, revealing their thoughts perfectly. Whereas Naipaul's fiction confines women to within an inferior and marginal framework, Morrison's narratives can help change African-Americans' position, especially African-American females, from margin to center. More importantly, the significance of Morrison's fiction is its capacity to combine gender issues with sexuality and social class concurrently. Morrison's novels determine truths about the human condition, and that is why her fiction is appealing to both white and black readers.

Toni Morrison tries to challenge the assumptions upon which many traditional beliefs about gender are built, especially the notion that gender identity is inborn, positioned at birth, and unalterable. Furthermore, Morrison has created a new discourse on gender and race, which rejects all modes of binary thought. She openly divulges her personal biases by noting that she grew up in a home defined by rigid gender definitions and emphasizing that she has had no experience rearing females. In her novels, especially the latest ones, Morrison transcends male/female, white/black dichotomies by presenting characters who resist the authorization of Black and White communities to suppress their ambiguities and the culturally approved roles assigned to them.

As for Naipaul's protagonists, sexuality becomes a pathological alternate for social intercourse and communication. An instantiation of their dysfunctional, dispassionate relationships, sexuality merely is "an expression of power, fear, and dominance" (King, 1993, 108) or the ultimate weapon in political power struggles. The characters' "social disaffection" translates as "sexual misadventure," thus "making sex and sexual promiscuity the novel's frame for political misadventure and misalliance" (Mustafa, 1995, 126–127). If all of Naipaul's novels indirectly treat sexuality and eroticism as emotionally scathing and rarely satisfying, this singularly naturalistic yet symbolic political representation of intersexuality becomes a vehicle for demolishing the hegemonic dichotomies in dominant societies.

Morrison disrupts dominant patriarchy and succeeds in her quest to open a broader landscape in American and European literature. Moreover, although Morrison uses black women's communities to defy white patriarchy and to resist black male oppression, Naipaul celebrates masculinity and phallic patriarchal power through the sexual affairs between white women and postcolonial men. Naipaul maintains phallic authority as a resisting strategy practiced by postcolonial men to oppress and dominate white culture, signified by white women. I have presented gender as a highly malleable construction that enables Morrison's characters (and humans in general) to achieve significant social and personal mobility, despite the trauma and destabilization that other aspects of their identities may cause. Alternatively, Naipaul shows deep-rooted gender bias as he delineates male characters with a patriarchal mindset performing normative stereotypical gender roles as he has subscribed to a phallocentric ideology in his delineation of gender roles and images.

Chapter Six

Naipaul and Morrison

Some Conclusions and New Comparative Outlooks

I want to pay tribute to V.S. Naipaul, who passed away on the 11th of August, 2018. Throughout his career, Naipaul courted controversy in terms of what he said about the Caribbean and its history. However, no matter how argumentative he became, he never ceased to engage in a fearless—if loaded—conversation about belonging, identity, and the enduring colonial past with other Caribbean and postcolonial writers. The works on which his reputation will firmly rest give an unparalleled analysis of what it is to be a postcolonial migrant. In his works, Naipaul captured the deep chords of migrant life—the first journey powered by dreams, the ambition to arrive and stay that is always at odds with a longing to return home, and the discovery on the return that the place of origin has permanently changed. He vividly exemplified that people are all changed by the intersection of land and language, and that persistence rather than courage is often required to make a change. For four decades, Naipaul explored the legacy of colonialism, gathering a series of awards as he shifted between fiction and nonfiction books. Awarding Naipaul the Nobel Prize in Literature in 2001, the Swedish Academy praised him for "having united perceptive narrative and incorruptible scrutiny in works that compel us to see the presence of suppressed histories."

I want to pay another tribute to Toni Morrison, who passed away on the 6th of August, 2019. Although Morrison has left our physical realm, the many treasures she left us will bear fruit for generations to come. Toni Morrison was a gigantic intellect, a brilliant illuminator of her African-American nation's stories, a heart-breaking journalist, and a revolutionary author. She revolutionized American literature. While writing fiction, she quilted her language with plot, society, and history in a strikingly original fashion to heighten the possibilities of the literary imagination. Nowadays, Toni

Morrison has her place in American history—a history that she herself influenced profoundly. Morrison opened up the American literary canon and paved the way for other African-American writers. Her prose widened the boundaries of African-American literature and enriched all fiction writing. She was awarded the Nobel Prize in 1993 because her "novels characterized by visionary force and poetic import, give life to an essential feature of American reality." Morrison's work is characterized by magical realism and a persistent eye toward the wounds of African-American history. She unloaded race as a social construct, excavating the deep psychological tolls of sexism and racism. Morrison once maintained: "The function of freedom is to free someone else" and her writings have freed many souls and minds. Her impact will be sensed for centuries to come.

This book has defined comparative literature as a discipline that has its origins in Western academia, and it still carries that dominance. However, in the postcolonial era, this tendency to normalize Western superiority is being challenged at various levels. The book has dealt with the complexities that comparative literature encounters within postcolonial spaces. When comparative literature's primary focus has been European literature, it entails more introspection of the existing layers of the power structure regarding language and literature in postcolonial countries. In this globalized, cosmopolitan world, the influence and power of English are taken into question in the context of translation in comparative literature. This book has argued that the study of comparative literature in the postcolonial context challenges the power structure of the discipline itself to be present in the study of literature and languages as the context demands.

Most important, comparing and relating V.S. Naipaul and Toni Morrison has helped, to a large extent, to mold comparative literature in a postcolonial context and to examine the new approach of the postcolonial comparative. At the beginning of the study, I hyperbooked that Toni Morrison could be discussed from a postcolonial perspective. To pursue this assumption, I compared Morrison to Naipaul, who is considered a postcolonial author, through relating both of them to Frantz Fanon's theory of identity. Therefore, exploring and comparing Naipaul's and Morrison's novels in a postcolonial framework was one of the primary concerns of the study. It is also significant to bear in mind that comparing and relating Toni Morrison and V.S. Naipaul has widened comparative literature into a postcolonial context outside of its typical Eurocentric focus.

In this book, I have claimed that a postcolonial comparative approach has created a dialogue between the literature of the marginalized and the literature of the dominant powers. After writing five chapters of the book, I have discovered that postcolonial literature is comparative; it is more comparative than other literature because its comparativism defines it at its very core.

There is a need, however, for a dialogue between writers, theorists, and scholars working across cultures and languages so that a postcolonial comparative approach might emerge. Therefore, I argue that postcolonial literature cannot be anything but comparative since it is written from the position of always already having been placed in comparison with other literature. Moreover, using historical and cultural contextualization and close textual analysis as the primary methodology has helped relate and compare the two writers in light of Fanon's postcolonial theory of identity.

This book started out with an inquiry into the life of Naipaul and Morrison and their creative work. Thematic and formal preoccupations have been informed by the authors' personal experiences and the social relations in which they have been engaged. Naipaul and Morrison regularly refer to actual people, and historical and social realities consequently place their novels in a definite time and place. I have tried to deconstruct the binary opposition between marginalized groups and dominant powers based on postcolonial theories of mimicry, hybridity, and the uncanny proposed by Frantz Fanon, Robert Young, and Homi K. Bhabha.

While addressing the first stage of Fanon's theory, I have demonstrated that Naipaul's and Morrison's theme of mimicry or unqualified assimilation is a crucial component in their earliest novels, *The Mimic Men* and *The Bluest Eye*. Besides, mimicry or assimilating into the culture of the dominant power is considered one of the main reasons that bring about the fragmented identities of the characters in Naipaul's and Morrison's earliest novels. Therefore, I have found that mimicry creates a fractured identity of marginalized people, and this incomplete identity leads to self-fragmentation and further estrangement. I have maintained that the racially marginalized and previously colonized are locked into their choices and deeds as they long for their hopeless wishes. Fanon's first phase of "unqualified assimilation" is shown in Naipaul's and Morrison's novels but in a very different way. For Naipaul, the stage of mimicry is predictable; it is a dilemma that constitutes postcolonial experience, and even though it makes it easier for postcolonial migrants to cope with the dominant culture, part of the colonized's past experience has to be sacrificed in the process. Although *The Bluest Eye* and *The Mimic Men* can be related to Fanon's first phase of mimicry, Morrison's mimicry is different from Naipaul's. While Morrison represents submission and resistance, Naipaul only represents the submissive side of mimicry.

After discussing mimicry in the second chapter, the book has discussed the second phase of recalling the past, which Naipaul and Morrison carried in their identity and recreated in their novels. By analyzing their historical fictional novels, Morrison's *Beloved*, and Naipaul's *The Enigma of Arrival*, I have shed light on the second phase of Fanon's theory, where he maintains that indigenous intellectuals grow dissatisfied with assimilating the dominant power, and instead celebrate the authentic traditions and practices of their original culture. Indigenous intellectuals present the past, memory, folk traditions, customs, rituals, myth, and legends of their nation, and try to use these concepts as an initial step toward identity. Both Morrison and Naipaul have reached the second stage of Fanon in which indigenous writers recall their past as a way of celebrating their cultural identity. Although Naipaul has actual colonial experience and physically travels to his original lands (Trinidad and India), his past is still enigmatic and vague. Naipaul is always hesitant, lost, fragmented, and dislocated because he denies his past and his traditions. Nevertheless, Morrison, who neither experienced actual colonial domination nor ever traveled to her African homeland, went deep to reach her roots, and restored her ancestors' folklore and culture to use the past to form a communal space in the present.

I have also highlighted Frantz Fanon's third phase of celebrating a cultural identity within his theory of identity. Hybridity reflects Fanon's fighting stage, where indigenous writers create new revolutionary literature. In this literature, indigenous writers attempt to hybridize their folklore with the dominant culture to celebrate newly created identities, and this merging is explicit in Naipaul's and Morrison's structure of their later novels. Furthermore, indigenous writers shed light on their folklore and culture to expose the new generations to their original culture. Besides, according to Fanon, indigenous writers guide their nations to a new way of becoming. In so doing, Naipaul and Morrison guide their people to hybridity as a revolutionary way of belonging in dominant societies to resist marginalization. I have explained that Naipaul and Morrison, in their later novels, *Half a Life*, *Magic Seeds*, and *Home*, have attempted to show hybridity as an anticolonial tool regarding identity, culture, and language, because in hybridity, 'the sense of mixing' breaks down and resists any type of essentialism created by the dominant powers.

Contrary to popular notions, hybridity is not a term that resolves and dissolves the tension between two cultures. It is always the splitting and doubling that disallows the easy self-apprehension of the dominant and colonial power. Therefore, I have argued that hybridity is not mimicry, but that mimicry can lead to hybridity. It is not a mere mixture or merging between two cultures. Morrison and Naipaul renegotiate their hybrid identities, but differently. For both of them, hybridity is a new way of becoming. The vague state of the subaltern within but outside the mainstream of the dominant culture creates a double-consciousness. This duality is not at all times an irritation, but it can be a blessing. It leads to a specific perspective which allows for openness, and the embracing of contradiction and paradox and broad completeness, even of one's deepest fears. The concept of hybridity as a product of the double-consciousness is discussed to present how cultural hybridity is considered a means to resist the discrimination created by the dominant culture.

Morrison succeeds in being her people's awakener, as Fanon asserts in his third stage, as she depicts an image of American society that can be a home for her and her nation, but while keeping and glorifying her past, culture, and tradition. Naipaul, as a postcolonial writer, also succeeds in guiding his people to a new solution to belong and land safely. He crystallizes his traditions and rituals, not to disparage them, but to improve them and to help in developing his nation. Naipaul and Morrison present the resolution for their people's eternal dilemma of home by summarizing their literary journeys in their later novels, *Half a Life*, *Magic Seeds*, and *Home*. Naipaul wants indigenous people to live like magic seeds that can be cultivated anywhere. These magic seeds can adapt to any soil and any terrain. Also, Morrison finds home when she hybridizes and quilts the fragments of her ancestral past with the current present of her African-American nation.

However, the question here may be: is hybridity considered the end of the struggle for indigenous people? I believe that through hybridity, marginalized groups will start celebrating their newly created identity within dominant societies. In other words, the history of colonialism and the Middle Passage has left ineradicable scars on the social, cultural, and symbolic worlds of postcolonial and African-American people, which no formal process of decolonization can ever entirely erase. Hybridity is a way in which postcolonial or subaltern people have challenged the established codes of their identities. Marginalized people have adopted hybridity regarding language, culture, and identity. The contradictions that have been experienced in the hybrid positions have created a third space in which postcolonial people and marginalized groups have negotiated and extended their positions. The negotiation of their identities in this third space has resulted in new ways of defining themselves, which have enabled them to express their ways of being in the various worlds to which they belong.

This book has also shown gender as one of the central aspects of the postcolonial world. However, I have connected his first stage of mimicry to gender oppression to clarify that mimicry of the dominant powers can lead to gender oppression, which leads to many forms of resistance. Naipaul and Morrison attempt to resist and defy hegemonic power. Morrison stresses the idea of black women's communities that resists black patriarchy. However, Naipaul represents allegoric sexual relationships between English women and postcolonial migrants, in which postcolonial men often vent their internal annoyance toward the dominant society, and their females often suffer. When subaltern men feel humiliated and suppressed by the dominant power, they project their anger onto the only beings they know are lower on the social scale—usually women. In other words, subaltern men try to compensate for their emasculation by mimicking and practicing domination to regain their self-image, which has been damaged by dominant groups.

What is much more imperative is that Morrison and Naipaul address gender issues in some of their novels. In some of her novels, Morrison attempts to deconstruct the traditional norms of gender as a tool of resistance to hegemonic power in dominant patriarchal societies. For example, in *Sula*, Morrison represents the title character challenging and resisting black phallic patriarchy by rejecting marital life and engaging in dissident sexual relationships, subverting the hegemony of heterosexuality which queer theory has exposed and criticized. Morrison considers gender to be a form of identity, but with the critical side note that there cannot be a gender identity before doing gendered acts. Therefore, since some of Morrison's female characters, such as Sula, do not perform conventional femininity, and it becomes questionable as to whether their desires are directed solely to men; this does not mean that they are transgendered or lesbian, but raises issues relating to bigender and quite possibly sexual dissidence, which can be further explored and researched.

Most of Naipaul's characters reinforce conventional gender norms and don't resist like Morrison's characters do. A notable feature in most of his novels is the mellowness and submission of the female characters. Naipaul is like Fanon: neither pays much attention to female images. Naipaul does not portray many women in his novels, but they are given chances to appear. The dominant protagonists in his novels are generally males. Even some titles of his novels have been named only after the name of his male protagonists. Therefore, Naipaul's normative view of gender roles opposes Morrison's revolutionary views of gender that deconstruct and resist patriarchal societies.

However, Naipaul presents bisexuality in his *Guerrillas*, and portrays this category in relation to politics. Being bisexual expresses the double-consciousness of postcolonial migrants who do not know where to belong. Meanwhile, creating the character of Jimmy Ahmed, an African bisexual Muslim leader, Naipaul resists the binary opposition created by Third World traditions, which often do not accept bisexuality and treat it as an aberration. Moreover, he challenges the Islamic religion, which prohibits bisexuality and queerness.

Therefore, while Morrison attempts to resist traditional views of gender through her denial of the binary opposition concerning sex and gender, Naipaul prefers to sustain his traditional views on gender normativity and celebrates patriarchy to resist the marginalization of postcolonial migrants in dominant societies. Morrison has attempted to deconstruct the hegemony of patriarchy. However, the most critical outcome after examining a selection of her fictional works is that there has to be a challenge to, or subversion of, the traditional definition of gender, which includes the main binary opposition of male/female. Morrison opens up the possibility of new research in her novels, presenting revolutionary thought to the whole world. In so doing, the book may provide a gateway to further studies on gender theory, queer theory, and their intersectional relationship with postcolonial literary theory.

Furthermore, the book has demonstrated that postcolonial theory asserts many aspects that have been related to Naipaul and Morrison, such as fragmentation, alienation, racism, mimicry, recalling the past, hybridity, race, oppression, and gender. While relating these aspects to both Naipaul and Morrison, I support Fanon when he states: "colonial racism is no different from any other racism" (Fanon, 1968, 88). Colonialism and racism are, therefore, intricately linked. When comparing Morrison's African-American novels and Naipaul's postcolonial novels, I have come to know that although they belong to different literary schools, they share a lot concerning the goal of destabilizing or resisting racial hierarchies and debates concerning the relationship between the colonizers and the colonized, which is similar, but not reducible, to the relationship between masters and slaves. Therefore, Toni Morrison, as an African-American writer, could be considered one of the renowned postcolonial feminist writers who has touched on the very idea of raising the voice of oppressed or marginalized groups. According to postcolonial theory, marginalized groups must speak back to the so-called norms, which are carved out by the dominant powers. Morrison's novels give a specific example of how the subaltern can speak. Her characters are symbols of such subalterns who can choose their way of living. Her novels show that all of her characters are considered a central part of African-American community, and their existence is necessary for bonding and connecting that society.

I have used a selection of novels by Morrison and Naipaul from each one's large body of work. I have preferred to go deeper into each writer's work using fewer novels to enrich the analysis. Also, as mentioned earlier in the chapter, this book has discussed gender in Naipaul's and Morrison's selected novels; however, because of time constraints and the scope of this book, I have not reviewed the new categories of gender or nonbinary gender in detail. These could prove fruitful for further research where one could shed light on the marginalization of specific gender groups. Moreover, Toni Morrison's latest novel, *God Help the Child* (2015), is outside of the scope of this book. In this novel, Morrison has negated what she said in her first novel, *The Bluest Eye*. In the latter, she stresses the dilemma of the black race, which is the ugliness of blackness and the beauty of whiteness. However, in her latest novel, *God Help the Child*, Morrison emphasizes the beauty of blackness and black pride. Morrison's latest novel, *God Help the Child,* could also provide rich material for relating to postcolonial theory.

As for Naipaul, I have dealt with gender binary in some of his novels; however, still, there are some which can be further studied. The book in no way professes to be the final word on Naipaul; it merely provokes future intellectual inquiry in this field. One may wish to examine the issues focused on in Naipaul's novels that have been treated marginally, such as relating minority issues of gender issues to politics. As mentioned earlier in the chapter, gender will form my next area of research. I want to focus on replacing and reshaping the traditional definition of gender to include nonbinary genders, as that would include gender identity beyond the traditional male/female binary. In consideration of time constraints and the scope of this book, I could add Fanon and his (in)attention to gender in future studies. Gender is a fertile field to be studied in detail so that postcolonial comparative can be related to gender issues with reference to postcolonial feminist writers such as Fadia Faqir, Assia Djebar, Diana Abu Jaber, Ahdaf Sweif, Urvashi Butalia, Gloria Naylor, Alice Walker, and others, within the postcolonial comparative approach developed in this book.

In the first chapter of this book, I referred to scholars such as Susan Bassnett, Gayatri Spivak, Haun Saussy, Edward Said, Robert Young, and Homi Bhabha, all of whom emphasize the importance of the global scope of comparative literature to include the literature of the marginalized and subjugated groups through the impact of apartheid, slavery, colonialism, and other forms of supremacy. However, in recent years, there have been further studies about comparative literature that support the globalism of the discipline. They do not ask only for the need to extend comparative analysis to marginalized groups, but also call for a more profound reconfiguration of the very tools and methods of literary analysis (see Behdad and Thomas, 2014; Cheah, 2016; Damrosch et al., 2009; Damrosch, 2020; Dziub and Surlapierre, 2019; Franco, 2021; Gasperi and Pivato, 2018; Kaakinen, 2017; and Young, 2013). According to this logic, the comparative analysis of reading positions should not merely add more contexts of reception into the discussion, but should examine critically the very premises that operate in an analytical approach to reading. Therefore, I agree with Alfred Lopez's point about the future of comparative literature in the twenty-first century: "in order for comparative literature to survive and flourish in the 21st century, it must paradoxically accept its own annihilation as it now stands, as it has defined itself since 1877" (Lopez, 2007, 7). Accordingly, the comparison between Naipaul and Morrison weaves comparative literature into postcolonial literature, which did not formerly exist in the main Eurocentric concern of comparative literature. Besides, this book has contributed to this rethinking of the field through a reconsideration of comparative literature as postcolonial literature, which will assist comparative literature to become more politicized when addressing marginalized literatures alongside canonical Euro-American literature.

Furthermore, this book has contributed to the field of World Literature, as it has analyzed up-to-date novels by Naipaul and Morrison. According to David

Damrosch in *What Is World Literature?*: "World Literature still consists of a huge corpus of works. These works, moreover, stem from widely disparate societies, with very different histories, frames of cultural reference, and poetics" (Damrosch, 2003, 2). I have positioned comparative literature in a postcolonial framework and have suggested that the discipline should shed its traditional Eurocentric approach by going global and paying more extensive attention to different societies, with very different histories, frames of cultural reference, and poetics. This is similar to Damrosch when stating that a work enters World Literature through a double process: firstly, by being read as literature, and secondly, by being circulated out into a broader world beyond its linguistic, national, and cultural points of origin (Damrosch, 2003, 3). In other words, literary work can enter into World Literature and then fall out of it again if it shifts beyond an entrance point along either axis—the literary or the worldly. The shifts that a literary work may endure, moreover, do not reflect the unfolding of some internal logic of the literary work in itself, but come about through often complex dynamics of cultural change and contestation with other literatures.

This book should also work as a starting point to new comparative studies that can interpret and reread Morrison's literary texts in general and her novels in particular from new feminist perspectives. Morrison always calls for female empowerment, as do some eco-feminist Arab female writers who write in the Arabic language, such as Miral Etahawy (Egypt), Samiha Khris (Jordan), Bothayna Khedr (Sudan), and Raja'a Elalem (Saudi Arabia). In further research, Morrison could be compared to them and be read from an eco-feminist angle. Eco-feminism connects the abuse and domination of women with that of the environment and argues that there is a strong relationship between women and nature that comes from their shared history of oppression and domination by patriarchal societies.

Nature and women are significant themes in Toni Morrison's novels, which highlight the appropriateness of applying this theory to her novels. For example, *The Bluest Eye*, *Beloved*, and *Sula* are usually studied by psychoanalytic, postcolonial, and feminist critics. Nevertheless, Morrison's eco-feminist concern for nature has rarely been studied. Some of her novels could represent theories of eco-feminism and the early thoughts of Toni Morrison when compared to eco-feminist Arab women writers. Moreover, comparing Morrison to these writers will lead their fiction to be read in different contexts, and these texts being translated into different languages.

On the other hand, Morrison's novels could also be translated into Arabic to enrich Arabic literature as well as American and European literatures. Thus, the book shows that a literary work manifests differently abroad than it does in its original home as it illuminates ongoing projects for the future.

Also, cultural studies of postcolonialism can help brighten postcolonial themes present in our rich Arabic literature. Thus, this book may also pave the way to combine postcolonial themes within Morrison's literary texts and in postcolonial literature from other parts of the world. For example, while Morrison exposes the mechanism through which slavery sought to legitimize itself by categorizing African people as inferior, colonialism in the Middle East has similarly attempted to perpetuate itself by categorizing Arabian race as inferior.

From the 1960s onward, Arab-American and expatriate Middle Eastern female authors, especially the writers who have chosen to write from a feminist perspective, such as Nawal Saadawi (Egypt), Leila Ahmed (Egypt), Gada El-Samman (Syria), Khanata Banuna (Morocco), Assia Djebar (Algeria), Zainab Salbi (Iraq), and Sahar Khalifa (Palestine), have embraced topics that celebrate "broader social and political issues" in addition to topics that arouse women's "obsession with living up to the opportunities for self-realization or self-fulfillment" (Shaaban, 1993, 36). In addition to the themes discussed by the above authors, they ask about the relationship between the self and the other, "the private individual's relationship to history and/or culture from which she finds her experience of herself and her life excluded" (Buss, 2002, 3). Furthermore, by exploring the fiction which spans over half a century written by expatriate Anglophone or Francophone Arab women writers, further comparative studies can elaborate how Arab writers in diaspora sit alongside Toni Morrison, while surpassing the geographical confinement with all the inherent traumatic and victorious experiences, and still be actively involved with and immersed in the intellectual lives and political struggles of their homelands.

While exploring some works by expatriate Egyptian or Middle Eastern female writers, one can notice that their texts aim to subvert, destabilize, and deconstruct Egyptian or Middle Eastern phallocentric ideologies, patriarchal/colonialist practices, and traditions and totalizing imperialist histories. Moreover, postcolonial feminism has addressed and deconstructed the idea of the Third World woman, whereby women in the Third World are doubly oppressed: first for being a woman and second through the effects of colonialism. Consequently, they act like Toni Morrison when constituting a pivotal endeavor to revisit their forgotten histories and discover the communal and cultural memories associated with their present conditions of rootlessness and rootedness, autonomy and belonging.

Alternatively, Naipaul can also be compared to Arab and Middle Eastern female expatriate writers. Naipaul and Arab and Middle Eastern female writers explain how alienated they are in their home of origin—the place that was supposed to launch their identity and create a sense of belonging. For example, the Egyptian-American writer Leila Ahmed has the same feeling as Naipaul; in most of her novels, she feels like an alien in Egypt because she studied nothing about it at school, and neither did Naipaul. The Western educational system that they experienced never acknowledged Egyptian or Trinidadian cultural and educational heritage.

Most Arab and Middle Eastern female writers in the diaspora choose to write about their personal experiences, as Naipaul did in most of his novels, with many writing memoirs to criticize, and even to condemn, the cultural practices that stood like barriers in their way to constructing their ethnic identity and living in a home that would not always make them feel nationally alienated and physically displaced. Future comparative study research could shed light on a significant commonality among Naipaul and most expatriate Arab and Middle Eastern women writers: the inability to establish a safe home and/or to feel "at home" as they remained living in their homes of origin, given that their homes of origin often function as sources of violence, oppression, crisis, and internal displacement.

Combining Naipaul's and Morrison's novels with the novels of Arab female writers in diaspora would create global and new outlooks on their literary archaeology. In this global world, "geopolitical borders, similar to symbolic or discursive borders (race, gender, sexuality, class), are neither entirely fixed nor impenetrable, but are constructed and operate as relational sites of power, (re)negotiation, and struggle" (Spurlin, 2016, 105). Therefore, most expatriate Arab women writers have attempted to de-center their nations, deconstructing their fixity and various boundaries (cultural, historical, racial, geographical) by representing characters who not only exceed these boundaries, but who restructure their identities, although never, in the same way, each time. Alternative concepts of home and belonging are represented in the works of Arab women writers in diaspora, which is indispensable within the context of the postcolonial condition of exile and migration.

Most expatriate Arab female writers' novels and those of Toni Morrison are self-reflexive as they analyze their nation's historical narratives against people's individual experiences. From the beginning of her literary life, Morrison stressed race as a primary reason for racial discrimination. In her latest novel, *God Help the Child,* slavery and the Middle Passage still reflect the way that black female bodies are used, seen, and treated in American society in the twenty-first century. According to Toni Morrison, "race still matters" (Gras, 2016, 81). This is factual, and one can see how it causes the subalternity of the characters in her novels. *God Help the Child* has received many reviews, and most critics have acknowledged Morrison's past work and view *God Help the Child* as part of "Morrison's ongoing literary dialogue on race, beauty, childhood, and identity" (Kulpa, 2016, 230).

Thus, Morrison's themes are global. The subalternity of human beings, particularly children and females, whether they are of color or not, is one of the main themes of her novels, so "the Morrisonian [postcolonial] themes are there" (Mashaqi and Al Omari, 2018, 179; brackets added) such as slavery, homeliness, rootlessness, cultural clash, mimicry, questions of identity, language, magic realism, and marginalization. Some recent studies maintain that Morrison's narratives restore a subject position to the victims of slavery by reanimating the voices of the silenced. While postcolonial theory has gone a long way toward addressing the problem of the silenced 'Other,' very little attention has been paid to postcolonial significance of the American slave narrative (see Bennett et al., 2020; Dimitriadis and McCarthy, 2001; Durrant, 2004; Mashaqi and Al Omari, 2018; Sinha, 2008; Tagore, 2009; Wardi, 2021; and Wilson and Ringrose, 2016).

As for Naipaul, it is also evident from the book that, unlike most Third World writers from societies emerging from colonialism, Naipaul has his eyes targeted on subtle and often elusive factors, which he feels contribute significantly to the continuing deterioration of conditions in his Trinidadian society, and by extension, in postcolonial societies. The irreversibility of colonialism should be acknowledged, and more energy focused not on decrying the West for postcolonial society's predicaments but on overcoming individual limitations. The principle of self-examination is of paramount importance as a people's destiny rests wholesale in their own hands. Indeed, according to Naipaul, the individual must do everything within their radius to alter the material and spiritual conditions of their life. This book has shown how he depicts conservatism as a major obstacle to human progress. Whereas Bruce, Cudjoe, Nixon, and Mustafa, whom I have referred to in this book, maintain the same opinions about Naipaul's rootlessness and enigmatic past, recent studies similarly stress these ideas about him (see Jörngården, 2018; Meighoo, 2018; Misra, 2017; Radovic, 2015; Saradhambal, 2017; and Zou, 2015).

Overall, all of the novels discussed in this book have addressed the identity fragmentation that is brought about in self-other relationships in many shapes and forms, such as colonizers/colonized, master/slave, male/female, white/black, metropolitan/migrants, and binary gender/nonbinary gender. The book seeks to find a way to reimagine self-other relationships in an attempt to recover marginalized groups from subjugation and denial, and to cultivate better human relationships across cultures, races, religions, and regions for the future. To such intractable questions around postcolonial poetics, marginalized history, and identity, Naipaul's and Morrison's fiction do not offer any ready-made or simplistic answers, but they do efficiently unsettle the terms under which these questions are usually dealt with in postcolonial literature, as well as in intellectual history. Therefore, Naipaul's and Morrison's fiction constitute a significant part of a lifelong political project that opens up the human past and inscribes it into the infinite possibilities of the future.

This book has shown that postcolonialism can be viewed as an inherently comparative project in that it constitutes the sort of transnational literary space that has long been central to the dominant conceptions of comparative literature. Moreover, postcolonialism has been crucial to comparative literature. Not only has postcolonial theory brought the issue of colonialism to the forefront of literary studies in the West by exposing critically the ideological structures of aesthetic and scientific images of otherness in European thought through modern history, it has also enabled a mode of critical review that focuses on the complex ways in which knowledge and European literature have been implicated in relations of power. The postcolonial comparative has reconfigured the literary canon by creating a dialogue between the literature of the marginalized and dominant power; therefore, while framing comparative literature in a postcolonial framework, the works of indigenous writers such as Naipaul and Morrison have not only enlarged the literary canon, but have also helped to transform the very notion of literature itself.

Bibliography

Achebe, Chinua (1975). "The African Writer and The English Language," in Achebe, Chinua, *Morning Yet on Creation Day: Essays*. New York: Anchor Press, 91–103.
Aitken, Gillon (ed.) (1999). *V.S. Naipaul Between Father and Son: Family Letters*. New York: Vintage.
Aldridge, A. Owen (1980). "Introduction" in Tay, William, Chou, Ying-Hsiung, and Yuan, Heh-Hsiang (eds.), *China and the West: Comparative Literature Studies*. Hong Kong: The Chinese University Press, iii–xiii.
Allon, F. (2000). "Nostalgia Unbound: Illegibility and the Synthetic Excess of Place," *Continuum: Journal of Media and Cultural Studies*, 14(3), 275–87.
Alzubairi, Fatemah (2019.) *Colonialism, Neo-Colonialism, and Anti-Terrorism Law in the Arab World*. Cambridge: Cambridge University Press.
Apter, Emily (1995). "Comparative Exile: Competing Margins in the History of Comparative Literature," in Bernheimer, Charles (ed.), *Comparative Literature in the Age of Multiculturalism*. Baltimore: Johns Hopkins University Press, 86–95.
Ashcroft, Bill, Gareth Griffiths, and Helen Tiffen (eds.) (1989). *The Empire Writes Back Theory and Practice in Postcolonial Literatures*. London: Routledge.
——— (1995). *The Post-colonial Studies Reader*. London: Routledge.
——— (1999). *Post-colonial Studies: The Key Concepts*. London: Routledge.
Awkward, Michael (1988). "Roadblocks and Relatives: Critical Revision in Toni Morrison's *The Bluest Eye*," in McKay, Nellie Y. (ed.), *Critical Essays on Toni Morrison*. Boston: G. K. Hall & Co., 57–68.
Baker, A. Houston, and Charlotte Pierce-Baker (1985). "Patches: Quilts and Community in Alice Walker's Everyday Use," *Southern Review*, 21(3) July, 706–720.
Bandia, Paul (2010). "Literary Heteroglossia and Translation: Forms of Resistance in Euro-African Writing," in Tymoczko, Maria (ed.), *Translation, Resistance, Activism*. Amherst and Boston: University of Massachusetts Press, 168–89.
Bassnett, Susan (1995). *Comparative Literature: A Critical Introduction*. Oxford: Blackwell.
——— (2006). "Reflections on Comparative Literature in the Twenty-First Century," *Comparative Critical Studies*, 3(1–2), 3–11.

Battagla, Judy (2014). "Myth and Meaning-Making Showtime's *The L World*," in Whitt, David and Perlich, John (eds.), *Myth in the Modern World: Essays on Intersections with Ideology and Culture*. Jefferson, NC: McFarland Publications.

Behdad, Ali, and Dominic Thomas (2014). *A Companion to Comparative Literature*. Hoboken, NJ: John Wiley and Sons.

Bennett, Juda, Winnifred R. Brown-Glaude, Cassandra Jackson, and Piper Kendrix Williams, (eds.) (2020). *The Toni Morrison Book Club*. Madison: University of Wisconsin Press.

Bernheimer, Charles (1995). *Comparative Literature in the Age of Globalization*. Baltimore: Johns Hopkins University Press.

Bhabha, Homi K. (1985). "Signs Taken for Wonders: Questions of Ambivalence and Authority under a Tree Outside Delhi May 1817," *Critical Inquiry*, 12(1), 145–65.

——— (1990). "The Third Space: Interview with Homi Bhabha," interview with Jonathan Rutherford, in Rutherford, Jonathan (ed.), *Identity, Community, and Difference*. London: Lawrence and Wishart, 207–21.

——— (1992). "The World and the Home," *Social Text, Third World and Post-Colonial Issues*, 10(2–3), 141–53.

——— (1994). *The Location of Culture*. London: Routledge.

Bhandari, Sumedha (2017). *Toni Morrison's Art: A Humanistic Exploration of* The Bluest Eye *and* Beloved. Hamburg: Anchor Academic Publishing.

Bhardwaj, Shyama (2017). "Race and Gender in Toni Morrison's *The Bluest Eye*," *National Journal of Multidisciplinary Research and Development*, 2(3) September, 338–41.

Bloom, Harold (2010). *Toni Morrison's* The Bluest Eye. New York: Info Base Publishing.

Blunt, A. (2005). *Domicile and Diaspora: Anglo-Indian Women and the Spatial Politics of Home*. Malden: Blackwell.

Boehmer, Elleke (1995). *Colonial and Postcolonial Literature: Migrant Metaphor*. Oxford: Oxford University Press.

Bouson, J. Brooks (2000). *Quiet as it's Kept: Shame, Trauma, and Race in the Novels of Toni Morrison*. Albany: Sunny Press.

Boxill, Anthony (1976). "The Little Bastard World of V.S. Naipaul's *The Mimic Men* and *A Flag on the Island*," *The International Literature Review*, 3, 12–19.

Boyne, John (2017). "Women Are Better Writers Than Men: Novelist John Boyne Sets the Records Straight," *The Guardian*, December 12, 2017.

Braziel, Jana Evans, and Mannur, Anita (2003). *Theorizing Diaspora*. Hoboken, NJ: Wiley Blackwell.

Brown Green, Myrah (2009). *Pieced Symbols: Quilt Blocks from the Global Village*. North Carolina: Lark Books.

Burns, Lorna (2019). *Postcolonialism After World Literature: Relation, Equality, Dissent*. London: Bloomsbury Publishing.

Butler, Judith (1990). *Gender Trouble: Feminism and the Subversion of Identity*. New York: Routledge.

——— (1993). *Bodies That Matter*. London: Routledge.

——— (2004). *Undoing Gender*. New York and London: Routledge.

Buss, Helen M. (2002). *Repossessing the World: Reading Memoirs by Contemporary Women*. Waterloo, ON: Laurier University Press.
Carmean, Karen (1993). *Toni Morrison's World of Fiction*. New York: Whitestone Publishing Company.
Casey, Edward S. (1993). *Getting Back into Place: Toward a Renewed Understanding of the Place-world*. Bloomington: Indiana University Press.
Chambers, Iain (1990). *Border Dialogues: Journeys in Postmodernity*. New York: Routledge.
Cheah, Pheng (2016). *What Is a World? On Postcolonial Literature as World Literature*. Durham, NC: Duke University Press.
Clifford, James (1994). "Diasporas," *Cultural Anthropology*, 9(3), 302–38.
Cohen, Robin (2008). *Global Diasporas: An Introduction*. London: Routledge.
Cohn, Dorrit. (1978). *Transparent Minds: Narrative Modes for Presenting Consciousness in Fiction*. Princeton, NJ: Princeton University Press.
Collins, Patricia Hill (2002). *Black Feminist Thought: Knowledge, Consciousness, and the Politics of Empowerment*. London: Routledge.
Connell, John, Russell King, and Paul White (2002). *Writing Across Worlds: Literature and Migration*. London: White Routledge.
Cudjoe, Selwyn R. (1988). *V.S. Naipaul: A Materialist Reading*. Amherst: The University of Massachusetts Press.
Dahab, Farida Elizabeth (2004). "Translator's Introduction," in Chevrel, Yves (ed.), *Comparative Literature Today: Methods and Perspectives*. Translated by Farida Elizabeth Dahab. Kirksville, MO: The Thomas Jefferson University Press, xi–xv.
Damrosch, David (2020). *Comparing the Literatures: Literary Studies in a Global Age*. Princeton, NJ: Princeton University Press.
Damrosch, David, Natalie Melas, and Mbongiseni Buthelezi (2009). *The Princeton Source in Comparative Literature: From the European Enlightenment to the Global Present*. Princeton, NJ: Princeton University Press.
Damrosch, David (2003). *What is World Literature?* Princeton, NJ: Princeton University Press.
Davis, Cynthia (1999). "Self, Society, and Myth in Toni Morrison's Fiction," in Bloom, Harold (ed.), *Modern Critical Views: Toni Morrison*. Philadelphia: Chelsea House, 171–78.
Davis, Kimberly Chabot (1998). "Postmodern Blackness: Toni Morrison's *Beloved* and the End of History," *Twentieth-Century Literature*, 44(2), 242–62.
Devor, Aaron H. (2010). "Becoming Members of Society: Learning the Social Meanings of Gender. Gender Blending: Confronting the Limits of Duality" in Colombo, Gary, Cullen, Robert and Lisle, Bonnie (eds.), *Rereading America: Cultural Concepts for Critical Thinking and Writing*. Boston: Bedford, 383–92.
Dickinson, Philip (2016). *Romanticism and Aesthetic Life in Postcolonial Writing*. New York: Springer.
Dimitriadis, Greg, and Cameron McCarthy (2001). *Reading and Teaching the Postcolonial: From Baldwin to Basquiat and Beyond*. New York: Teachers College Press.

Dittmar, Linda (1990). "Will the Circle Be Unbroken?: The Politics of the Forms in *The Bluest Eye*," *Novel: A Forum on Fiction*, 23(2), 137–55.

Dixon, Melvin (1990). "Like an Eagle in the Air: Toni Morrison," in Bloom, Harold (ed.), *Modern Critical Views: Toni Morrison*. New York: Chelsea House, 93–104.

Dobbs, Cynthia (2011). "Diasporic Design of House, Home and Haven in Toni Morrison's *Paradise*," in Nicol, Kathryn, and Terry, Jennifer (eds.), *Toni Morrison: New Directions*. Pennsylvania: University of Connecticut, 109–26.

Dooley, Gillian (2005). "Naipaul's Women," *South Asian Review*, 26(1), 88–103.

Du Bois, W.E.B. (1994). "Of Our Spiritual Strivings," in *The Souls of Black Folks*. Avenel, NJ: Gramercy Books, 2–8.

Dueker, Kelly (2007). "When a Man Becomes a Woman (And Vice Versa)," A Web Case on *Beloved* by Toni Morrison, English Department, Millikin University, 1–7. Available at: http://www.millikin.edu/english/beloved/Dueker-feminist-essay1.html.

Durrant, Sam (2004). *Postcolonial Narrative and the Work of Mourning: J.M.Coetzee, Wilson Harris, and Toni Morrison*. Albany: State University of New York Press.

Duvall, John (2000). *The Identifying Fictions of Toni Morrison*. New York: Palgrave.

Dziub, Nikol, and Frédérique Toudoire Surlapierre (eds.) (2019). *Comparative Literature in Europe: Challenges and Perspectives*. Cambridge: Cambridge Scholars Publishing.

Eliot, T.S. (1920). "Tradition and the Individual Talent," The Sacred Wood. Available at: http://www.bartleby.com/200/sw4.html.

Elliott, Mary Jane Suero (2000). "Postcolonial Experience in a Domestic Context: Commodified Subjectivity in Toni Morrison's *Beloved*," *MELUS*, 25(3–4), 181–201.

El-Meligi, Eman (2012). *Symbolism in the Novels of Tawfiq Al-Hakim and V.S. Naipaul: A Comparative Study of Literary Technique*. New York: Edwin Mellen Books.

Eyerman, Ron (2004). "The Past in the Present: Culture and the Transmission of Memory," *Acta Sociologica*, 47(2), 159–69.

Eyre, M. Banning (1982). "Naipaul at Wesleyan," *The South Carolina Review*, 14(2), 115.

Fanon, Frantz (1952). *Black Skin, White Masks*. Translated by Charles Lam Markmann. New York: Grove Press.

——— (1968). *The Wretched of the Earth*. Translated by Constance Farrington. New York: Grove Press.

Farah, Nurridin (2009). "Souls in Exile: Memory, Creativity, and Opportunity," lecture notes, The Committee of Canadian-Somalis in Ottawa, Canada, delivered on December 12, 2009.

Fasold, Ralph, and Roger Shuy (eds.) (1970). *Teaching Standard English in the Inner City*. Washington, D.C.: Center for Applied Linguistics.

Faulkner, William (1954). *Sanctuary and Requiem for a Nun*. New York: Signet Books.

Feder, Lillian (2001). *Naipaul's Truth: The Making of a Writer*. Lanham, MD: Rowman & Littlefield.

Flood, Alison (2011). "V.S. Naipaul Finds No Woman Writer His Literary Match—Not Even Jane Austen," *The Guardian*, June 13, 2011.
Foucault, Michel (2003). *Abnormal*. Translated by Graham Burchell. New York: Verso.
Fowlie, Wallace (1981). *A Reading in Dante's Inferno*. Chicago: University of Chicago Press.
Franco, Bernard (2021). *CompLit: Comparative Literature and European Cultures/Litterature Comparee Et Cultures Europeennes*. Paris: Classiques Garnier.
Gandhi, M. K. (1967). *Non-Violent Resistance* (Satyagraha). New York: Schocken Books.
Gasperi, Giulia De, and Joseph Pivato (2018). *Comparative Literature for the New Century*. Quebec: McGill-Queen's Press.
Gauding, Madonna (2009). *The Signs and Symbols Bible*. New York: Sterling Publishing.
Geertz, Clifford (1988). *Works and Lives: The Anthropologist as an Author*. Cambridge: Polity Press.
Gibson, Donald B. (1989). "Text and Countertext in Toni Morrison's *The Bluest Eye*," *Literature, Interpretation, Theory*, 1(1–2), 19–32.
Gilkes, Cherly Townsend (1983). "From Slavery to Social Welfare: Racism and the Control of Black Women," in Swerdlow, Amy, and Lessinger, Hanna (eds.), *Class, Race, and Sex: The Dynamics of Control*. Boston: G. K. Hall, 288–300.
Gillis, John (1994). *Memory and Identity: The History of a Relationship. Commemorations. The Politics of National Identity*. Princeton, NJ: Princeton University Press.
Giovanni, Nikki (1971). *Gemini Autobiographical Statement on My First Twenty-Five Years of Being A Black Poet*. New York: Penguin.
Gorra, Michael (2008). *After Empire: Scott, Naipaul, Rushdie*. Chicago: University of Chicago Press.
Gras, Delphine (2016). "Post What? Disarticulating Post-Discourses in Toni Morrison's *God Help the Child*," *Humanities: An Open-access Journal*, 5(4), 80–98.
Grewal, Gurleen (1997). "Laundering the Head of Whitewash: Mimicry and Resistance in *The Bluest Eye*," in McKay, N.Y. and Earle, K. (eds.), *Approaches to Teaching Toni Morrison*. New York: Modern Language Association, 118–27.
——— (2013). "The Working Through of the Disconsolate: Transformative Spirituality in Paradise," in Fultz, Lucille P. (ed.), *Toni Morrison: Paradise, Love, A Mercy*. London: Bloomsbury, 40–54.
Griffith, Glyne A. (1996). *Deconstruction, Imperialism, and the West Indian Novel*. London: Routledge.
Gusdorf, Georges (1980). "Conditions and Limits of Autobiography," in Olney, James (ed.), *Autobiography: Essays, Theoretical and Critical*. Princeton, NJ: Princeton University Press, 27–48.
Gyetvai, Éva (2006). "The Figure Sula Makes: The Narrative Technique of Defragmentation," *49th Parallel, an Interdisciplinary E-Journal of North American*

and Canadian Studies, 17, 1–17. Available at: https://fortyninthparalleljournal.files.wordpress.com/2014/07/6-gyetvai-the-figure-sula-makes.pdf.

Haaken, Janice (1996). "The Recovery of Memory, Fantasy, and Desire: Feminist Approaches to Sexual Abuse and Psychic Trauma," *Signs*, 21(4), 1069–94.

Hall, Stuart (1993). "Cultural Identity and Diaspora," in Williams, Patrick and Chrisman, Laura (eds.), *Colonial Discourse and Post-Colonial Theory*. Cambridge: Cambridge University Press, 113–235.

——— (1996). "Who Needs Identity?," in Hall, Stuart and Du Gay, Paul (eds.), *Questions of Cultural Identity*. London: SAGE, 1–18.

Hamilton, Alex (1971). "Living a Life on Approval," *The Guardian*, October 4, 1971, 8.

Hamilton, Ian (1997). "Without a Place," in Jussawalla, Feroza (ed.), *Conversations with V.S. Naipaul*. Jackson: University Press of Mississippi, 120–26.

Hammonds, Evelynn M. (1997). "Toward a Genealogy of Black Female Sexuality: The Problematic of Silence," in Alexander, M. Jacqui, and Mohanty, Chandra Talpade (eds.), *Feminist Genealogies, Colonial Legacies, Democratic Futures*. London: Routledge, 170–83.

Harcourt, Wendy (2016). *Bodies in Resistance: Sex and Gender Politics in the Age of Neoliberalism*. New York: Springer.

Harris, Trudier (1991). *Fiction and Folklore: The Novels of Toni Morrison*. Knoxville, TN: University of Tennessee Press.

Hemenway, Robert (1982). "Sex and Politics in Naipaul," in *Studies in the Novel*, 14(2), 189–202.

Holloway, Karla F. C., and Demetrakopoulos, Stephanie (1987). *A New Dimensions of Spirituality: A Biracial and Bicultural Reading of the Novels of Toni Morrison*. New York: Greenwood Press.

Hoogvelt, A. (1997). *Globalisation and the Postcolonial World: The New Political Economy of Development*. London: Macmillan.

hooks, bell (1982). *Ain't I a Woman: Black Women and Feminism*. London: Pluto Press.

——— (1989). *Talking Back: Thinking Feminist, Thinking Black*. Boston: South End Press.

——— (1990). *Yearning, Race, Gender, and Cultural Politics*. Boston: South End Press.

——— (1992). *Black Looks, Race and Representation*. New York: Routledge.

——— (2000). *Feminist Theory from Margin to Center*. Boston: South End Press.

Horvitz, Deborah (1989). "Nameless Ghosts: Possessions and Dispossession in *Beloved*," *Studies in American Fiction*, 17(2), 157–67.

Huddart, David (2006). *Homi K. Bhabha*. Oxford: Abingdon.

Hutcheon, Linda (1995). "Circling The Downspout of the Empire," in Ashcroft, Bill, Griffiths, Gareth, and Tiffen, Helen (eds.), *The Post-colonial Studies Reader*. London: Routledge, 130–36.

Jain, Jasbir (2008). "Landscape of the mind: Unravelling of Naipaul's *The Enigma of Arrival*," *Caribbean Literatures*, 5(2), 115–24.

Jay, Paul (1984). "The Art of Fictional Representation," in Jay, Paul (ed.), *Being in the Text: Self- Representation from Wordsworth to Roland Barthes*. London: Cornell University Press.

Johansson, Evelina, and Mona Lilja (2013). "Understanding Power and Performing Resistance: Swedish Feminists, Civil Society Voices, Biopolitics and Angry Men," *NORA: Nordic Journal of Women's Studies*, 21(4), 264–79.

Jones, David Pryce (1982). *Introduction to V.S. Naipaul's Works*. Oxford: Oxford University Press.

Jörngården, Anna (2018). "'A Ruin Amidst Ruins': V.S. Naipaul Walking the English Countryside," *Modern Fiction Studies*, 64(2), 209–38.

Kaakinen, Kaisa (2017). *Comparative Literature and the Historical Imaginary: Reading Conrad, Weiss, Sebald*. Cham, Switzerland: Springer International Publishing.

Kalra, S., R. Kaur, and J. Hutnyk (2005). *Diaspora and Hybridity*. New Delhi: SAGE.

Kelley, Margot Anne (1994). "Sisters' Choices: Quilting Aesthetics in Contemporary African American Women's Fiction," in Torsney, Cheryl B., and Elsely, Judith (eds.), *Quilt Culture: Tracing the Pattern*. Columbia: University of Missouri, 49–67.

King, Bruce (1993). *V.S. Naipaul*. London: Palgrave Macmillan.

Krumholz, Linda (1993). "The Ghosts of Slavery: Historical Recovery in Toni Morrison's *Beloved*," *African American Review*, 26(3), 395–408.

Kuenz, Jane (1993). "The Bluest Eye: Notes on History, Community, and Black Female Subjectivity," *African American Review*, 27(3), 97–110.

Kulpa, Kathryn (2016). "Review of *God Help the Child* by Toni Morrison," *Magill's Literary Annual*, 7(1), 228–31.

Lacan, Jacques (1978). *The Seminar of Jacques Lacan*. New York: Norton.

Ladner, Joyce A. (1971). *Tomorrow's Tomorrow: The Black Woman*. Garden City, NJ: Doubleday.

Laing, Ronald (1990). *The Divided Self*. New York: Penguin Books.

Lane, J. Richard (2006). *Fifty Key Literary Theorists*. London: Routledge.

Laplanch, Jean and Jerry Pontalis (1968), "Fantasy and the Origins of Sexuality," *The International Journal of Psychoanalysis*, 49(1), 1–18.

Leach, Maria (ed.) (1949). *Funk & Wagnall's Standard Dictionary of Folklore, Mythology and Legend*. New York: Funk & Wagnalls.

Lee, Dorothy H. (1984). "The Quest for Self: Triumph and Failure in the Works of Toni Morrison," in Evans, Man (ed.), *Black Women Writers (1950–1980): A Critical Evaluation*. New York: Anchor Books, 346–60.

Lerner, Gerda (1972). *Black Women in White America*. New York: Vintage Books.

—— (1979). *The Challenge of Women's History*. Oxford: Oxford University Press.

Levine, Lawrance W. (1977). *Black Culture and Black Consciousness: Afro-American Folk Thought From Slavery to Freedom*. Oxford: Oxford University Press.

Levy, Judith (1995). *V.S. Naipaul: Displacement and Autobiography*. New York: Garland.

Lewis, Linden (2003). "Caribbean Masculinity," in Lewis, Linden (ed.), *The Culture of Gender and Sexuality in the Caribbean*. Gainesville: University of Florida, 94–125.

Lopez, J. Alfred (2007). "Introduction: Comparative Literature and the Return of the Global Repressed," *The Global South, Globalization and the Future of Comparative Literature*, 1(2), 1–15.

Loomba, Ania (1998). *Colonialism and Postcolonialism*. London: Routledge.

Loomba, Ania, Suyir Kaul, Antoinette M. Burton, Matti Bunzl, and Jed Esty (2005). "Beyond What? An Introduction," in Loomba, Ania, Kaul, Suvir, Burton, Antoinette M., Bunzl, Matti, and Esty, Jed (eds.), *Postcolonial Studies and Beyond*. Durham, NC: Duke University Press, 1–38.

Lucas, Rose (1991). "The Parturition of Memory in Toni Morrison's Beloved," *Australasian Journal of American Studies*, 1 (1), 39–47.

MacDonald, F. Bruce (1982). "The Artist in Colonial Society: *The Mimic Men* and *The Interpreters*," *Caribbean Quarterly*, 28(1), 20–31.

MacDowell, Deborah E. (1988). "The Self and the Other: Reading Toni Morrison's *Sula*," in McKay, Nellie Y. (ed.), *Critical Essays on Toni Morrison*. Boston: G.K. Hall & Co., 77–90.

Manjapra, Kris (2020). *Colonialism in Global Perspective*. Cambridge: Cambridge University Press.

Martin, Guy (1985). "The Historical, Economic and Political Bases of France's African Policy," *The Journal of Modern African Studies*, 23(2), 189–208.

Mashaqi, Sahar Abdelkarim Asad and Mohamed Khair Kifah Ali Al Omari (2018). "Postcolonial Approach to the Problem of Subalternity in Toni Morrison's *God Help the Child*," *International Journal of Applied Linguistics & English Literature*, 7(1), 177–83.

Mason, Theodore O. (1990). "Stories and Comprehension," in Bloom, Harold (ed.), *Song of Solomon in Modern Critical Views: Toni Morrison*. New York: Chelsea House Publishers, 171–88.

Massey, Darren (1994). *Space, Place and Gender*. Cambridge: Polity.

McKittrick, Katherine (2000). "Black and 'Cause I'm Black I'm Blue': Transverse Racial Geographies in Toni Morrison's *The Bluest Eye*," *Gender, Place and Culture—A Journal of Feminist Geography*, 7(2), 125–42.

McLeod, John (2000). *Beginning Postcolonialism*. Manchester: Manchester University Press.

Meighoo, Kirk (2018). "V.S. Naipaul: Commonwealth Citizen Extraordinaire," *The Round Table*, 107(5), 635–36.

Memmi, Albert (1965). *The Colonizer and the Colonized*. New York: The Orion Press.

Miller, James (2006). *Dante and the Unorthodox: The Aesthetics of Transgression*. Waterloo, Ontario: Wilfrid Laurier University Press.

Miller, Karl (1977). "V.S. Naipaul and the New Order," in Hamner, Robert, D. (ed.), *Critical Perspectives on V.S. Naipaul*. Washington, D.C.: Three Continents Press, 332–34.

Miner, Madonne M. (1990). "Lady No Longer Sings the Blues: Rape, Madness, and Silence in The Bluest Eye," in Pryse, Marjorie, and Hortense, J. (eds.), *Conjuring Black Women, Fiction and Literary Tradition*. Bloomington: Indiana University Press, 176–91.

Misra, Nivedita (2017). "From Tramp to Traveller: V.S. Naipaul Mirrors Immigrant Experiences in a Free State," *Transnational Literature*, 9(2), 1–11. Available at http://fhrc.flinders.edu.au/transnational/home.html

Moglen, Helene (1993). "Redeeming History: Toni Morrison's Beloved," *Cultural Critique*, 24, 17–40.

Mohanty, Chandra Talpade, Ann Russo, and Lourdes Torres (1991). *Third World Women and the Politics of Feminism*. Bloomington: Indiana University Press.

Moore-Gilbert, B. (1997). *Postcolonial Theory: Contexts, Practices, Politics*. London: Verso.

Morris, Robert K. (1975). *Paradoxes of Order: Some Perspectives on the Fiction of V.S. Naipaul*. Missouri: University of Missouri Press.

Morrison, Toni (1973). *The Bluest Eye*. London: Vintage Books.

—— (1973). *Sula*. New York: Alfred A. Knopf.

—— (1974). "Behind the Making of The Black Book," *Black World*, 23(4), February, 86–90.

—— (1977). "Intimate Things in Place: A Conversation with Toni Morrison," Interview with Robert Stepto, *The Massachusetts Review*, 18(3), 473–89. Available at: www.jstor.org/stable/25088764

—— (1987a). *Beloved*. New York: Alfred A. Knopf.

—— (1987b). "The Site of Memory," in Zinnser, William (ed.), *Inventing the Truth: The Art and Craft of Memoir*. Boston: Houghton Mifflin, 103–24.

—— (1988). "In the Realm of Responsibility: A Conversation with Toni Morrison," Interview with Marsha Darling, *The Women's Review of Books*, 5(6), 5–6. Available at: https://www.jstor.org/stable/4020269

—— (1989). "The Pain of Being Black," Interview with Bonnie Angelo, *Time*, May, 120–23.

—— (1997). *Paradise*. New York: Alfred A. Knopf.

—— (1998). "Home," in Lubiano, Wahneema (ed.), *The House That Race Built*. New York: Vintage Books, 3–12.

—— (2012a). *Home*. New York: Alfred A. Knopf.

—— (2012b). "Toni Morrison on Love, Loss, and Modernity," Interview with Ariel Leve, *The Telegraph*, July 17, 2012. Available at https://www.telegraph.co.uk/culture/s/authorinterviews/9395051/Toni-Morrison-on-love-loss-and-modernity.html

—— (2015). *God Help the Child*. New York: Alfred A. Knopf.

Mukherjee, Meenakshi (2001). "A House for Mr.Naipaul," *Front Line, India's National Magazine*, 18(22), 1–5.

Mustafa, Fawzya (1995). *V.S. Naipaul*. Cambridge: Cambridge University Press.

Naipaul, V.S. (1962). *The Middle Passage*. London: Macmillan.

—— (1967). *The Mimic Men*. London: Andre Deutsch.

——— (1968). "Writing is Magic," Interview with Francis Wyndham, *Sunday Times*, 57.
——— (1971). *In a Free State*. London: Andre Deutsch.
——— (1973). "The Novelist V.S. Naipaul Talks about his Work to Ronald Bryden," Interview with Roland Bryden, *The Listener*, 89, March, 367–70.
——— (1975). *Guerrillas*. London: Andre Deutsch.
——— (1979). *A Bend in the River*. Harmondsworth, UK: Penguin.
——— (1981). *Among The Believers*. London: Andre Deutsch.
——— (1987). *The Enigma of Arrival*. New York: Viking Press.
——— (1997). *Beyond Belief: An Excursion Among Converted Peoples*. New York: Random House.
——— (2001). *Half a Life*. New York: Alfred A. Knopf.
——— (2004a). *Magic Seeds*. New York: Alfred A. Knopf.
——— (2004b). "Two Worlds," in *Literary Occasions Essays*. New York: Knopf, 181–95.
Nandy, Ashis (1983). *The Intimate Enemy: Loss and Recovery of Self Under Colonialism*. Oxford: Oxford University Press.
Naylor, Gloria (1994). "A Conversation: Gloria Naylor and Toni Morrison," in Taylor-Guthrie, Danille (ed.), *Conversations with Toni Morrison*. Jackson: University Press of Mississippi, 188–217.
Nixon, Rob (1988). "London Calling: V.S. Naipaul and the license of Exile," *South Atlantic Quarterly*, 87(1), 1–37.
Oyewumi, Oyeronke (2005). "Colonizing Bodies and Minds: Gender and Colonialism" in Desai, Gaurav, and Nair, Supriya (eds.), *Postcolonialisms: An Anthology of Cultural Theory and Criticism*. New Brunswick: Rutgers University Press, 339–61.
Page, Philip (1996). *Dangerous Freedom: Fragmentation and Fusion in Toni Morison's Novels*. Jackson: University Press of Mississippi.
Parker, Emma (2001). "A New Hystery: History and Hysteria in Toni Morrison's Beloved," *Twentieth-Century Literature*, 47(1), 1–19. Available at: https://www.jstor.org/stable/827854
Proust, Marcel (2001). *The Past Recaptured*. Translated by Andreas Mayor. New York: Vintage.
Radovic, Stanka (2015). "Savors of Place: V.S. Naipaul's Enigma of Departure," *Journal of Postcolonial Writing*, 51(1), 108–20.
Rai, Sudha (1982). *V.S. Naipaul: A Study in Expatriate Sensibility*. New Delhi: Arnold-Heinemann.
Rao, Raja (1971). *Kanthapura*. Delhi: Orient Paperback.
Ray, Mohit Kumar (2002). *V.S. Naipaul: Critical Essays*. West Indies: Atlantic Publishers & Dist.
Reviere, Susan L. (1996). *Memory of Childhood Trauma: A Clinician's Guide to the Literature*. New York: The Guilford Press.
Robbins, B., M. L. Pratt, J. Arac, R. Radhakrishnan, and Edward Said (1994). "Edward Said's Culture and Imperialism: A Symposium," *Social Text*, 40, 1–24.
Rosenberg, Ruth (1987). "Seeds in Hard Ground: Black Girlhood in The Bluest Eye," *Black American Literature Forum*, 21(4), 435–45.

Rowe-Evans, Adrian (1971). "The Writer as Colonial," *Transition*, 40, 56–62.
Rubenstein, Roberta (2001). *Home Matters: Longing and Belonging, Nostalgia and Mourning in Women's Fiction*. New York: Palgrave.
Rushdy, Ashraf H. A. (1999). "Daughters, Signifying History: The Example of Toni Morrison's Beloved," in Andrews, William L., and McKay, Nellie (eds.), *Toni Morrison's Beloved: A Case*. New York: Oxford University Press, 37-66.
——— (2004). "The Neo-Slave Narrative," in Graham, Maryemma (ed.), *Cambridge Companion to the African American Novel*. Cambridge: Cambridge University Press, 87–105.
Russell, Kathy, Midge Wilson, and Ronald Hall (1992). *The Color Complex: The Politics of Skin Colour among African Americans*. New York: Doubleday.
Safran, William (1991). "Diasporas, Modern Societies, Myth of Homeland and Return," *Diaspora*, 1(1), 83–99.
Said, Edward (1978). *Orientalism: Western Conceptions of the Orient*. London: Routledge.
——— (1993). *Cultural and Imperialism*. London: Chatto and Windus.
——— (2000a). "Jane Austen and Empire," in Bayoumi, Moustafa, and Rubin, Andrew (eds.), *The Edward Said Reader*. New York: Vintage Books, 347–68.
——— (2000b). "Reflections on Exile," in Said, Edward (ed.), *Reflections on Exile and Other Literary and Cultural Essays*. London: Granta Books, 173–86.
Saradhambal, K.S. (2017). "Evolution of Feminine Space in V.S. Naipaul's Selected Novels," International Conference on Globalization, Women Empowerment and Education, Vivekanandha College of Arts & Science for Women, Kolkota: International E-Journal of Trend in Research and Development (IJTRD), 1–16.
Saussy, Haun (2006). *Comparative Literature in an Age of Globalization*. Baltimore: Johns Hopkins University Press.
Schiff, Stephen (1997). "The Ultimate Exile," in Jussawalla, Feroza (ed.), *Conversations with V.S. Naipaul*. Jackson: University Press of Mississippi, 135–53.
Schlant, Ernestine (1999). *The Language of Silence*. London: Routledge.
Seward, Adrienne Lanier, and Tally, Justine (2014). *Memory and Meaning: Toni Morrison*. Jackson: University Press of Mississippi.
Shaaban, Bouthaina (1993). "Arab Women Writers: Are There Any?," *Washington Report on Middle East Affairs*, 11(7), 36.
Sinha, Sunita (2008). *Postcolonial Women Writers: New Perspectives*. New Delhi: Atlantic.
Smith, Kevin Paul (2007). *The Postmodern Fairytale Folkloric Intertexts in Contemporary Fiction*. London: Palgrave Macmillan.
Smith, Valerie (2012). *Toni Morrison: Writing Moral Imagination*. Hoboken, NJ: Wiley-Blackwell.
Spivak, Gayatri Chakravorty (1988). "Can the Subaltern Speak?," in Nelson, Gary, and Grossberg, Lawrence (eds.), *Marxism and Interpretation of Culture*. Chicago: Illinois Press, 271–313.
——— (2003). *Death of a Discipline*. New York: Columbia University Press.

Spurlin, William J. (2016). "Contested Borders: Cultural Translation and Queer Politics in Contemporary Francophone Writing from the Maghreb," *Research in African Literatures*, 47(2), 104–20.

Stallone, Dianna R. (1984). "Decriminalization of Violence in the Home: Mediation in Wife Battering Cases," *Law & Inequality Journal*, 2(2), 493–519.

Staples, Robert (1987). *The Urban Plantation: Racism & Colonialism in the Post-Civil Rights Era*. San Francisco: Black Scholar Press.

Strehle, Susan (2008). *Transnational Women's Fiction: Unsettling Home and Homeland*. New York: Palgrave Macmillan.

Su, John J. (1998). "Haunted by Place: Moral Obligation and the Postmodern Novel," *The Centennial Review*, 42(3), 598–614.

Suranyi, Agnes (2007). "The Bluest Eye and Sula: Black Female Experience from Childhood to Womanhood," in Tally, Justine (ed.), *The Cambridge Companion to Toni Morrison*. Cambridge: Cambridge University Press, 11–26.

Tagore, Proma (2009). *Shapes of Silence: Writing by Women of Colour and the Politics of Testimony*. Quebec: McGill Queen's Press.

Tai, Chuen-Shin (2016). "Mapping Postmodern in Toni Morrison's Beloved," *International Journal of Culture and History*, 2(4), 226–29.

Taniyan, Reyhan Özer (2015). "V. S. Naipaul's Magic Seeds: Jack and the Beanstalk Revisited," in Celikel, Mehmet Ali, and Taniyan, Baysar (eds.), *English Studies: New Perspectives*. New Castle: Cambridge Scholars Publishing, 270–79.

Tatar, Maria (2003). *The Hard Facts of the Grimms' Fairy Tales*. Princeton: Princeton University Press.

Thieme, John (1975). "V. S. Naipaul's Third World: A Not So Free State," *Journal of Commonwealth Literature*, 10(1), 10–22.

——— (1984). "A Hindu Castaway: Ralph Singh's Journey in The Mimic Men," *Modern Fiction Studies*, 30, 505–18.

——— (1987a). *The Web of Tradition: Uses of Allusion in V.S. Naipaul's Fiction*. Hertford, UK: Hansib.

——— (1987b). "Thinly-Veiled Autobiography," *Third World Quarterly*, 9(4), 1376–78.

Thrope, Michael (1976). *V.S. Naipaul*. Essex: Longman.

Tyson, Lois (1999). *Postcolonial and African American Criticism, Critical Theory Today: User-Friendly Guide*. New York: Garland.

Varisco, M. Daniel (2007). *Reading Orientalism: Said and the Unsaid*. Seattle: University of Washington.

Velassery, Sebastian (2005). *Casteism and Human Rights: Toward An Ontology of the Social Order*. Singapore: Marshall Cavendish Academic.

Wall, Cheryl A. (2005). *Worrying the Line: Black Women Writers, Lineage, and Literary Tradition*. Chapel Hill: North Carolina University Press.

Wang, Yurong and Li Lin (2014). "The Exploration of a Sense of Belonging: An Explanation of Naipaul's Novel Half a Life and Magic Seeds," *International Journal of Literature and Arts*, 2(5), 187–91.

Wardi, Anissa Janine (2021). *Toni Morrison and the Natural World: An Ecology of Color*. Jackson, MS: University Press of Mississippi.

Washington, Mary Helen (1987). *Invented Lives: Narratives of Black Women, 1860–1960*. New York: Anchor Press, Doubleday.

Weiss, Timothy F. (1992). *On the Margins: The Art of Exile in V. S. Naipaul*. Amherst: University of Massachusetts Press.

Wilson, Janet, and Chris Ringrose (eds.) (2016). *New Soundings in Postcolonial Writing: Critical and Creative Contours*. Leiden: Brill.

Wilson, Sharon Rose (2008). *Myths and Fairy Tales in Contemporary Women's Fiction: From Atwood to Morrison*. New York: Palgrave Macmillan.

Wirth-Nesher, Hana (1984). "The Curse of Marginality: Colonialism in Naipaul's Guerrillas," *Modern Fiction Studies*, 30(3), 531–45.

Young, Charles S. (2012). "POWs: The Hidden Reason for Forgetting Korea," in Casey, Steven (ed.), *The Korean War at Sixty: New Approaches to the Study of the Korean War*. New York: Routledge, 155–71.

Young, Robert J. (1995). *Colonial Desire: Hybridity, in Theory, Culture and Race*. New York: Routledge.

——— (2001). *Postcolonialism: An Historical Introduction*. New Jersey: Wiley-Blackwell.

——— (2013). "The Postcolonial Comparative," *PMLA*, 128(3), 683–89.

Yule, George (1996). *Pragmatics*. Oxford: Oxford University Press.

Zou, Min (2015). *The Transcription of Identities: A Study of V.S. Naipaul's Postcolonial Writings*. Bielefeld: Transcript Verlag.

Index

African Folklore, 25, 26, 93, 95, 97, 98, 116–18
African-American, xi, xiii, xiv, xv, xvi, xviii, 18–20, 22, 23, 25–28, 37, 41, 42, 44, 45, 50–52, 55, 57–59, 63–67, 71, 72, 78, 79, 81, 85, 87, 89, 91–100, 103–5, 110–14, 116–18, 122, 127–29, 131, 132, 134, 138, 139, 143–45, 147, 150–52, 155, 157, 160, 161, 166, 167, 169, 170, 173, 175
Ambivalence, xv, 32–34, 47, 60, 75, 80, 92, 95, 104, 115, 134, 184
Ania Loomba, xiii, 22, 102, 190
Arab-American, 178
Arab Women, 178–79, 193
Arab writers, 178
Arab, 177–79, 183, 193, 197
Arabia, 177
Arabian, 178
Arabic, 177, 178
Assimilate, xiii, 24, 31, 33, 37, 39, 40, 68, 69, 108
Assimilation, xiv, 24, 31, 32, 67, 70, 171

Beloved (*B*), vii, xvii, 25, 69, 71–79, 81, 82, 84, 85, 87–89, 91, 93–97, 99, 100, 108, 132, 146, 147, 150–52, 154–56, 163, 171, 177, 184–86, 188–94
Bend in the River (*BR*), 146, 148, 192
BEV. *See* Black English vernacular
Binary, xvi, xvii, 64, 102, 107, 116, 124, 134–38, 155, 157, 162, 167, 171, 174–76, 180
Bisexual, 138, 147–49, 174
Bisexuality, 138, 148, 149, 174
Black English vernacular (BEV), 55–57
Black women's communities, xvii, xviii, 26, 27, 95, 128, 137, 141, 145, 154–56, 160–62, 168, 173
Bluest Eye (*BE*), xvii, 24, 31, 34–37, 39, 44, 45, 48–50, 57, 59, 62, 64, 65, 140, 141, 147, 163, 165, 166, 171, 175, 177, 183, 184, 186, 187, 189, 190, 191, 194, 195

Casteism, 26, 102, 116, 118, 119, 195
Chinua Achebe, 55, 183
Colonialism, xii, xiii, xiv, xvi, 9, 11, 16–20, 22, 25–27, 29, 31–34, 36, 61, 67, 74, 86, 88, 102, 103, 127, 130, 134, 137, 139, 144, 148, 154, 163, 169, 173, 175, 176, 178, 180, 181, 183, 190, 192, 194, 195, 197

Comparative literature, ix, xi, xii, xiii, xvi, xviii, 9–20, 25, 28, 29, 170, 176, 177, 181, 183–85, 187, 189–90, 193

Comparative, vii, ix, xi, xii, xiii, xvi, xviii, 9–20, 23, 27–29, 169–71, 176–79, 181, 183–90, 195

Creole society, 21

Cross-cultural, xi, xvi, 2, 10, 44, 99, 103, 107, 133

Decolonization, 13, 29, 68, 134, 173

Diaspora, xi, xiv, 12, 18, 22, 23, 69, 73, 75, 112, 178, 179, 184, 185, 188, 189

Edward Said, xii, 14–17, 19, 28, 47, 81, 176, 183, 193

Emasculation, 153–56, 159, 161, 162, 166, 174

Empowerment, 118, 128, 129, 138, 148, 153, 154, 159, 161, 162, 177, 185, 193

Enigma of Arrival (*EA*), vii, xvii, 25, 69, 71, 73–92, 95, 96, 98–100, 105, 148, 171, 189, 192

Exile, 21, 23, 36, 47, 50, 70, 71, 81, 83, 97, 98, 108, 110–12, 179, 183, 187, 192, 193

Extraterritorial, 84, 107, 115

Frantz Fanon, xiii, xiv, xv, xvi, xvii, 24–26, 29, 31, 32, 45, 54, 67–70, 80, 82, 86, 92, 100–103, 106, 108, 115, 119, 122–24, 127–29, 131–33, 135, 141, 142, 148, 162, 170–76, 186

Folklore, xv, 25, 26, 55, 86, 92–95, 97, 98, 100, 101, 116–18, 172, 174, 188, 189

Fragmentation, xiv, xv, xviii, 18, 24, 26, 32, 35, 36, 43, 45, 47, 48, 50, 52, 53, 57, 61–63, 68, 78, 82, 84, 87, 89, 95, 97, 101, 104, 105, 112, 116, 118, 128, 132, 143, 155, 171, 175, 180, 192

Fragmented Identities, iii, vii, xi, xiii, 23, 26, 31, 36, 58, 76, 133, 139, 155, 167

Free State (*FS*), 146, 148, 192

Gayatri Spivak, xii, 13, 14, 17, 18, 28, 161, 162, 194

Gender, vii, xiii, xiv, xv, xvi, xvii, 12, 18, 19, 24, 26, 27, 44, 106, 111, 128, 129, 135–51, 153–64, 167, 168, 173–76, 179, 180, 184, 185, 188, 190

God Help the Child, 175, 179, 187, 189, 190, 192

Guerrillas (*G*), 146–48, 153, 164, 165, 174, 192, 195

Half a Life (*HL*), vii, xvii, 25, 101, 104–10, 112, 113, 115, 118, 123–25, 129, 130, 133, 154, 158, 159, 163, 166, 172, 173, 192, 195

Heterosexuality, 128, 136, 164, 174

Home (*H*), vii, xvii, 26, 101, 104–6, 108, 110–13, 115, 116, 119, 121, 122, 124, 125, 127–31, 133, 154, 159, 163, 172, 173, 191

Homi Bhabha, xii, xv, 17, 24, 28, 33–35, 41, 42, 44, 47, 56, 60, 63, 67, 80, 101–7, 113–15, 125, 132, 144, 171, 176, 184, 188

Homosexuality, 136, 149, 150

House for Mr Biswas, 148

Hybrid, xii, 12, 16, 42, 72, 80, 96, 98–99, 104–9, 113, 115–16, 120–24, 129, 131–33, 172–73

Hybridity, vii, xv, xvii, 18, 26, 76, 101–9, 115–16, 119–25, 129, 132–34, 171–73, 189, 195

Hybridization, 12, 15, 61, 91, 101, 102, 103, 104, 115, 116, 117, 118, 122, 124, 143, 172, 173

Identity, vii, xiii, xiv, xv, xvi, xvii, 11, 14, 16–22, 24–26, 28, 31–36, 38–42, 44, 46, 48, 49, 51, 53, 54, 57–63, 66, 67, 69–71, 73, 75–83, 85–89,

91–93, 95, 97–101, 103, 104, 105, 108–18, 124, 125, 128, 129, 132–38, 141, 143, 145, 149, 152, 154, 155, 157, 161–63, 166, 167, 169–74, 176, 178–80, 184, 185, 187, 188, 195
In-betweenness, 43, 44, 55, 73, 75, 76–81, 84, 86, 87, 89, 92, 95, 96, 98, 99, 103, 132
Intersexuality, 168
Islamic religion, 149, 174

Judith Butler, 135–37, 144, 156, 157, 185

Liminal space, 125

Magic Seeds (*MS*), vii, xvii, 25, 101, 104–8, 110, 113, 115–25, 129, 130, 133, 154, 158, 159, 163, 166, 172, 173, 192, 195
Masculinity, xvii, 137–40, 143, 145, 153, 154, 157, 162, 165, 168
Mercy, 163, 187
Middle passage, xvi, 4, 67, 73, 81, 94, 118, 122, 134, 145, 152, 153, 173, 179, 192
Mimic Men (*MM*), vii, 24, 31, 34–38, 44–50, 53, 54, 58–60, 67, 68, 140, 141, 148, 163, 164, 171, 184, 190, 192, 194
Mimicry, vii, xv, 16, 19, 21, 24, 26, 28, 31–37, 43–44, 46–49, 53–64, 67–70, 108–9, 112, 132, 134, 139, 142, 144, 155, 162, 171–73, 175, 180, 187
Mockery, 33–34
Morrison, i, xi, xiii, xiv, xv, xvi, xvii, xviii, 10, 19–28, 31–39, 41, 42, 44–106, 108, 110–19, 121–35, 137–40, 143–81, 184–95
Multiculturalism, 122, 130, 183
Muslim, 138, 147–49, 174

Naipaul, iii, vii, xi, xiii, xiv, xv, xvi, xvii, xviii, 10, 19–32, 34–38, 42–44, 46–49, 51–63, 66–71, 73–100,

102–10, 112–16, 118–27, 129, 132–35, 137–41, 143–51, 153–55, 157–59, 161–81, 183–95
Narrative Hybridity, 123
Neo-colonialism, 21, 29, 183

Orientalism, 15, 16, 193

Patriarchal power, xvii, 137, 153, 162
Patriarchy, 137, 138, 141, 151, 154, 155, 168
Phallic, xvii, 27, 137, 139, 162, 166
Postcolonial comparative, xi, xii, xiii, xvi, xviii, 10, 12–15, 17–20, 23, 28, 29, 170, 171, 176, 181, 195
Postcolonial literature, vii, xii, xv, 9–13, 17–19, 28, 29, 54, 170, 171, 176, 178, 180, 183–85
Postcolonialism, i, iii, xiii, xiv, xv, 9–11, 15, 16, 18, 20, 22, 23, 28, 33, 88, 95, 102, 112, 129, 178, 181, 185, 190, 192, 195

Queerness, 138, 149, 174

Racism, xvi, 64, 105, 111, 125, 127–29, 151, 161, 170, 175, 187, 194
Rememory, 72, 73, 75, 79, 80
Robert Young, xii, xv, 104, 171, 176, 195

Sex, 126, 135, 136, 137, 139–42, 147, 150, 152, 153, 162, 164, 165, 167, 168, 174, 187
Sexism, 127, 157, 170
Sexist ideology, 157
Sexist language, 163
Sexuality, 18, 27, 137, 139, 144, 146, 148, 149, 151, 153, 165, 167, 168, 179, 188, 189
Slavery, xiii, xvi, 20, 23, 59, 61, 67, 71–75, 77, 78, 80, 81, 84–87, 89, 93, 94, 97–100, 111, 117, 121, 145, 147, 151–53, 155, 156, 160, 176, 178, 179, 187, 189, 190

Stereotype, 17, 33, 127, 152, 156, 161, 166
Sula (*S*), xvii, 27, 137, 145, 154, 157, 174, 177
Susan Bassnett, xii, 10, 12–14, 17, 18, 176, 183

Third space, 47, 104, 105, 132, 134, 173, 184
Trauma, 33, 36, 66, 72, 79, 89, 91, 92, 98, 100, 102, 105, 110, 116, 117, 127–29, 131, 132, 152, 153, 166, 168, 184, 188
Traumatic, 67, 73, 75, 78, 81, 85, 89, 94, 97–100, 111, 115, 118, 128, 131, 132, 151, 152, 178

Unhomeliness, vii, 17, 44, 78, 101, 105–8, 114, 115, 117, 123, 124, 129, 132

Women's empowerment, 154, 157
World literature, 17, 177, 185

About the Author

Alshaymaa Mohamed Ahmed is assistant professor of English and comparative literature in the Humanities Department at the College of Language and Communication, Arab Academy for Science Technology and Maritime Transport (AASTMT) in Cairo, Egypt. She received her BA in English language and literature from Ain Shams University, Cairo, Egypt. She also obtained her MA thesis in comparative literature from Ain Shams University as well. She was awarded her PhD in English and comparative literature, Arts and Humanities department at Brunel University, London, UK. Moreover, she was awarded the vice-chancellor prize of doctoral research for her achievement in her PhD, Brunel University, London, UK. She is a member of the International Comparative Literature Association (ICLA). She is also a member of the American Comparative Literature Association (ACLA) and the British Comparative Literature Association (BCLA). Her main academic interest is in postcolonial and feminist writings and discourses associated with colonialism, especially as they relate to Africa and the Middle East.

www.ingramcontent.com/pod-product-compliance
Lightning Source LLC
Chambersburg PA
CBHW020119010526
44115CB00008B/895